FOR OUR SALVATION

For Our Salvation

Two Approaches to the Work of Christ

GEOFFREY WAINWRIGHT

WILLIAM B. EERDMANS PUBLISHING COMPANY
GRAND RAPIDS, MICHIGAN

Published jointly 1997 in the United States of America by
Wm. B. Eerdmans Publishing Co.
255 Jefferson Ave. S.E., Grand Rapids, Michigan 49503
and in Great Britain by
Society for Promoting Christian Knowledge
Holy Trinity Church
Marylebone Road
London NW1 4DU

Printed in the United States of America

02 01 00 99 98 97   7 6 5 4 3 2 1

Library of Congress Cataloging-in-Publication Data

Wainwright, Geoffrey, 1939- .
For our salvation : two approaches to the work of Christ /
Geoffrey Wainwright.
p.   cm.
Collection of author's lectures given before various assemblies of
theological students, pastors, and interested laypeople.
Includes bibliographical references.
ISBN 0-8028-0846-8 (pbk. : alk. paper)
1. Jesus Christ — Person and offices. 2. Incarnation. 3. Atonement.
4. Senses and sensation — Religious aspects — Christianity. I. Title.
BT220.W195   1997
232 — dc21   96-49761
CIP

British Library Cataloguing-in-Publication Data

A catalogue record for this book is available from
the British Library

SPCK ISBN 0-281-05123-2

For
Dominic Mark
and
Wesley Michael
and
unto the third and the fourth generation

Contents

Contents

Preface

This book brings together two sets of lectures given before various assemblies of theological students, pastors, and interested laypeople. The reception accorded them at their original delivery encourages the hope that they may also receive a welcome in printed form from a readership of similar composition.

Like the lectures, the book is addressed from faith to faith: the reality of the gospel and the truths of Christian doctrine are taken for granted by the author and among the audience (hence the free use of the inclusive "we"). Without the slightest claim to exhaustivity in the presentation of biblical and traditional material, the chapters aim to set out two approaches to the saving work of Christ that are firmly grounded in the Scriptures and in the thought, imagination, and practice of the church catholic and evangelical. Without entering into every detail of current challenges and contemporary issues, I wish also to propose some broad perspectives for the interpretation, propagation, and application of the classic proclamation and teaching. The greater need is for reimmersion in Scripture and Tradition; at least, it is only when that need is met that the task of further transmission can properly be handled.

Either set of chapters may be read first. Under "Senses of the Word," the purpose is to explore the range and density of the biblical accounts of God's self-communication for the sake of a comprehensive doctrine of the incarnation and of the redemptive work of the Word made flesh. Informal theological use is made of modern accounts of cognition and signification to help in the job of giving a Christian schooling to the human senses such as is needed in our sensate culture. It is, above all, the liturgy of the church that is taken as the medium for discipline and enjoyment. In this half of the book, it is perhaps the more catholic side of Christianity that is being called on for the benefit of the evangelical.

Under "The Threefold Office," the aim is to suggest the ecumenical background and potential of a pattern of thought that is perhaps most characteristic of the Reformed tradition. The prophetic, priestly, and royal offices of Christ, precisely in their soteriological thrust, provide — especially in combination — important categories for christology, theological anthropology, and ecclesiology. They also show how Christianity addresses the perennial human questions, recurrent certainly in our time, of knowledge and meaning, of power and authority, and (right in the middle of them) the pain of alienation and the possibility of redemption.

Behind both approaches to the work of Christ exhibited in this book stands the confession of the Nicene Creed: the faith in Jesus Christ, "God from God," "through whom all things were made," who "for us" and "for our salvation," "by the Holy Spirit took flesh from the Virgin Mary and was made man," who "for our sake was crucified under Pontius Pilate," and "on the third day rose again" and "ascended into heaven, and is seated at the right hand of the Father," and who "will come again in glory to judge the living and the dead," and whose "kingdom will have no end."

The rhetorical style of the lecture has been largely retained, as well as the combination of broad display and occasional close illustration appropriate to that genre. In a few places, I have borrowed content from other writings of mine and placed it in new contexts. Footnotes serve chiefly to give references and are very seldom used to enter into scholarly debate. Scripture quotations are almost always taken from the Revised Standard Version, which to my mind remains the best translation of the Bible for general purposes. Patristic citations are made according to Migne, which is still the most regularly accessible source (the *Patrologia Graeca* is abbreviated as *PG,* and the *Patrologia Latina* as *PL*); the connoisseurs will know where else to look.

The lectures were given in various forms and forums: "Senses of the Word" as Voigt Lectures at McKendree College for the Central and Southern Illinois Conferences of the United Methodist Church, as Theta Phi Lectures at Asbury Theological Seminary, and as Kershner Lectures at the Emmanuel School of Religion, Johnson City; "The Threefold Office" as Swander Lectures at Lancaster Theological Seminary, as Currie Lectures at the Presbyterian Theological Seminary in Austin, as Payton Lectures at

Preface

Fuller Theological Seminary, and as Anderson Lectures at the Presbyterian College in Montreal. I am grateful to the officers, faculties, ministers, students, and associates of those respective institutions at the time, and particularly: Bishop Woodie White; President Maxie Dunnam, Provost Robert Mulholland, and Dr. David Bauer; President Robert Wetzel and Professor Frederick Norris; Interim President Robert Fauth and Dean Elizabeth Nordbeck; Acting President Ellis Nelson and Dean Robert Shelton; President David Allan Hubbard, Provost Larry DenBesten, and Dean Robert P. Meye; and Dean William Klempa.

My thanks are also due to my former student Philip Butin, who put his familiarity with Calvin at my disposal; to my present student Telford Work, who read proofs and made helpful comments; to my colleague Karen Westerfield Tucker, who not only spotted some gaps and suggested several transitions in my text but also composed the tune for a largely unused Watts hymn; to Michael Root, of the Lutheran Institute for Ecumenical Research in Strasbourg, who supplied me with a copy of an otherwise inaccessible text by Martin Bucer; and to Jon Pott, Charles Van Hof, Jennifer Hoffman, Milton Essenburg, and Stephanie Hartings, my collaborators at Eerdmans.

Duke University   GEOFFREY WAINWRIGHT
Lady Day, 1996

PART I

SENSES OF THE WORD

Faith Assisted by Sense

1. My Savior God, my Sov-'reign Prince reigns far a-bove the skies; but brings his gra-ces down to sense, and helps my faith to rise.
2. My eyes and ears shall bless his name, they read and hear his word; my touch and taste shall do the same when they re-ceive the Lord.
3. Bap-tis-mal wa-ter is de-signed to seal his cleans-ing grace; while at his feast of bread and wine he gives his saints a place.
4. But not the wa-ters of a flood can make my flesh so clean, as by his spir-it and his blood he'll wash my soul from sin.
5. Not choic-est meats, nor no-blest wines so re-fresh, as when my faith goes through the signs and feeds up-on the flesh.
6. I love the Lord that stoops so low to give his word a seal; but the rich grace his hands be-stow ex-ceeds the fig-ures still.

TEXT: Isaac Watts (1674-1748)
MUSIC: *Sensus fidei* by Karen Westerfield Tucker (1996).

I

The Word Made Flesh

Each Christmas Eve, the service of lessons and carols in the chapel of King's College, Cambridge, comes to its climax with the reading of the opening verses from Saint John's Gospel. The music has resounded under the finest fan vaulting in Christendom. Singing faces have been illuminated by the light of a thousand candles, whose wispy smoke tickles the nostrils and the palate. The gentle heat from the tapers and the damp cold of a late fenland afternoon make alternating impressions on the skin. Then one's entire body shivers as the voice of the provost intones:

> In the beginning was the Word, and the Word was with God, and the Word was God. The same was in the beginning with God. All things were made by him; and without him was not any thing made that was made. In him was life, and the life was the light of men. And the light shineth in darkness, and the darkness comprehended it not. . . . And the Word was made flesh and dwelt among us (and we beheld his glory, the glory as of the only-begotten of the Father) full of grace and truth.

The ninth lesson ended, the faithful are summoned by *Adeste Fideles* to "come and behold him." The dean blesses the congregation in the name of him who "by his incarnation gathered into one things earthly and heavenly." The organ strikes up the Mendelssohn tune for Charles Wesley's "Hark! The Herald Angels Sing." The service is over, and one tries to linger for a last glimpse of the Rubens altarpiece, *The Adoration of the Magi.*

3

"And the Word became flesh and dwelt among us, full of grace and truth; we have beheld his glory, glory as of the only Son from the Father": that is the central affirmation of the Christian faith; or, perhaps better, one formulation of the central article of the faith. Saint Paul put it in very similar terms: "It is the God who said, 'Let light shine out of darkness,' who has shone in our hearts to give the light of the knowledge of the glory of God in the face of Christ" (2 Cor. 4:6). Both Saint Paul and Saint John knew that the incarnation had entailed the crucifixion of the Lord of glory (1 Cor. 2:8; Phil. 2:5-11), that the glory of Christ included his elevation on the cross (John 3:14; 7:39; 8:28, 54; 12:16, 23, 32-34; 13:31f.; 17:1-5). The crucial point was that God had entered, personally and at cost, into our fallen world for our salvation: "God so loved the world that he gave his only Son, that whoever believes in him should not perish but have eternal life. For God sent the Son into the world, not to condemn the world, but that the world might be saved through him" (John 3:16f.); for "when the goodness and loving kindness of God our Savior appeared, he saved us, . . . so that we might be justified by his grace and become heirs in hope of eternal life" (Titus 3:4-7). In what follows, we shall draw on a wide range of the New Testament witness concerning the work of Christ for our salvation; but the leitmotif will remain that set by John 1:14: "The Word became flesh *(ho logos sarx egeneto)*." We shall identify the Word; we shall examine the event of the Word's becoming flesh; and we shall unfold the consequences that this given mode of God's redemptive self-communication to us has for our response as embodied creatures called to share the life of God.

I. THE WORD . . .

It is possible to read the Fourth Gospel against the background of a Greek philosophy and culture. In that case, Saint John's use of *logos* will recall the Stoic *logos,* the divine principle of rationality, the *logos spermatikos* which is scattered like seed throughout the universe, keeping things in orderly being, preventing the cosmos from degenerating into chaos. This "word," says Saint John, has now been "made flesh" (John 1:14) — and, as Jesus Christ, has expired on the cross (John 19:30). That this universal divine principle should have been concentrated into a single human being is already "foolishness to the Greeks," without the additional "nonsense" of his crucifixion (cf. 1 Cor. 1:23); yet for believers, Christ crucified is "the power of God and the wisdom of God" (1 Cor. 1:24).

While Greek patterns of thought, drastically revolutionized, may form part of Saint John's repertory for identifying the Subject of the incarnation and the Agent of our redemption, a more immediately accessible conceptuality is to be found in the Old Testament, whose writings would be known to the Fourth Evangelist, whether in Greek or in Hebrew, and which has remained canonical Scripture in the liturgical and doctrinal life of the church. A biblical understanding of the divine Word bears the following features:[1]

First, God's Word is creative. Each stanza of the creation narrative in Genesis 1 takes the pattern of "And God said, Let there be," and each time "it was so." The psalmist summarizes and applies the story thus (Ps. 33:6-9):

> By the word of the LORD the heavens were made,
>   and all their host by the breath of his mouth.
> He gathered the waters of the sea as in a bottle;
>   he put the deeps in storehouses.
> Let all the earth fear the LORD,
>   let all the inhabitants of the world stand in awe of him!
> For he spoke, and it came to be;
>   he commanded, and it stood forth.

Christian hymn writers have continued that tradition. Thus Isaac Watts, in "I Sing the Almighty Power of God":

> He formed the creatures with his word,
> And then pronounced them good.[2]

---

1. Here I am greatly indebted to Eduard Lohse, "Deus dixit: Wort Gottes im Zeugnis des Alten und Neuen Testaments," in his *Die Einheit des Neuen Testaments: Exegetische Studien zur Theologie des Neuen Testaments* (Göttingen: Vandenhoeck & Ruprecht, 1973), pp. 9-28. Too late for consideration came the rich study of Maurice Cocagnac, *L'énergie de la Parole biblique* (Paris: Cerf, 1996).

2. Isaac Watts, "Praise for Creation and Providence," from *Divine Songs Attempted in Easy Language for the Use of Children* (London, 1715).

Or John Wesley, in his extended metrical paraphrase of the Lord's Prayer:

> Father of all! whose powerful voice
> Called forth this universal frame . . .
>
> Thou by thy word upholdest all. . . .[3]

Echoing Romans 4:17, Charles Wesley invokes the One who "speaketh worlds from nought."[4]

Second, God's Word not only creates and sustains what is made but is powerful and efficacious within the world and in history. Isaiah 55:10f. is a classic text in this connection:

> For as the rain and the snow come down from heaven,
>   and return not thither but water the earth,
> making it bring forth and sprout,
>   giving seed to the sower and bread to the eater,
> so shall my word be that goes forth from my mouth;
>   it shall not return to me empty,
> but it shall accomplish that which I purpose,
>   and prosper in the thing for which I sent it.

That is spoken through the same Isaiah in whom full monotheism comes to final expression (Isa. 45:18):

> For thus says the LORD,
> who created the heavens
>   (he is God!),
> who formed the earth and made it
>   (he established it;
> he did not create it a chaos,
>   he formed it to be inhabited!):
> "I am the LORD, and there is no other."

---

3. John Wesley, "The Lord's Prayer Paraphrased," from John and Charles Wesley, *Hymns and Sacred Poems* (Bristol, 1742).

4. Charles Wesley, "Father of Jesus Christ, My Lord," from John and Charles Wesley, *Hymns and Sacred Poems* (Bristol, 1742).

Third, in human history the election of Israel takes place by and under the Word of God. First Abraham is addressed (Gen. 12:1-3):

Now the LORD said to Abram, "Go from your country and your kindred and your father's house to the land that I will show you. And I will make of you a great nation, and I will bless you, and make your name great, so that you will be a blessing. I will bless those who bless you, and him who curses you I will curse; and in you all the families of the earth shall be blessed."

Then, in Exodus 3–4, God calls to Moses out of the burning bush, tells him that he is the God of Abraham, Isaac, and Jacob, reveals his name of "I AM" or "the LORD," and sends Moses and Aaron off to the children of Israel in Egypt with these remarkable words: "And you [Moses] shall speak to him [Aaron] and put the words in his mouth; and I will be with your mouth and with his mouth, and will teach you what you shall do. He shall speak for you to the people; and he shall be a mouth to you, and you shall be to him as God." And on Mount Sinai, when Israel has been safely delivered from Egypt, the Lord gives to his people his commandments in the shape of the "ten words," the "decalogue," which are the "words of the covenant" (Exod. 34:27f.). God's choice and his commandments stand (Deut. 26:16-19).

In the subsequent history of Israel, therefore, God's Word comes, fourthly, in prophetic mode: to summon the people to faithfulness, to utter judgment on disobedience, to offer forgiveness to the repentant, to promise restoration and renewal by God's mercy. Prophecies are characteristically introduced or concluded by "Thus says the LORD." Knowing that "the Lord GOD does nothing, without revealing his secret to his servants the prophets," Amos can testify to the compelling voice of the Lord:

The lion has roared;
who will not fear?
The Lord GOD has spoken;
who can but prophesy? (3:7f.; cf. 1:2)

God's Word through a true prophet can be terrifying: "Is not my word like fire, says the LORD, and like a hammer which breaks the rock in pieces?" (Jer. 23:29). It can also announce God's intention to intervene redemptively for the sake of his people (Isa. 35:1-10; 43:14-21; 51:9-11), with an even greater deliverance than from Egypt (Jer. 23:7f.), a raising of the dead to life (Ezek. 37), and a new covenant written on their hearts (Jer. 31).

The New Testament continues to speak of the power of God's Word to penetrate to the core of human affairs: "The word of God is living and active, sharper than any two-edged sword, piercing to the division of soul and spirit, of joints and marrow, and discerning the thoughts and intentions of the heart. And before him no creature is hidden, but all are open and laid bare to the eyes of him with whom we have to do" (Heb. 4:12f.). The radically new thing is that God's Word has now entered the world as Jesus Christ, as the Letter to the Hebrews itself makes clear: "In many and various ways God spoke of old to our ancestors by the prophets, but in these last days he has spoken to us by a Son" (1:1f.). This Jesus, who "although he was a Son," "learned obedience through what he suffered" (5:8) and has "tasted death for every one" (2:9), is none other than the One "through whom also [God] created the world" (1:2; cf. 11:3), who upholds "the universe by his word of power" (1:3). "Appointed the heir of all things," he has "in these last days" (1:2) inaugurated "a kingdom that cannot be shaken" (12:28; cf. 9:26b-28).

The old pattern is taken up into the new context by the Word made flesh. Jesus calls people from their homes — to follow him (Mark 1:16-20; 8:34-38; Matt. 8:18-22 = Luke 9:57-62; Matt. 10:34-39), and he will accompany his apostles when they scatter to the ends of the earth in order to make disciples for him from every nation (Matt. 28:16-20; cf. Acts 1:8). In the Sermon on the Mount (Matt. 5–7), Jesus reveals the character of God and sets forth the deepest meaning of the law — with "I say unto you." He warns of judgment (Matt. 10:14f.; 11:20-24; Luke 10:10-15; Matt. 12:36f.; Matt. 24:37-44 = Luke 17:26-30; John 5:22-29; 16:8-11), invites sinners to repentance (Matt. 4:17 = Mark 1:15; Luke 5:32), and pronounces forgiveness (Matt. 9:2-8 = Mark 2:3-12 = Luke 5:18-26). He bequeaths a "new covenant" (Matt. 26:28; Mark 14:24; Luke 22:20; 1 Cor. 11:25), issues a "new commandment" (John 13:34; 15:12), and promises the divine indwelling that will enable his people to keep it (John 14:15-24). Accomplishing an "exodus" at Jerusalem (Luke 9:31; John 19:30), he rises from the dead and offers new life. The wind and the waves have obeyed his voice (Matt. 8:23-27 = Mark 4:36-41 = Luke 8:22-25), and the risen Jesus tells his disciples where to catch fish (John 21:1-14). The eschatological work of the Word made flesh is to bring "a new creation" (2 Cor. 5:17; cf. Rom. 4:16-25; 8:11; 1 Cor. 15:42-56).

Having thus identified *the Word* that was made flesh, we may now look more closely at the fact that the divine Word was *made flesh*.

2. . . . MADE FLESH

That the divine Word should have been made flesh is a sheer act of God's grace, but retrospectively we may find it at least congruous with the corporeal forms through which God spoke according to the Old Testament. If the higher Greek philosophy was suspicious of materiality, Hebrew faith by contrast confessed the material creation as made by God. As such, it could serve as the vehicle of God's self-communication, which was received by human beings in all their bodily existence. We may observe this by examining the way in which the scriptural writers use terminology with the Hebrew root *dbr*.

Expressions with the root *dbr* are usually translated by "word" when they occur as nouns and by "to speak" when they occur as verbs. But Old Testament usage of *dbr* covers a range of meaning more complex than simply "spoken words." *Dbr*-expressions can designate also a thing, an act, an event. Thus Genesis 15:1 reads: "After these things *(dᵉbarim)* the word of the LORD *(dᵉbar-YHWH)* came to Abram." *Dᵉbarim* are not only spoken but done: "The servant told Isaac all the things *(kal-ha-dᵉbarim)* he had done" (Gen. 24:66). In the Historical Books, a whole reign can be described as the "words" or "deeds" of that king, meaning "all that took place" while he ruled (for example, the "acts of Solomon [*dibre Sᵉlomoh*]," 1 Kings 11:41). Saul, Jonathan, and David know about "the king's business" or "matter" *(dᵉbar ha-melek)* (1 Sam. 21:8/9; cf. 20:39; 21:2/3).

In line with that linguistic usage, a prophet may *see* the "word" of the Lord, and what he sees is an object or a gesture. Thus Amos "saw" words concerning Israel (1:1): the Lord "showed" him locusts eating the grass of the land (7:1), a devouring fire (7:4), a plumb line held by the Lord himself (7:7), a basket of late summer fruit (8:1);[5] Amos saw the

---

5. The Lord makes wordplays: the summer fruit *(qayits)* signifies that the end *(qets)* has come upon Israel.

Lord standing on the altar, saying, "Smite the capitals" (9:1). According to Jeremiah 1:11-14:

> The word of the LORD *(dᵉbar-YHWH)* came to me, saying, "Jeremiah, what do you see?" And I said, "I see a rod of almond." Then the LORD said to me, "You have seen well, for I am watching over my word *(dᵉbari)* to perform it."[6] The word of the LORD came to me a second time, saying, "What do you see?" And I said, "I see a boiling pot, facing away from the north." Then the LORD said to me, "Out of the north evil shall break forth upon all the inhabitants of the land."

Clearly, *dbr,* even the *dᵉbar-YHWH,* carries a certain material density. The "Word of God" took solid flesh as Jesus of Nazareth.

To speak of Jesus Christ as "the Word of God" is to name his person. This person came to expression in the thick texture of his human life. His "flesh" is constituted not only by his body, born of Mary, but by an entire range of words and deeds, by his interactions with his historical contemporaries, and by the events which surround and mark his career. Discussion of his spoken words will be reserved for the next chapter, under the heading "Listen to Him." To catch the whole scope precisely of the *incarnation,* however, we need to note that Jesus performed healings by words or gestures or a complex of both: he touched the leper and said, "Be clean" (Matt. 8:2f. = Mark 1:40f. = Luke 5:12f.); he touched the hand of Peter's mother-in-law, and the fever left her (Matt. 8:14f. = Mark 1:30f.; cf. Luke 4:38f., where Jesus "rebuked the fever"); he took Jairus's daughter, given up for dead, by the hand, and the girl arose (Matt. 9:25; cf. Mark 5:41 = Luke 8:54, where Jesus told her to "arise"); he touched the eyes of two blind men, saying, "According to your faith be it done to you," and their eyes were opened (Matt. 9:27-29), a cure he performed also on other occasions (Matt. 20:29-34; Mark 10:46-52; Luke 18:35-43; John 9:1-7); he told a man to stretch out his withered hand, and it was restored (Matt. 12:10-13 = Mark 3:1-5 = Luke 6:6-10).

Moreover, Jesus did not only tell parables but he also enacted them. Sometimes he interpreted these gestures by the spoken word; at other times he appears to have let the actions speak for themselves. Seeing great crowds as "sheep without a shepherd" (Mark 6:34), he fed large numbers with a few loaves and fish (Matt. 14:13-21 = Mark 6:31-44 = Luke 9:10-17; Matt.

6. Again, a pun: *shaqed* (almond) and *shoqed* (watching).

15:32-38 = Mark 8:1-9; cf. John 6:1-14, which is followed by an expository discourse on the bread of life). At the wedding feast in Cana, he turned water into wine (John 2:1-11). As his death drew near, he rode into Jerusalem on a donkey (Matt. 21:1-11 = Mark 11:1-10 = Luke 19:29-38), and he was hailed as coming in the name of the Lord (though his disciples did not understand this until later, says John 12:12-16). He cleansed the temple that had become "a den of robbers" instead of "a house of prayer" (Matt. 21:12f. = Mark 11:15-17 = Luke 19:45f.), coupling his action (according to John 2:13-22) with a promise, understood only later, to replace the temple with his own risen body. On the eve of his passion, Jesus washed the feet of his disciples, explaining his action as "an example," that they ought all the more "to wash one another's feet" (John 13:1-17). That same night, he gave them the bread as his body and the cup of wine as his blood (Matt. 26:26-29 = Mark 14:22-25; Luke 22:14-20; 1 Cor. 11:23-26).

Under the solidity of his flesh, we have to reckon also those focal events which marked out the life and history of Jesus as the incarnate Word. Jesus was conceived and carried and born of a maiden mother (Luke 1:31, 42; 2:7; Matt. 1:25). He was baptized in the waters of the Jordan by John (Matt. 3:13-17; Mark 1:9f.; Luke 3:21f.; cf. John 1:29-34). He was transfigured on the mountain, so that "his face shone like the sun" (Matt. 17:1-8 = Mark 9:2-8 = Luke 9:28-36). He underwent a passion that culminated in his crucifixion (Matt. 27:1-50; Mark 15:1-37; Luke 23:1-46; John 18:28–19:30). His body was taken down from the cross and buried in a tomb (Matt. 27:57-61; Mark 15:42-47; Luke 23:50-56; John 19:38-42). On the third day the tomb was found empty, and he was seen in his risen body by several groups of his disciples (Matt. 28; Mark 16; Luke 24; John 20–21; 1 Cor. 15:3-8). He ascended to heaven (Luke 24:51; Acts 1:9-11).

Given this utterly corporeal character of the human life lived by the Word of God for the redemption of the world, it is entirely congruous that he should choose to keep coming to his church by material means for the sake of our salvation.

3. THE WORD OF LIFE

The First Letter of John (1:1-3) harks back to the prologue of John's Gospel in describing the continuing conveyance of the Word of life:

That which was from the beginning, which we have heard, which we have seen with our eyes, which we have looked upon and touched with our hands, concerning the word of life — the life was made manifest, and we saw it, and testify to it, and proclaim to you the eternal life which was with the Father and was made manifest to us — that which we have seen and heard we proclaim also to you, so that you may have fellowship with us; and our fellowship is with the Father and with his Son Jesus Christ.

Writing under the title "The Word of Life," the Joint Commission between the Roman Catholic Church and the World Methodist Council has placed this Johannine text at the head of its entire treatment of the theme of revelation as it seeks to set theological perspectives for the doctrinal agreement that will be needed to bring about "full communion in faith, mission, and sacramental life." The Commission expounds the biblical passage in this way:

This sacred text starts from the particularity of the God of Israel's self-revelation in Christ: the divine Word, who was in the beginning with God and has led the history of the chosen people, has been made flesh in Jesus. That sheer self-gift of God is a word of life to humankind: God so loved the world that he gave his only Son, that whoever believes in him should not perish but have eternal life. In Christ, in his words, his deeds, his entire existence, God has been revealed in audible, visible, palpable form; God has been received by human ears, eyes, and hands. What the first believers have taken in, they then bear witness to and transmit, for the message spreads the offer of a life shared with God. The modes of the announcement will appropriately reflect, echo and hand on what was seen, heard and touched in the embodied manifestation of God in Jesus Christ. Accepted in faith, the words, signs and actions of the Gospel will become the means of communion with the one true God, Father, Son, and Holy Spirit. The divine life into which the Spirit introduces believers will be a common life, as each transmits and receives what is always the gift of God.

In this passage from Scripture, we find already indicated all the main themes of the Commission's deliberations and report: the gift of the revelation of the Triune God; the human response of faith; the proclamation, as missionary message, of what has been received in faith; word and sacrament as the intelligible and tangible means of grace;

communion with the Triune God as the very life of the Church, the community of believers which in God's name offers to the world the salvation that the Church already anticipates with joy.[7]

Although the theological frameworks in which it is expressed may vary, it is a commonplace in the historic Christian faith that Christ addresses himself, and indeed gives himself, to his people by spoken words and by sacramental actions. Take, for example, Calvin in the Geneva Catechism. Christians need to "hear" the Holy Scriptures and "to attend with special regularity the gatherings where the doctrine of salvation is expounded in the company of the faithful"; for "through the gospel, according to Paul, Christ is communicated to us (1 Corinthians 1:21)." To the preaching are joined the sacraments. Given our "earthly body," they function as "symbols or mirrors, to exhibit to us the appearance of spiritual and heavenly things in a kind of earthly way. . . . It is to our interest that all our senses be exercised in the promises of God, by which they are the better confirmed to us." Divinely instituted, the sacraments get their virtue entirely from the will of God to use them as "instruments" of the Spirit's work. They are beneficial only when received in faith, which in turn they strengthen. Under those conditions, the sacraments are "an aid, by which we may be directed straight to Christ, and from him seek salvation and real felicity." Christ "communicates his benefits to us in no other way than in making himself ours." In the Lord's Supper, there are "two things," which are related as "sign" and "reality": first, "the bread and the wine, which are seen by our eyes, handled by our hands, and perceived by the taste; and second, Christ, by whom our souls are inwardly fed, as by their own proper nourishment." And "even the resurrection of the body is there confirmed to us, as by a given pledge, since the body itself shares in the symbol of life."[8]

---

7. Joint Commission between the Roman Catholic Church and the World Methodist Council, *The Word of Life: A Statement on Revelation and Faith* (Lake Junaluska, N.C.: World Methodist Council, 1996), nos. 2-3.

8. See *Calvin: Theological Treatises*, ed. and trans. J. K. S. Reid (Philadelphia: Westminster, 1954), pp. 88-139 (in particular pp. 129-39). I am reading Calvin in the strongly sacramental way favored by Brian A. Gerrish, *Grace and Gratitude: The Eucharistic Theology of John Calvin* (Minneapolis: Fortress, 1993). It must be admitted that it is possible to find in Calvin a weaker sense of material instrumentality. Less surprisingly perhaps, Martin

The liturgical movement of the twentieth century has both reflected and helped to bring about an ecumenical convergence, in theory and in practice, toward a principal Sunday assembly in which the Scriptures are read and proclaimed and the Lord's Meal is celebrated. Documentation of the convergence is found in the Faith and Order text of the World Council of Churches on *Baptism, Eucharist, and Ministry* and in the authorized responses of some two hundred churches to this so-called Lima text.[9] The highly positive reply of the United Methodist Church affirms, of this "central act of the Church's worship," that "God's effectual word is there revealed, proclaimed, heard, seen, and tasted."[10] As we have already noted, the First Letter of John (not to mention John Calvin) would have authorized also the verb "touched"; and, greatly daring, the Second Letter to the Corinthians might even, as we shall note later, justify the verb "smelled."

The next three chapters will, in fact, be devoted to demonstrating in more detail, from the Scriptures and from the traditional liturgies and practices of the church, how Christ the Word addresses and gives himself to us in our fivefold sensate existence for our salvation. First, we are summoned to "hear him," for

> He speaks, and, listening to his voice,
> New life the dead receive,
> The mournful, broken hearts rejoice,
> The humble poor believe.[11]

Luther held that things and gestures may become spiritual through use by the Word, the Spirit, and faith — "be it seeing, hearing, speaking, touching, begetting, bearing, eating, drinking, or anything else": so in his 1527 treatise "That These Words of Christ, 'This Is My Body,' Still Stand Firm," in *Luther's Works*, vol. 37, ed. R. H. Fischer (Philadelphia: Muhlenberg, 1961), p. 92. On corporeality in the Lutheran tradition, see Oswald Bayer, *Leibliches Wort: Reformation und Neuzeit im Konflikt* (Tübingen: Mohr, 1992).

9. See *Baptism, Eucharist, and Ministry,* Faith and Order Paper no. 111 (Geneva: World Council of Churches, 1982); *Churches Respond to BEM: Official Responses to the "Baptism, Eucharist, and Ministry" Text,* ed. Max Thurian, 6 vols. (Geneva: WCC, 1986-88); and *Baptism, Eucharist, and Ministry, 1982-1990: Report on the Process and Responses,* Faith and Order Paper no. 149 (Geneva: WCC, 1990).

10. *Churches Respond to BEM,* vol. 2 (1986), pp. 177-99, in particular p. 188.

11. From the hymn by Charles Wesley familiar as "O for a Thousand Tongues to Sing"; extracted from "Glory to God, and Praise and Love," which was published in John and Charles Wesley, *Hymns and Sacred Poems* (London, 1740).

Then we shall be invited to "taste and see the goodness of the Lord." Used traditionally as a verse to accompany the Holy Communion, the psalmist's words also provoke reflection on the visual communication of Christ and his gospel, so comprehensively intended:

> O that the world might taste and see
> The riches of his grace;
> The arms of love that compass me
> Would all mankind embrace.[12]

For, finally, the "fragrance" of the gospel, to speak with the apostle Paul, is that of Christ, whom the Evangelists show so generous in extending his saving "touch." None of this attention to the corporeal character of Christ and his gospel should detract from either their rationality and intelligibility or their rootage in the transcendent mystery of God, and these aspects will be thematically acknowledged in the last chapter of this half of the book.

We are not yet, however, quite ready for all that. After having thus far concentrated on the corporeality of Christ as the Word of God, we now must call corresponding attention to the carnality of those into whose condition he entered and enters.

4. RECEIVED BY THE SENSES

God's revelation is always received, as Saint Thomas Aquinas notes, "after the manner of the receiver."[13] Humans are embodied creatures; and, while we are more than our senses, we receive through our senses.

> The hearing ear and the seeing eye,
> the LORD has made them both. (Prov. 20:12)

12. From Charles Wesley's "Jesus! The Name High Over All," published in Charles Wesley, *Hymns and Sacred Poems* (Bristol, 1749).

13. It is a constant axiom, with minimal variations in the formulation, throughout Thomas's *Commentary on the Sentences,* his *Summa Theologiae,* and the *Quaestiones Disputatae:* "Quod in aliquo recipitur, recipitur in eo per [*or:* secundum] modum recipientis."

In the course of his fundamental treatment of signification in *De Doctrina Christiana*,[14] Saint Augustine gives prominence to the sense of sight and, even more, to the sense of hearing. A nod, a motion of the hand, an actor's gestures are all "signs given to sight," as also "banners and military standards visibly indicate the will of the captains": "all these things are like so many visible words." The trumpet, the flute, and the harp "make sounds which are not only pleasing but also significant"; but it is above all "words" which "pertain to the ears." Turning to the other senses, Augustine gives examples from the Gospels, to each of which we shall ourselves later revert: "Our Lord gave a sign with the smell of the ointment with which his feet were anointed; and the taste of the sacrament of his body and blood signified what he wished; and when the woman was healed by touching the hem of his garment, something was signified." While all five senses are thus recognized, the signs which have superiority for Augustine are "words," whether spoken or written: "I could express the meaning of all signs of the type here touched upon in words, but I would not be able at all to make the meanings of words clear by these signs." Accordingly, while the sensual range of semiotics is broad, the character of humankind as a linguistic animal is to be maintained in a way which is both more precise and more comprehensive.

Since embodiment belongs to our very nature as human beings, it is natural that our Creator should address us by way of our physical senses. But our senses are affected by our fallen condition, which is expressed in what the apostle Paul pejoratively calls "the flesh."[15] Saint Athanasius describes our plight as a misdirection of the senses: human beings "have turned their eyes no longer upward but downward"; "having rejected the contemplation of God," they "seek about for God in nature and in the world of sense, feigning gods for themselves"; they "fix their senses" on creatures rather than the Creator. Into this condition, the Word of God has come redemptively: "Willing to profit humankind, he sojourns here as a man, taking to himself a body like theirs, from things of earth, so that they who would not know him from his providence and rule over all

14. In particular, Augustine, *De Doctrina Christiana* II.3.4 (Migne, *Patrologia Latina* 34:37-38). Translation from *St. Augustine: On Christian Doctrine,* trans. D. W. Robertson, Jr. (New York: Macmillan, 1958), pp. 35f.; cf. *Augustine: De Doctrina Christiana,* ed. and trans. R. P. H. Green (Oxford: Clarendon Press, 1995), pp. 58-61.

15. See, for the various usages of "flesh" in Saint Paul, W. David Stacey, *The Pauline View of Man* (London: Macmillan; New York: St. Martin's Press, 1956), and for the present usage in particular, pp. 160-73.

16

things, may even from the works done by his body know the Word of God which is in the body, and through him the Father." His method and purpose was to make men "center their senses on himself," for by this "transfer to him" they then would be able to share in the restoration and renewal that came by way of his death and resurrection.[16]

The need for the rectification of our senses, and God's gift of it, has liturgically been recognized in the multiform anointings of some traditional rites of Christian initiation. An early example may be taken from the postbaptismal chrismation as described and expounded by Saint Cyril of Jerusalem:

> First you were anointed on the forehead so that you might lose the shame which Adam, the first transgressor, everywhere bore with him, and so that you might "with unveiled face behold the glory of the Lord" [2 Cor. 3:18]. Next you were anointed on the ears, that you might acquire ears which will hear those divine mysteries of which Isaiah said, "The Lord has given me an ear to hear with" [Isa. 50:4 (LXX)]. Again, the Lord Jesus in the gospel said, "He who has ears to hear, let him hear" [Matt. 11:15]. Then you were anointed on the nostrils, so that after receiving the divine chrism you might say "We are the aroma of Christ to God among those who are being saved" [2 Cor. 2:15]. After that, you were anointed on the chest, so that "having put on the breastplate of righteousness, you might stand against the wiles of the devil" [Eph. 6:11, 14]. Just as Christ after his baptism and visitation by the Holy Spirit went out and successfully wrestled with the enemy, so you also, after your holy baptism and sacramental anointing, put on the armor of the Holy Spirit, confront the power of the enemy, and reduce it, saying "I can do all things in Christ who strengthens me" [Phil. 4:13].[17]

This beginning of the transformation of our senses is needed for our response to God's self-gift in revelation and redemption. The response bears at least three facets. It is, first, a return offering of ourselves to God. "Present

---

16. Athanasius, *On the Incarnation of the Word,* especially chs. 13-16 (Migne, *Patrologia Graeca* 25:117-25; hereafter cited as *PG*).

17. Cyril of Jerusalem, *Mystagogical Catecheses* III.4 (Migne, *PG* 33:1092), quoted from Edward Yarnold, *The Awe-Inspiring Rites of Initiation: Baptismal Homilies of the Fourth Century* (Slough, Buckinghamshire: St. Paul Publications, 1972), pp. 81f.

your bodies," says Saint Paul, "as a living sacrifice, holy and acceptable to God, which is your *logikē latreia*" (Rom. 12:1), that is, "your worship according to the *Logos.*" As the "minds" of believers are "renewed" through conformity to "the will of God" (Rom. 12:2), so their bodies become "temples of the Holy Spirit" dwelling within them (1 Cor. 6:19f.). Second, love toward God is matched by love toward the neighbor, which finds expression in the onward transmission of the gospel in mission and service. This means that our bodily capacities, by which we ourselves have received the gifts of God, are in turn employed to mediate the gifts to others: as hearers of the Word, we now speak it; as those who have tasted the goodness of the Lord, we minister to the nourishment of others; as those who have glimpsed the glory of the Lord, we endeavor to show it to others; as those anointed with the gospel's fragrance, we become the aroma of Christ to others; as those touched by Christ's healing hand, we seek to extend a blessing to others in their needs. And third: the gradual transformation of our senses prepares us for the final resurrection when we shall start to enjoy those things which, even now, our eyes have not seen, our ears heard, nor our hearts conceived, but which God has in store for those who love him (cf. 1 Cor. 2:9).

The transformation of our senses by the Word of God takes on a particular poignancy in our contemporary North American and West European culture. We live in a very sensate and sensualist society. We are in some ways absorbed in our senses, a people defined by materialism and sexuality. Yet in other ways we are curiously detached from our bodies, as though we were not really affected by what happens to us in our bodies or what we do in them. The contradiction between indulging our senses and disowning our bodies is only an apparent one. If our bodies are not us, then we are not responsible in and for them; and that irresponsibility may assume the character either of license or, indeed, of withdrawal. The same phenomenon occurred in the gnosticism of the second century. Saint Irenaeus countered its threat to Christianity by retelling the authentic biblical tale of the divine Word's history *ad extra* as the single sweep of universal creation, the making of humankind, the incarnation in Jesus the Christ, the constitution of the church, the institution and practice of the sacraments, and the awaited resurrection of the body.[18] Having emphasized that the bread and cup of the Lord's Supper are "part of that creation to which we belong," made by "the Word through whom the tree bears fruit

---

18. For an introduction, see Jacques Fantino, *La Théologie d'Irénée. Lecture des Écritures en réponse à l'exégèse gnostique* (Paris: Éditions du Cerf, 1994).

and the fountains flow and the earth yields first the blade, then the ear, then the full corn in the ear,"[19] Irenaeus in a typical passage makes the connections between our embodied condition, the flesh and blood of Christ, the Eucharist, and the new creation of the end times:

> Since, then, the cup and the bread receive the Word of God and become the eucharist of the body and blood of Christ, and from them the substance of our flesh grows and subsists: how can they [the Gnostics] deny that the flesh is capable of the gift of God which is eternal life, that flesh which is fed by the body and blood of the Lord and is a member of him? For blessed Paul says in his Letter to the Ephesians: "We are members of his body, of his flesh and of his bones." He does not say this of a spiritual and invisible sort of man (for a spirit has no flesh and bones), but of man in his real constitution of flesh and nerves and blood. It is this which receives nourishment from the cup which is his blood, and growth from the bread which is his body. And as the wood of the vine planted into the ground bears fruit in its season, and the grain of wheat falls into the ground and molders and is raised manifold by the Spirit of God who upholds all things; and afterwards through the wisdom of God they come to be used by men, and having received the Word of God become the eucharist which is the body and blood of Christ: so also our bodies, nourished by the eucharist, and put into the ground, and dissolved therein, will rise in their season, the Word of God giving them resurrection to the glory of God the Father.[20]

Perhaps the best execution of the equivalent intellectual task in our time has been that of Hans Urs von Balthasar. In his description of "the pattern of redemption," the "theological aesthetics" comes nearest to providing the comprehensive framework into which the considerations of the next few chapters need to be set.[21] Selectively but characteristically, my aim is to show from the Scriptures and from the Tradition of the church, especially in its liturgical manifestations, how the Word of God addresses us through our senses, revealingly, judgingly, redeemingly, and thus provides our senses and us with the schooling that we sorely need at this time and place.

19. Irenaeus, *Against the Heresies* IV.17.5; IV.18.4 (Migne, *PG* 7:1023; 1027).
20. Irenaeus, *Against the Heresies* V.2.3 (*PG* 7:1125-27).
21. For an introduction, see Edward T. Oakes, *Pattern of Redemption: The Theology of Hans Urs von Balthasar* (New York: Continuum, 1994).

2

Listen to Him

Perhaps the greatest multimedia event of all time was the transfiguration of our Lord, traditionally located on Mount Tabor. The visual predominated, as you will see; but notice also the tactile. It is, however, the auditory that we shall pick up on in this chapter. Here is the familiar story, in Saint Matthew's version (17:1-8):

> And after six days Jesus took with him Peter and James and John his brother, and led them up a high mountain apart. And he was transfigured before them, and his face shone like the sun, and his garments became white as light. And behold, there appeared to them Moses and Elijah, talking with him. And Peter said to Jesus, "Lord, it is well that we are here; if you wish, I will make three booths here, one for you and one for Moses and one for Elijah." He was still speaking, when lo, a bright cloud overshadowed them, and a voice from the cloud said, "This is my beloved Son, with whom I am well pleased; listen to him." When the disciples heard this, they fell on their faces, and were filled with awe. But Jesus came and touched them, saying, "Rise, and have no fear." And when they lifted up their eyes, they saw no one but Jesus only.

Our interest lies not so much in the remarks of Peter, who seems to have found himself at a loss, nor even in the conversation, unreported in its contents, between Jesus and the prophets of Mount Sinai and Mount Carmel. It is the voice from the clouds that chiefly captures our attention. The Father takes up what he had said at the baptism of Jesus — "This is

20

my beloved Son, with whom I am well pleased" — and now adds: "Listen to him!"

1. The Words of the WORD

Much of the Gospels is, in fact, occupied with the spoken words of the Word made flesh. As you will know, there has been a revival of interest in "Q," the hypothetical "source *(Quelle)*" postulated by nineteenth-century German Protestant scholarship in order to account for closely similar passages in Matthew and Luke that have no equivalent in Mark and are therefore underivable from that supposedly first of the Synoptic Gospels. Whether in oral or in written form, "Q" or "Proto-Q" or "Ur-Q" — or whatever stage they are at in the so-called Jesus Seminar — is reckoned by many to give us our earliest access to Jesus, and it is predominantly a "sayings-source" (called indeed by some scholars at one time "the *logia*").[1] The same would be true of the uncanonical Gospel of Thomas, which is improbably favored by a few as an even older source of knowledge about Jesus.[2] However all that may be, the canonical Gospels as we have them contain many reported sayings and discourses of Jesus.

There are, for instance, the aphorisms that often (though not always) constitute the punch line of what the form critics called "pronouncement

1. The "Jesus Seminar" is composed of a group of North American scholars who try to determine, by so-called historical-critical principles, the degrees of authenticity attaching to the reported words and deeds of Jesus in the canonical Gospels; see *The Five Gospels: The Search for the Authentic Words of Jesus* (New York: Macmillan, 1993). The Jesus Seminar will probably not lie down too readily, even though it has been demolished by Luke Timothy Johnson, *The Real Jesus: The Misguided Quest for the Historical Jesus and the Truth of the Traditional Gospels* (San Francisco: Harper, 1996). The approach to the Gospels represented in the present book operates rather on the following principles: (1) the canonical Gospels offer basically trustworthy accounts of Jesus and his impact; (2) the diversity in the Gospels is better read with an eye or an ear to harmony than to dissonance; (3) the different literary and rhetorical genres of the gospel materials are to be respected; (4) there should be no *a priori* exclusion of "the miraculous" as the Enlightenment defined it in order to dismiss it.

2. Particular importance is attached to the apocryphal Gospel of Thomas by, e.g., John Dominic Crossan, *The Historical Jesus: The Life of a Mediterranean Jewish Peasant* (San Francisco: Harper, 1991), which the dust jacket claims to be "the first comprehensive determination of who Jesus was, what he did, what he said."

stories": such pithy, provocative sayings include "You cannot serve God and mammon" (Matt. 6:24 = Luke 16:13), "Judge not, that you be not judged" (Matt. 7:1 = Luke 6:37), "Whoever does the will of my Father in heaven is my brother, and sister, and mother" (Matt. 12:50 = Mark 3:35 = Luke 8:21), "It is easier for a camel to go through the eye of a needle than for a rich man to enter the kingdom of God" (Matt. 19:24 = Mark 10:25 = Luke 18:25), "Render therefore to Caesar the things that are Caesar's, and to God the things that are God's" (Matt. 22:21). Then there are the parables that highlight features of God's impending reign and call for decision in the face of it. There are teaching discourses, concerning either the character of God and the human conduct that appropriately corresponds to it (as in the Sermon on the Mount) or the person of Jesus and his role in the salvation of the world (as in the Fourth Gospel). A few prayers of Jesus are recorded (Matt. 11:25f. = Luke 10:21; Mark 14:36 = Matt. 26:39, 42, 44 = Luke 22:42; Luke 23:34, 46; John 11:41; 17:1-26), and he appears to have had the habit of withdrawing in order to pray (Mark 1:35; Matt. 14:23 = Mark 6:46; Luke 5:16; 6:12; 9:28). Jesus uttered prophecies, as concerning the fall of Jerusalem (Matt. 24 = Mark 13 = Luke 21:5-36) and his own passion, death, and resurrection (Matt. 16:21 = Mark 8:31 = Luke 9:22; Matt. 17:22f. = Mark 9:31; Matt. 20:17-19 = Mark 10:32-34; Luke 17:25; 18:31). He blessed (Matt. 5:1-12; Luke 6:20-22), and he chided (Luke 6:24-26; 11:42-52; Matt. 23:13-36). He pronounced forgiveness (Matt. 9:2-8 = Mark 2:3-12 = Luke 5:18-26; 7:36-50). He rebuked and expelled demons (Mark 1:23-27 = Luke 4:33-36; Matt. 8:28-32 = Mark 5:1-13 = Luke 8:26-33). His healings employed words that were so memorable they were preserved in Aramaic ("Ephphatha," Mark 7:34; "Talitha cumi," Mark 5:41); and his voice raised the widow's son at Nain (Luke 7:14f.) and called Lazarus forth from the tomb (John 11:43; 12:17). Jesus summoned people to follow him (Matt. 4:18-22 = Mark 1:16-20; Matt. 9:9 = Mark 2:14 = Luke 5:27f.). He conversed with his disciples (Matt. 13:10-23, 36-43; Matt. 16:5-12 = Mark 8:14-21; Matt. 16:13-20 = Mark 8:27-30 = Luke 9:18-22) and commissioned them to speak and act in his name (Matt. 10:1-42; Luke 9:1-6; 10:1-20). Jesus instituted rites and practices (Matt. 26:26-29 = Mark 14:22-25 = Luke 22:14-20; Matt. 28:19; John 13:14).

In the Fourth Gospel there is a particularly close identification between the Word and his words.[3] According to John 6:68f., Simon Peter

---

3. There is no need to limit oneself here to a study of the occurrence of the term *rhēmata* (words, sayings). All the vocabulary of speech comes into account.

answered Jesus on one occasion: "Lord, to whom shall we go? You have the words of eternal life; and we have believed, and have come to know, that you are the Holy One of God." R. Bultmann comments:

> His words are utterances about himself; *for his word is identical with himself.* What is said of his word is also said of himself: his words are "life," they are "truth" (6:63; 17:17); but so is he himself — "I am the way, and the truth, and the life" (14:6). Whoever hears his word and believes Him who sent him has Life (5:24), but that is what he himself is — "I am the resurrection and the life; he who believes in me, though he die, yet shall he live" (11:25). His "words" (12:48; 17:8), his "testimony" (3:11, 32f.), must be "accepted" — so must he (1:12; 5:43; cf. 13:20). To reject him is identical with not accepting his words (12:48). That his own "abide" in him and he in them means the same thing as that his words "abide" in them (15:4-7). He is the judge (5:22, 27) — so is his word (12:48). No wonder, then, that the evangelist can confer upon him for his pre-existent period the mythological title: Word *(Logos)!*[4]

Moreover, there is in the Fourth Gospel a close identification between the words of Jesus and his works. Thus John 8:28: "When you have lifted up the Son of man, then you will know that I am he, and that I *do* nothing on my own authority but *speak* thus as the Father taught me" (emphasis added; cf. 14:10). In John 15:22 and 15:24, the "speaking" of Jesus and his "doing" appear in parallel: "If I had not come and spoken to them, they would not have sin. . . . If I had not done among them the works which no one else did, they would not have sin." In John 17, work *(ergon)*, words *(rhēmata)*, and word *(logos)* appear as equivalents: "I glorified thee on earth, having accomplished the work which thou gavest me to do" (v. 4), "I have given them the words which thou gavest me" (v. 8), "I have given them thy word" (v. 14) — which is "truth" (v. 17)![5] Thus it may be said that there is a mutual coinherence between the words and the deeds of the divine Word made flesh. The

---

4. R. Bultmann, *Theology of the New Testament,* trans. Kendrick Grobel (New York: Scribner, 1952-55), 2:63f. Bultmann oddly refuses to find in "the words of Jesus in John" any "instruction in christology" or the "metaphysics of his person"; he does, however, allow that his *deeds* show him to be the salvation-bringer (cf. John 5:36; 10:24f.).

5. Cf. Bultmann, *Theology of the New Testament,* 2:60f.

spoken words illuminate the works — and indeed the Work that he performs and is. The deeds enact his words — and even the Word that he brings and is.

This coinherence allows us to say that what the Word speaks is an effective word. It draws its strength from the fact that Jesus himself, his words, and his deeds are an announcement of the dawning reign of God (Origen calls him "*autobasileia,* the kingdom in person").[6] When messengers come from the imprisoned John the Baptist asking whether Jesus is the Christ, Jesus replies: "Go and tell John what you hear and see: the blind receive their sight and the lame walk, lepers are cleansed and the deaf hear, and the dead are raised up, and the poor have good news preached to them" (Matt. 11:2-5; cf. Luke 7:18-22). But the spoken and enacted word of Jesus is not magic, producing its results among humans, as it were, automatically. It calls for faithful hearing (itself admittedly a gift) — within a context of understanding and meaning which it finds or creates (as will be developed in the final chapter of this half of the book). So, after telling the parable of the sower, Jesus says generally, "Whoever has ears to hear, let him hear," and to his disciples in particular: "To you it has been given to know the secrets of the kingdom of God" (Luke 8:4-10; cf. Matt. 13:1-11; Mark 4:1-11).

Since this eschatological message of Jesus engages the judgment and the salvation of the world, he makes provision for its spread. During his earthly ministry he sent his chosen twelve out to preach that "the kingdom of heaven is at hand" and to "heal the sick, raise the dead, cleanse lepers, cast out demons" (Matt. 10:5-7; cf. Luke 9:1f.), and again seventy others with a similar message (Luke 10:1, 9), saying to them, "He who hears you hears me, and he who rejects you rejects me, and he who rejects me rejects him who sent me" (Luke 10:16). After Christ's resurrection, this local mission became universalized: repentance and forgiveness of sins are to be preached far and wide (Luke 24:45-49; cf. John 20:21-23); his commissioned followers are to be his witnesses to the ends of the earth (Acts 1:8); they are to make disciples from all nations (Matt. 28:19; cf. Mark 13:10).

6. Origen, *Commentaries on Matthew* XIV.7, on Matt. 18:23, referring also to Matt. 5:3 (Migne, *Patrologia Graeca* 13:1197).

2. The Proclamation of the Gospel

The classical sequence of the missionary proclamation and the response to it is laid out by the apostle Paul in Romans 10:13-17:

> For, "every one who calls upon the name of the Lord will be saved" [Joel 2:32; cf. Acts 2:21]. But how are men to call upon him in whom they have not believed? And how are they to believe in him of whom they have never heard? And how are they to hear without a preacher? And how can men preach unless they are sent? As it is written, "How beautiful are the feet of those who preach good news!" [Isa. 52:7]. But they have not all obeyed the gospel; for Isaiah says, "Lord, who has believed what he has heard from us?" [Isa. 53:1; cf. John 12:38]. So faith comes from what is heard, and what is heard comes by the preaching of Christ.

Thus there is a Savior; the Savior commissions the preacher; the preacher brings the message; the message may evoke a response of faith; the believers call on the name of the Lord, who is the Savior.

Since "faith comes by hearing," the spoken word is clearly indispensable;[7] but it is no ordinary word: "When you received the word of God which you heard from us, you accepted it not as the word of men but as what it really is, the word of God" (1 Thess. 2:13). In fact, "our gospel came to you not only in word, but also in power and in the Holy Spirit" (1 Thess. 1:5). And the positive response it elicits is also divinely empowered: "No one can say 'Jesus is Lord' except by the Holy Spirit" (1 Cor. 12:3). Both the preaching and the faith depend on the same Spirit who rests upon the Son and whom the incarnate Son promised to his followers. With that recognition of the role of the Holy Spirit in the process, we may now look more closely at the proclamation of the gospel, and then, in turn, at the response of faith.

The New Testament often uses the term *logos* (word) for the gospel proclaimed, which sometimes comes across in English translation as "mes-

---

7. *Hē pistis ex akouēs:* the RSV emphasizes the content ("faith comes from what is heard"), while other translations emphasize the process ("faith comes by hearing"). In any case, there is an intimate connection between the medium and the message. And what the RSV translates as "by the preaching of Christ" is literally "by the (spoken) word of Christ" *(dia rhēmatos Christou).*

25

sage." Preaching to Jews and God-fearers in Pisidian Antioch, Paul declares that the promise of a descendant to David has been fulfilled in Jesus the Savior, crucified and risen, through whom forgiveness of sins is proclaimed — and the apostle has been sent with "the word of this salvation" (Acts 13:16-41, in particular v. 26). In Ephesians 1:13, the "gospel of your salvation" is set in apposition to "the word of truth": having heard this, believers have been sealed with the promised Holy Spirit. The message can, therefore, also be called "the word of life," to which Christians hold fast (Phil. 2:16; cf. 1 John 1:1-3). It is such because it is first "the word of the cross" (1 Cor. 1:18) and so "the word of the reconciliation" that God has effected in Christ between the world and himself (2 Cor. 5:17-21, in particular v. 19).

The passage in 2 Corinthians makes of the apostles "ambassadors for Christ" (5:20). This creates a very close association, a kind of effective identity, between the content of the message and the proclamation of it, for the "word of reconciliation" includes the summons: "Be reconciled to God" (5:20). In language reminiscent of other passages concerning the "mystery" of God's saving purpose which has now been revealed in the incarnation of Christ and in the preaching about him (Rom. 16:25-27; 1 Cor. 2:7-10; Eph. 1:9f.; 3:1-21; Col. 1:24–2:3; 1 Tim. 3:16), Paul's letter to Titus speaks somewhat similarly of the "manifestation" of "the word" of divine salvation in a way that oscillates between the coming of Christ himself and the proclamation that the apostle has been commanded and entrusted to make (1:1-3; cf. 2:11-14; 3:4-7). A further instance of this dynamic relation between content and act is found in 1 Corinthians 9:14-18, which prompts Eduard Lohse to this comment: "Because the good news is effective proclamation, Paul uses the word *euangelion* not only to designate the content of the preaching but also to speak of the exercise of proclaiming, and thus to make clear that the gospel not only testifies to the event of salvation but is itself a saving event, entering into people's lives, transforming them, and creating communities of believers."[8] Lohse notes that the "word" of God is in fact characteristically linked by the New Testament writers with such verbs as "to announce" *(angellein)*, "to proclaim" *(kērussein)*, and "to bear witness" *(marturein)*, all of which indicate that

---

8. Eduard Lohse, "Deus dixit: Wort Gottes im Zeugnis des Alten und Neuen Testaments," in his *Die Einheit des Neuen Testaments: Exegetische Studien zur Theologie des Neuen Testaments* (Göttingen: Vandenhoeck & Ruprecht, 1973), pp. 20f.

"the content of the message that is announced is an event which reaches effectively into people's lives precisely through its proclamation."[9] The top and bottom of all this appears to be that Christ himself, now crucified and risen, speaks through his "ambassadors"; the proclamation of the gospel is a vehicle of his active presence.

This conviction, corresponding to the testimony of the New Testament writers, has been clearly expressed in the dogmatic tradition of the church. A famous marginal note to the Second Helvetic Confession (1566) ✓ declares: "Praedicatio verbi divini est verbum divinum."[10] The Lutheran Reformers affirm the ministerial pronouncement of forgiveness to be efficacious to the believer because the voice is in fact Christ's: "Hearing the Gospel and hearing absolution strengthens and consoles the conscience. Because God truly quickens through the Word, the keys truly forgive sin before Him, according to the statement, 'Whoever hears you, hears me' [Luke 10:16]."[11] Teaching on the nature of the liturgical assembly, the Second Vatican Council declares that Christ "is present in his word, since it is he himself who speaks when the Holy Scriptures are read in the Church."[12]

Liturgically, the spoken proclamation of the gospel has in fact been multiform. Sunday by Sunday, passages from the canonical Gospels have

---

9. Lohse, "Deus dixit," p. 11.

10. Second Helvetic Confession, 1.4: "The preaching of the Word of God *is* the Word of God"; see *La Confession helvétique postérieure,* ed. Jaques Courvoisier (Neuchâtel: Delachaux & Niestlé, 1944), p. 42.

11. Apology of the Augsburg Confession, XII.39f. (see *The Book of Concord: The Confessions of the Evangelical Lutheran Church,* trans. and ed. T. G. Tappert [Philadelphia: Fortress, 1959], p. 187). The Apology (VII-VIII.28, 47) also takes "Whoever hears you hears me" as a promise of Christ securing the church in the face even of unworthy ministers of grace through word and sacrament (Tappert, pp. 173, 177).

12. Constitution on the Sacred Liturgy, *Sacrosanctum Concilium,* 7. This paragraph enumerates several other vehicles of Christ's presence in the liturgical assembly: "the person of his minister," "the eucharistic species," the act of baptism (for, following Saint Augustine, "when anybody baptizes, it is really Christ who baptizes"), and "lastly, he is present when the Church prays and sings, for he has promised, 'where two or three are gathered together in my name there am I in the midst of them' (Matthew 18:20)." The Council stopped just short of mentioning also the sermon as a vehicle of Christ's presence (a draft had proposed saying "when the Holy Scriptures are read and expounded [*et explicantur*]"); see Franziskus Eisenbach, *Die Gegenwart Jesu Christi im Gottesdienst. Systematische Studien zur Liturgiekonstitution des II. Vatikanischen Konzils* (Mainz: Matthias-Grünewald-Verlag, 1982), in particular pp. 177-79, 497-501, 523-31.

been read by ministers from the pulpit or the ambo in the midst of the gathered community, and the congregational responses at the announcement and conclusion of the readings have hailed the Word made flesh, present anew in the Spirit:

> Glory to you, Lord Christ.
> Praise to you, Lord Christ.

In the homily, those appointed to preach in Christ's name have given voice to "the things of Christ" as they have heard the Holy Spirit declare them (cf. John 16:13-15). As part of the "proclamation of the Lord's death until he comes" (cf. 1 Cor. 11:26), the Eucharistic Prayer in the Lord's Supper has traditionally rehearsed the purpose and acts of God for our salvation, notably in its "preface," which can also be called a "praedicatio" (publication, proclamation) or a "contestatio" (witness, testimony, attestation).[13] A specially beautiful version is found in the "praeconium pascale" (a "praeconium" is a proclamation by the public crier or herald), which is sung in the Night of Easter to accompany the "Light of Christ":

> It is truly right
> that with full hearts and minds and voices
> we should praise the unseen God, the all-powerful Father,
> and his only Son, our Lord Jesus Christ.
> For Christ has redeemed us with his blood,
> and paid for us the price of Adam's sin
> to our eternal Father!
> This is our passover feast,
> when Christ, the true Lamb, is slain,
> whose blood consecrates the homes of all believers.
> This is the night when first you saved our ancestors:
> you freed the people of Israel from their slavery
> and led them dry-shod through the sea. . . .
> This is the night when Jesus Christ
> broke the chains of death

---

13. See J. A. Jungmann, *The Mass of the Roman Rite,* trans. F. A. Brunner (New York: Benziger, 1951-55), 2:102, 107, 115. "Praefatio" derives from *prae-fari,* to speak before an audience; so that "preface" is not to be taken in the sense of a mere preliminary.

and rose triumphant from the grave. . . .
May the Morning Star which never sets find this flame still burning:
Christ, that Morning Star, who came back from the dead,
and shed his peaceful light on all mankind,
your Son who lives and reigns for ever and ever.[14]

Such active presence of the divine Word is not, of course, confined to the liturgical assembly. It occurs first, indeed, in the missionary proclamation; for without evangelization there would be no gathered people for the worship of God. A hymn by the Anglican priest John Marriott (1780-1825) makes the connection between the creative Word and the spread of the gospel of Christ:

Thou whose almighty Word
Chaos and darkness heard,
And took their flight:
Hear us, we humbly pray,
And where the Gospel day
Sheds not its glorious ray,
Let there be light![15]

Just as the psalmist pictures Israel as publishing the name and deeds of the Lord among the nations (e.g., Pss. 9:1-2, 11; 40:5, 9-10), so the First Letter of Peter tells Christians, who now include Gentiles: "You are a chosen race, a royal priesthood, a holy nation, God's own people, that you may declare the wonderful deeds of him who called you out of darkness into his marvelous light" (2:9). As "witnesses to Christ" (cf. Acts 1:8), we have the promise of his presence in the task of making disciples from all nations, baptizing them in the name of the Father and of the Son and of the Holy Spirit and teaching them to observe all that Christ has commanded (Matt. 28:16-20).

14. *The Roman Missal,* trans. the International Commission on English in the Liturgy, quoted here from *The Sacramentary* (New York: Catholic Book Publishing Co., 1974), pp. 173-86.
15. The hymn was written about 1813 and published posthumously.

3. The Response of Faith

The classic response of faith, made in the Holy Spirit, is "Jesus is Lord" (1 Cor. 12:3). The process is more fully described earlier in the same chapter of Romans quoted above (10:8-13):

> What does [Scripture] say? The word is near you, on your lips and in your heart (that is, the word of faith which we preach); because, if you confess with your lips that Jesus is Lord and believe in your heart that God raised him from the dead, you will be saved. For man believes with his heart and so is justified, and he confesses with his lips and so is saved. The scripture says, "No one who believes in him will be put to shame." For there is no distinction between Jew and Greek; the same Lord is Lord of all and bestows his riches upon all who call upon him. For, "every one who calls upon the name of the Lord will be saved."

The parallelisms in this passage make clear that the confession of the lips is properly matched by faith in the heart. That is basic to whatever oral response is made to the proclamation of the gospel. And lip service is to be accompanied not only by faith in the heart but also by matching deeds: *akouē* ("hearing," or "what is heard") calls for *hupakouē* ("obedience"). These points are clear enough in both the Gospels (Matt. 7:21) and the Epistles (Heb. 13:15f.):

> "Not every one who says to me, 'Lord, Lord,' shall enter the kingdom of heaven, but he who does the will of my Father who is in heaven."

> Through [Christ] then let us continually offer up a sacrifice of praise to God, that is, the fruit of lips that acknowledge his name. Do not neglect to do good and to share what you have, for such sacrifices are pleasing to God.

With those safeguards in mind, we may concentrate for a moment on the spoken response of faith.

A passage in Paul's Second Letter to the Corinthians sets a paradigm (4:13-15). Echoing the psalmist (116:10), the apostle shows how the believer is immediately led to speak out, and this testimony becomes the vehicle whereby God's grace reaches to others, who then join the eucharistic chorus:

Since we have the same spirit of faith as he had who wrote, "I believed, and so I spoke," we too believe, and so we speak, knowing that he who raised the Lord Jesus will raise us also with Jesus and bring us with you into his presence. For it is all for your sake, so that as grace extends to more and more people it may increase thanksgiving, to the glory of God.

In another passage (Rom. 15:5-6), Saint Paul declares that the due praise of God requires that Christians live in harmony with one another:

May the God of steadfastness and encouragement grant you to live in such harmony with one another . . . that together you may with one voice glorify the God and Father of our Lord Jesus Christ.

The spoken response of faith finds corporate expression in the liturgy of the church. The classical rites of baptism all make the baptizands profess the Christian faith, whether through an affirmative response to the minister's questions ("Do you believe in God, the Father almighty . . . ? Do you believe in Jesus Christ, his only Son, our Lord . . . ? Do you believe in the Holy Spirit . . . ?") or in the repetition of the creed. The baptismal profession is recalled by every later recital of the creed, as in the Byzantine liturgy of the Eucharist where the introductory summons echoes Romans 15:5f.: "Let us love one another, that with one mind we may confess the Father, the Son, and the Holy Spirit." The eucharistic anaphora, or great thanksgiving, is the church's supreme "sacrifice of praise."

Then there is prayer, both individual and communal. The monastic office typically begins:

O Lord, open my lips:
And my mouth shall proclaim your praise.

Saint Benedict's *Rule* tells the monks that, as they "magnify the Lord at work in them" *(operantem in se Dominum magnificant)*, "mind and voice must be in agreement" *(ut mens nostra concordet voci nostrae).*[16] Such prayer

---

16. St. Benedict, *Rule for Monks,* prologue:30; and chap. 19:7; see Adalbert de Vogüé and Jean Neufville, *La Règle de saint Benoît* (Paris: Éditions du Cerf, 1971-72), 1:420; 2:536.

is in fact the privilege of all Christians and of every Christian, as Isaac Watts recognizes in "Jesus Shall Reign where'er the Sun":

> People and realms of every tongue
> Dwell on his love with sweetest song;
> And infant voices shall proclaim
> Their early blessings on his name.[17]

More will be said in chapter 5 about the response of song.

The spoken response of faith is not only liturgical or euchological in character; it also itself bears ethical dimensions. Here we may be advised by the Epistle of Saint James. God the Father, "of his own will," "brought us forth by the word of truth that we should be a kind of first fruits of his creatures" (1:18). We are to "be doers of the word, and not hearers only" (1:22). Piety is certainly active — "Religion that is pure and undefiled before God and the Father is this: to visit orphans and widows in their affliction, and to keep oneself unstained from the world" (1:27) — but one of the things that can undo piety is the tongue: "If any one thinks he is religious, and does not bridle his tongue but deceives his heart, this man's religion is vain" (1:26). Since the Letter of James is hardly a favorite with the compilers of lectionaries, it may be worth quoting here the entire passage in which the writer so graphically describes the member that is capable of so much evil as well as good (3:2-12, NRSV):

> Anyone who makes no mistakes in speaking is perfect, able to keep the whole body in check with a bridle. If we put bits into the mouths of horses to make them obey us, we guide their whole bodies. Or look at ships: though they are so large that it takes strong winds to drive them, yet they are guided by a very small rudder wherever the will of the pilot directs. So also the tongue is a small member, yet it boasts of great exploits. How great a forest is set ablaze by a small fire! And the tongue is a fire. The tongue is placed among our members as a world of iniquity; it stains the whole body, sets on fire the cycle of nature, and is itself set on fire by hell. For every species of beast and bird, of reptile and sea creature, can be tamed and has been tamed by the human species, but no one can tame the tongue — a restless evil, full of deadly poison.

17. Isaac Watts, *The Psalms of David, Imitated in the Language of the New Testament* (London, 1719).

With it we bless the Lord and Father, and with it we curse those who are made in the likeness of God. From the same mouth come blessing and cursing. My brothers and sisters, this ought not to be so. Does a spring pour forth from the same opening both fresh and brackish water? Can a fig tree, my brothers and sisters, yield olives, or a grapevine figs? No more can salt water yield fresh.

"Bless those who curse you," says Jesus, "pray for those who abuse you" (Luke 6:28). "Bless those who persecute you," says Paul, "bless and do not curse them" (Rom. 12:14). "Let him who boasts, boast of the Lord" (1 Cor. 1:31; 2 Cor. 10:17).

Having looked at the words of the Word, at the proclamation of the gospel, and at the spoken response of faith, we may bring this chapter on the oral and aural dimensions of our salvation to a close by some resumptive remarks that tie together the Word incarnate, the Word recorded, and the Word preached.

4. Savior, Scripture, and Sermon

It is a characteristic practice of Christian speech, particularly perhaps in the Augustinian tradition, to hold together — under "the Word of God" — the Word made flesh for our salvation, the Scriptures that bear original and permanent witness to the incarnate Word, and the sermons that bring home to each new generation the good news of our redemption as the Scriptures announce it. Thus Karl Barth, in setting out the governing criterion of his *Church Dogmatics,* wrote of "the Word of God in its threefold form" — "The Word of God as Preached," "The Written Word of God," and "The Revealed Word of God" — while maintaining "the unity of the Word of God." Equating "revelation" with "the Word became flesh," Barth expounds the relationships within the threefold form thus:

> The revealed Word of God we know only from the Scripture adopted by Church proclamation or the proclamation of the Church based on Scripture.
>
> The written Word of God we know only through the revelation which fulfils proclamation or through the proclamation fulfilled by revelation.

33

The preached Word of God we know only through the revelation attested in Scripture or the Scripture which attests revelation.[18]

Bearing in mind our special interest in the density of the *dabar* and the solidity of the flesh which the divine Word assumed, the connections between the Savior, the Scriptures, and the sermon may be traced along several lines: historical, pneumatological, anthropological, and liturgical.

Historically, the Scriptures record the promise of Christ's coming, the event of Christ's coming, and the earliest Christians' testimony to the advent of Christ. The scriptural record interweaves speech and act from those past times, event and interpretation. The firm location of Jesus Christ — his person, his words, his deeds, his death and resurrection — in the framework of creation and in the texture of human history is the condition of his saving relevance to us who live in succeeding generations. The speech-event of the sermon, resting on the scriptural witness and addressed to a particular assembly, is the classic way in which the gospel reaches people in all the concrete circumstances of their life and times. It prolongs the story of redemption by including in it those who receive it in faith.

Pneumatologically, the Spirit who "spake by the prophets" under the Old Testament is the same Holy Spirit who rests upon the Son and animated his incarnate life (his words, his deeds, the obedience of his passion, and the victory of his resurrection), and who then inspired the faith and witness of the disciples, apostles, and evangelists whose testimony to Jesus Christ and his impact is set down in the Scriptures of the New Testament. The same Holy Spirit now "takes the things of Christ" and "declares" them (cf. John 16:14f.) as the preacher proclaims the scriptural message (1 Thess. 1:5) and the faith of hearers is elicited (1 Cor. 12:3). It is a traditional principle of Christian hermeneutics that the Scriptures must be read and interpreted by the same Spirit in which they were written.[19]

Anthropologically, speech and act are interlaced modes of communication. Actions may sometimes, as the proverb goes, speak louder than words. Speech may be an effective act. The spoken word may interpret

18. Karl Barth, *Church Dogmatics* I/1, trans. G. W. Bromiley (Edinburgh: T. & T. Clark, 1975), pp. 88-124 (the quotation occurs on p. 121).

19. Thus, for example, Thomas à Kempis: "Omnis scriptura legi debet eo Spiritu quo scripta est" (*The Imitation of Christ* I.5). John Wesley liked to quote this text; see, for example, *The Works of the Rev. John Wesley*, ed. Thomas Jackson (London: Wesleyan Conference Office, 1872), 9:154 and 14:253.

a deed; the deed may enact an intention, a purpose, a message. For our salvation, Jesus Christ is both speaker and doer. The Scriptures record his words and his deeds. The Scriptures result from the writing down of speech. Reading from them in church restores to them the character of an event. The act of preaching from them prolongs that event, whose purpose is to give access again and again to the event of Christ and allow the Savior to address his hearers and to include faithful respondents into his death and resurrection.[20]

Liturgically, we may note several dimensions that modern scholarship has found to characterize the worship of the church that gathers "in Christ's name" (cf. Matt. 18:20).[21] Christian worship is *anamnetic:* it "recalls" the original saving event of Christ in such ways as to allow believers to become part of it; and the open reading of the Scriptures in the assembly, the preaching of sermons faithful to them, and the observance of practices whose institution the Scriptures record are among the instruments of the "anamnesis." Christian worship is also *epicletic:* it "invokes" the Holy Spirit upon the congregation, its ministers, the words to be read and said and heard, the actions to be performed and received, in order that the participants may enjoy saving communion with God through Christ. And so Christian worship is also both *doxological* and *eschatological:* it is an anticipated realization of humankind's "chief end," which is, in the concise terms of the Westminster Catechism, "to glorify God and enjoy him for ever"; and the testimony of the Scriptures supplies both the content and the forms by which we praise even now the Lamb upon the heavenly throne and share already in his wedding banquet.

Now, that should whet the appetite for the next chapter, wherein we "taste and see the goodness of the Lord."

---

20. Some of Paul's letters, for example, seem to have been meant from the start to be read aloud in the congregations (cf. Col. 4:16); see Pieter J. J. Botha, "Letter Writing and Oral Communication in Antiquity: Suggested Implications for the Interpretation of Paul's Letter to the Galatians," in *Scriptura* 42 (1992): 17-34. According to the "Muratorian canon," it seems that "being read in church" was a factor in establishing the canonical status of the early Christian writings that constitute our New Testament; see Geoffrey Wainwright, *Doxology: The Praise of God in Worship, Doctrine, and Life* (New York: Oxford University Press, 1980), pp. 163-65.

21. See Peter Brunner, *Worship in the Name of Jesus,* trans. M. H. Bertram (St. Louis: Concordia, 1968).

3

Taste and See

"O taste and see that the LORD is good!": Psalm 34:8 is a traditional communion verse, said or sung at the distribution of the bread and wine in the church's liturgy of the Lord's Supper. It had already been picked up in the First Letter of Peter, an epistle that has seemed to many exegetes to echo the rites of initiation whereby Christians are baptized and partake for the first time of the Eucharist: "Like newborn babes, long for the pure milk of the Word *(to logikon gala),* that by it you may grow up to salvation; for you have tasted the goodness of the Lord" (2:2-3; cf. KJV). There is an allusion to Psalm 34:8 also in the Letter to the Hebrews, where the writer warns that it will be impossible to restore to repentance from apostasy "those who have once been enlightened, who have tasted the heavenly gift, and have become partakers of the Holy Spirit, and have tasted the goodness of the word of God and the powers of the age to come" (6:1-6).

In the first half of this chapter, we shall treat the part played by food and drink in the communication of the Word made flesh, and hence by the sense of taste in our reception of the Word. That means principally the Lord's Supper, and the related practice of the love feast; but attention will be paid also to the place of milk and honey in the ritual tradition of Christianity. Then in the second half of the chapter we shall move to vision and the sense of sight, for in his goodness the Lord gave himself to be seen in the Word incarnate; and although in the interval we "walk by faith, not by sight" (2 Cor. 5:7; cf. John 20:29), our eyes are already being prepared for the day when we shall know him "face to face" (1 Cor. 13:12) and "see him as he is" (1 John 3:2).

1. The Lord's Supper and the Love Feast

According to John 6, the Word made flesh spoke of himself as "the bread from heaven" and "the bread of life"; and the promise there made of eternal life to those who "eat his flesh and drink his blood" is given the possibility of concrete realization through faithful participation in the Meal that Matthew, Mark, Luke, and Paul record Jesus as instituting, on the eve of his passion and redemptive death, with the bread and wine — "This is my body," "This is my blood" — to be eaten and drunk "in remembrance of me."

Controversy has marked the history of Christian thought on the nature of the identity between Christ and the bread that is eaten and the wine that is drunk in the Lord's Supper. Seeking as far as possible to avoid such controversy, we are encouraged by the theme of the present chapter to trace the role of Christ as Word in this matter.

Between the incarnation of the Word and the consecration of the bread and wine there is, according to Justin Martyr in the middle of the second century, an analogy, and even a kind of effective extension:

> We do not receive these things as common bread or common drink; but just as our Savior Jesus Christ, being incarnate through the Word of God, took flesh and blood for our salvation, so too we have been taught that the food over which thanks have been given by a word of prayer *(di' euchēs logou)* which is from him, (the food) from which our flesh and blood are fed by transformation, is both the flesh and blood of that incarnate Jesus. For the apostles, in the records composed by them which are called gospels, have handed down thus what was commanded of them: that Jesus took bread, gave thanks, and said, "Do this for the remembrance of me; this is my body"; and likewise he took the cup, gave thanks and said, "This is my blood"; and gave to them alone.[1]

A similar train of thought was continued in the passages quoted from Saint Irenaeus at the end of the first chapter.[2]

When evidence of an epiclesis appears in early eucharistic prayers, it is sometimes the Logos who is invoked. The prayer of Sarapion, an

---

1. Justin Martyr, *First Apology*, 66 (Migne, *Patrologia Graeca* 6:428-29; hereafter cited as *PG*), translation from R. C. D. Jasper and G. J. Cuming, *Prayers of the Eucharist: Early and Reformed*, 3d ed. (New York: Pueblo, 1987), p. 29.

2. See above, p. 19.

Egyptian bishop and friend of Saint Athanasius around the middle of the fourth century, reads as follows:

> Let your holy Word come on this bread, O God of truth, that the bread may become the body of the Word; and on this cup, that the cup may become blood of the Truth.[3]

Ancient Gaulish and Spanish prayers also sometimes invoke the Word as an agent of eucharistic consecration: "May thy holy Word come down, we pray, O almighty God, upon these things which we offer thee";[4] "Send thy Word from heaven, O Lord, to wipe away faults and to hallow the oblations."[5]

The classic Roman doctrine is that the consecration is effected by the words of Christ — "This is my body," "This is my blood" — spoken by the priest *in persona Christi*. The teaching of the Eastern Orthodox Church is that the consecration is not complete until the Holy Spirit has been invoked to "make" or "show" the bread and the cup to be the body and blood of Christ.

At the English Reformation, Thomas Cranmer's First Prayer Book of 1549 invoked both the Word and the Spirit:

> . . . and with thy Holy Spirit and word vouchsafe to bless and sanctify these thy gifts and creatures of bread and wine, that they may be unto us the body and blood of thy most dearly beloved Son Jesus Christ, who in the same night that he was betrayed, took bread . . .[6]

---

3. Jasper and Cuming, *Prayers of the Eucharist,* pp. 77f. (cf. p. 75 for an interpretation). Saint Athanasius himself, in the fragment of a baptismal sermon, says: "When the great prayers and holy supplications have been sent up, the Word descends into the bread and cup, and they become his body" (Migne, *PG* 26:1325 and 86:2401).

4. *Missale Gallicanum,* in Migne, *Patrologia Latina* 72:342, 345; hereafter cited as *PL.*

5. M. Férotin, *Liber Mozarabicus Sacramentorum* (Paris, 1912; republished Farnborough, Hampshire: Gregg International, 1969), col. 200.

6. Jasper and Cuming, *Prayers of the Eucharist,* p. 239. Cranmer here seems to echo phraseology from the Sarum Breviary, in the Sunday matins in the octave of Corpus Christi, and ultimately derivable from Paschasius Radbertus, whereby consecration "in verbo efficitur Creatoris et in virtute Spiritus sancti"; see E. C. Ratcliff, "The Liturgical Work of Archbishop Cranmer," in his *Liturgical Studies,* ed. A. H. Couratin and D. H. Tripp (London: SPCK, 1976), pp. 184-202 (here p. 195 and note). At the equivalent point in the Prayer Book of the (Protestant) Episcopal Church in the USA, "Word" was printed with an initial capital from 1793 onwards; see Marion J. Hatchett, *The Making of the First American Book of Common Prayer* (New York: Seabury Press, 1982), pp. 135, 187 n. 19.

Eucharistic theology being a controversial matter throughout sixteenth-century England, the canny reply of Queen Elizabeth I when asked for her view of Christ's presence is to be appreciated:

> 'Twas God the Word that spake it,
> He took the bread and brake it;
> And what the Word did make it,
> That I believe and take it.

In twentieth-century eucharistic theology, the role of Christ as creative Word has enjoyed renewed attention. According to the Genevan Reformed theologian F. J. Leenhardt, for example, when Christ gives the bread with the words "This is my body," then the bread is no longer in its deepest constitution what the baker made it, but what the Word has made it. For a thing is what it is in the will and purpose of God; and if the Word has declared the divine intention that this bread be the body of Christ, then that is what the bread henceforth is.[7] Another feature of liturgical revisions in the twentieth century has been the introduction of a pneumatological epiclesis, in one form or another, into rites of the Western tradition; and this may be greeted as a welcome recognition of the inseparability of the Word and the Spirit such as we have detected in our investigation of the incarnation.

Admitting that the bread and the wine of the Eucharist are a gift to us of the Word for the sake of a salutary communion with himself, we may now turn to the scriptural testimony for a thicker description of the way in which food and drink were for him in his earthly ministry a means of communicating the gospel and anticipating the celebration of God's kingdom. The story could, of course, be taken right back to the Passover and the covenant meal on Mount Sinai (Exod. 12–13 and 24), and even to the Garden of Eden.[8] But we may light on the

---

7. F. J. Leenhardt, "This Is My Body," in O. Cullmann and F. J. Leenhardt, *Essays on the Lord's Supper,* trans. J. G. Davies (Richmond: John Knox, 1958), pp. 24-85, in particular p. 48. An interesting nuance is introduced by the Armenian liturgy: "Then taking the bread in his holy divine immortal immaculate and *creative* hands, he blessed . . ." (F. E. Brightman, *Liturgies Eastern and Western* [Oxford: Clarendon Press, 1896], pp. 436f.); cf. the fragment of a sixth-century Persian prayer: "He took bread and wine which his own will had made, and he sanctified it . . ." (Brightman, p. 515).

8. See the development of Alexander Schmemann reported later in this book, pp. 147-48.

eschatological vision set forth in Isaiah 25:6-9, for this is the kind of imagery needed to make full sense of Jesus' teaching and practice in this matter:[9]

> On this mountain the LORD of hosts will make for all peoples a feast of fat things, a feast of wine on the lees, of fat things full of marrow, of wine on the lees well refined. And he will destroy on this mountain the covering that is cast over all peoples, the veil that is spread over all nations. He will swallow up death for ever, and the Lord GOD will wipe away tears from all faces, and the reproach of his people he will take away from all the earth; for the LORD has spoken. It will be said on that day, "Lo, this is our God; we have waited for him, that he might save us. This is the LORD; we have waited for him; let us be glad and rejoice in his salvation."

Now, when Jesus came announcing the dawning reign of God, his "parables of the kingdom"[10] and related sayings often pictured a feast (Matt. 8:11 = Luke 13:29; Matt. 22:1-10 = Luke 14:15-23; cf. Matt. 25:10, 21, 23; Luke 12:37); and his practice of eating and drinking with publicans and sinners, which gained him such notoriety, was an enacted offer of forgiveness and salvation (Matt. 9:10-13 = Mark 2:15-17 = Luke 5:29-32; Matt. 11:19 = Luke 7:34; Luke 15:1f.; 19:1-10). When Jesus fed the multitudes, he took the part of the messianic shepherd-king having compassion on his flock (Matt. 14:13-21 = Mark 6:30-44; Matt. 15:32-39 = Mark 8:1-10; Luke 9:11-17; John 6:3-15). To his closest followers he left a ritual meal, with the promise that they would sit at his table in the kingdom (Matt. 26:29 = Mark 14:25 = Luke 22:18, 30). After his death and resurrection, he made himself "known to them in the breaking of the bread" (Luke 24:28-35; cf. Acts 2:42), visited them in the course of their dinner (Luke 24:36-43; Mark 16:14; cf. Acts 10:40f.), and prepared breakfast for them by the lakeside (John 21:9-13). According to the seer John, this communion with Christ continues, at least in analogous mode, for the exalted Lord still says, "Behold, I stand at the door and knock; if any one hears my voice and opens the door, I will come in to him and eat with him, and he with me" (Rev. 3:20).

9. For more detail, see Geoffrey Wainwright, *Eucharist and Eschatology* (London: Epworth Press, 1971; New York: Oxford University Press, 1981).

10. See C. H. Dodd, *Parables of the Kingdom,* rev. ed. (New York: Scribner's, 1961).

And: "Blessed are those who are invited to the marriage supper of the Lamb" (Rev. 19:9).[11]

It is the traditional teaching and experience of the church (though interpretations vary) that at the Lord's Supper Christ is both "host and food" (that phrase is used by Zwingli, *"hospes et epulum"*).[12] Amid the language of "nourishment" and "delight," we may call special attention, following our theme of the senses, to "the taste." In a prayer from the Gregorian Sacramentary, the communicants, "having been filled by the gift of salvation," pray that "what gladdens us by its taste may by its effect renew us *(ut cuius laetamur gustu, renovemur effectu)*."[13] Some of the most remarkable language in this range is found in the *Hymns on the Lord's Supper* of John and Charles Wesley, especially in the third section entitled "The Sacrament a Pledge of Heaven."[14] Thus in hymn 101:

> How glorious is the Life above
> Which in this Ordinance we taste;
> The Fulness of Celestial Love,
> That Joy which shall for ever last!

Or in hymn 108:

> For all that Joy which now we taste
> Our happy hallow'd souls prepare,

11. In the postresurrection stories, the use of the verb *sunalizō* at Acts 1:4 opens up an interesting line of thought. It may be translated "staying together" or "eating together." In the latter case, the connection is with the noun *hals* (salt). Taste and wisdom are proverbially linked (the Latin *sapere* means both to taste and to know). In the African and Roman rite, salt (perhaps originally salted bread) was given to catechumens: Saint Augustine relates in his *Confessions* (I.11.17), "I was signed with His cross and seasoned with His salt"; cf. Alois Stenzel, *Die Taufe. Eine genetische Erklärung der Taufliturgie* (Innsbruck: Rauch, 1958), pp. 171-75.

12. U. Zwingli, *De canone missae epicheresis* (1523); cf. Jasper and Cuming, *Prayers of the Eucharist*, p. 186.

13. See H. Lietzmann, *Das Sacramentarium Gregorianum nach dem Aachener Urexemplar* (Münster im Westfalen: Aschendorff, 1921), p. 28 (prayer 39:3); Jean Deshusses, *Le Sacramentaire grégorien: ses principales formes d'après les plus anciens manuscrits* (Fribourg: Éditions Universitaires, 1971), pp. 135, 236, 298 (prayers 173, 564, 793).

14. A facsimile of the original 1745 edition (Bristol, Felix Farley) has been published by the Charles Wesley Society (Madison, N.J., 1995).

O let us hold the Earnest fast,
This pledge that we thy Heaven shall share,
Shall drink it New with thee above,
The Wine of thy Eternal Love.

One last quotation, from hymn 110, will bring us back to the Bread of Life in John 6:

Jesus, on thee we feed,
Along the desert Way,
Thou art the living Bread
Which doth our spirits stay,
And all who in this Banquet join
Lean on the Staff of Life Divine.

Standing, historically and theologically, in a somewhat puzzling relation to the sacramental Eucharist is the love feast (*agapē* in Greek, which is simply the most characteristic Christian term for love). From 1 Corinthians 11 it appears both that the Eucharist took place in connection with a fellowship meal *and* that the inappropriate behavior of the Christians at Corinth was such as could explain the eventual separation of the sacrament from the broader meal. (Just as the mere fact of eating and drinking in the presence of Jesus during his earthly ministry was no guarantee of salvation, as Luke 13:22-30 makes clear, so also the Lord's Supper could be abused to the condemnation of the participants, as Paul tells them in 1 Corinthians 11:17-34. Jude 12 speaks of carousals that disfigure the love feasts.) From the end of the second century, Tertullian provides from North Africa a description of the Christian "supper" *(coena)* which sounds rather different from the Sunday assembly described by Justin Martyr in the Roman church forty or fifty years earlier (Justin lists readings from "the writings of the prophets" and "the memoirs of the apostles," homily, general prayers, presentation of the bread and wine, prayer of thanksgiving by the presider, communion), although we cannot be sure whether "the sacrament of the bread and the cup" (which Tertullian certainly knows)[15] was celebrated separately from

---

15. *Panis et calicis sacramentum,* in *Adversus Marcionem* V.8 (Migne, *PL* 2:520); cf. *eucharistiae sacramentum,* in *De corona,* 3 (*PL* 2:99) and *Adversus Marcionem* IV.34 (*PL* 2:473), and *corpus Domini,* in *De idololatria,* 7 (*PL* 1:745) and *De oratione,* 19 (*PL* 1:1287).

the love feast. This is how Tertullian depicts what he explicitly calls a love feast:[16]

> Our supper explains itself by its name, which is the Greek word for love. Whatever it costs, our outlay in the name of piety is gain, for it is the needy that we benefit by that banquet. . . . First we taste *(praegustetur)* of prayer to God before we recline to food; we eat only what suffices hunger, and drink only such as befits such as are chaste. We satisfy appetite as those who remember that even during the night they have to worship God. We converse as those who know that they are in the hearing of their Lord. After water for washing the hands, and the lights have been brought in, every one is called forward to sing praises to God, either from the Holy Scriptures or of his own composing. And this is a proof of the measure of the drinking. As we began, so the feast is concluded with prayer. We depart not like a pack of ruffians, nor in gangs of vagabonds, nor to break out into licentiousness, but with as much regard for our modesty and chastity as if we had been taking in a moral lesson rather than a supper.

By the late fourth century, the Eucharist and the *agapē* had certainly been separated, as is shown by the picture Saint John Chrysostom retrojects onto apostolic practice from his own time in Antioch and Constantinople: "When the assembly *(synaxis)* was over, after the communion of the mysteries, they all went to a common banquet *(euōchia),* the rich bringing their provisions with them, and the poor and destitute being invited by them, and all feasting in common."[17]

Although obviously susceptible to abuse, it is apparent that the love feast — the *convivium Domini* — at its best captured two features of the common life in Christ — the "conviviality" — that properly mark Christianity: mutual care (and especially care for the needy), and joy in the Lord.[18] It is, therefore, no surprise that the love feast should be revived among Christian communities that in certain times and places experience

---

16. Tertullian, *Apologeticus,* 39:16-19 (Migne, *PL* 1:538-41).

17. John Chrysostom, *Homily 27 on 1 Corinthians* (Migne, *PG* 61:223-24).

18. See Bo Reicke, *Diakonie, Festfreude und Zelos in Verbindung mit der altchristlichen Agapenfeier* (Uppsala: Lundequistska Bokhandeln, 1948); A. B. du Toit, *Der Aspekt der Freude im urchristlichen Abendmahl* (Winterthur: Keller, 1965); X. Léon-Dufour, *Le partage du pain selon le Nouveau Testament* (Paris: Seuil, 1982).

a renewal after apostolic patterns. Early Methodism was such a case.[19] The regular love feast figured there as part of a network of mutual encouragement, prayer, and concern, of shared "conversation on the work of God," and of active engagement on behalf of the sick and poor; it went concomitantly with a revival, at least in England, of eucharistic observance. Down to my childhood in the village Methodism of Yorkshire, the love feast survived in the form of the "faith tea," and I suppose that a distant trace is still to be found in the "potluck supper."

Some have found a connection between the *agapē* and use of milk and honey in the ritual history of Christianity.

2. MILK AND HONEY

In describing the rites of baptism, Tertullian tells how, on emerging from the water, "we are taken up as new-born children and taste first of all *(praegustamus)* a mixture of milk and honey."[20] What twentieth-century scholarship has identified as the *Apostolic Tradition* of Hippolytus gives more details, from the early third century in Rome, of the holy communion that concluded the baptismal service of (in all probability) Easter Night:

> And then the offering shall be presented by the deacons to the bishop; and he shall give thanks over the bread for the representation, which the Greeks call "antitype," of the body of Christ; and over the cup of mixed wine for the antitype, which the Greeks call "likeness," of the blood which was shed for all who have believed in him; and over milk and honey mixed together in fulfilment of the promise which was made to the fathers, in which he said, "a land flowing with milk and honey," in which also Christ gave his flesh, through which those who believe are nourished like little children, making the bitterness of the heart sweet by the gentleness of his word *(in suauitate verbi amara cordis dulcia efficiens);* and over water, as an offering to signify the washing, that the inner man also, which is the soul, may receive the same things as the

19. See Frank Baker, *Methodism and the Love-Feast* (London: Epworth Press, 1957).
20. Tertullian, *De corona*, 3 (Migne, *PL* 2:99); cf. *Adversus Marcionem* I.14 (*PL* 2:587); also Clement of Alexandria, *Paidagogos* I.6 (Migne, *PG* 8:309).

body. And the bishop shall give a reason for all these things to those who believe.

And when he breaks the bread, in distributing fragments to each, he shall say: "The bread of heaven in Christ Jesus." And the recipient shall answer: "Amen." And if there are not enough presbyters, the deacons also shall hold the cups, and stand by in good order and reverence: first, he who holds the water; second, the milk; third, the wine. And they who receive shall taste *(gustent)* of each thrice, he who gives it saying: "In God the Father almighty," and the recipient shall say "Amen"; "And in the Lord Jesus Christ," "Amen"; "And in the Holy Spirit and the holy Church," "Amen." So shall it be done with each one.[21]

In the Latin West, provision continued to be made for the blessing of milk and honey at Easter and (another baptismal occasion) Pentecost.[22]

J. A. Jungmann points to an earlier pagan Roman custom of the gift of milk and honey to a child as a sign of reception into the family.[23] In Christian baptismal usage, the reference is, of course, to the Promised Land, the Lord's gift of Canaan to Israel now being taken as the "type" of the salvation brought by Christ, into which the baptized are being introduced and which will one day be completed in what Bernard of Cluny, by way of John Mason Neale, called

Jerusalem the golden,
With milk and honey blessed.[24]

21. G. J. Cuming, *Hippolytus: A Text for Students* (Bramcote, Nottingham: Grove Books, 1976), p. 21; cf. Gregory Dix and Henry Chadwick, *The Treatise on the Apostolic Tradition of St. Hippolytus of Rome*, rev. ed. (London: SPCK, 1968).

22. See, for Easter, *The Pontifical of Egbert, Archbishop of York*, ed. W. Greenwell (Durham: G. Andrews, for the Surtees Society, 1853), p. 129, and, for Pentecost, the Leonine Sacramentary (L. C. Mohlberg, *Sacramentarium Veronense* [Rome: Herder, 1956], p. 26 [prayer 205]).

23. Josef A. Jungmann, *The Early Liturgy* (Notre Dame, Ind.: University of Notre Dame Press, 1959), p. 139.

24. John Mason Neale's version of "Urbs Sion aurea," from Bernard of Cluny's *Hora novissima*, overtranslates the phrase *patria lactea;* honey is not mentioned in the original, but the context is full of sweetness.

As part of the recovery of feminine imagery in the Christian tradition, Elisabeth Moltmann-Wendel has observed that "milk is the product of the mother and honey comes from bees governed by their queen," and "in the cultures of the ancient Near East milk and honey are common images for the food of the gods, the food of paradise, the food of life."[25] In the Old Testament, the taste of the manna in the wilderness, the "bread from heaven," "was like wafers made with honey" (Exod. 16:31). For the psalmist, the "ordinances of the LORD" are "sweeter also than honey and drippings of the honeycomb" (Ps. 19:9-10), and he exclaims (Ps. 119:103):

> How sweet are thy words to my taste,
> sweeter than honey to my mouth!

When Ezekiel ate the scroll with the words of God written on it, bitter as they were, "it was in my mouth as sweet as honey" (3:3; cf. Rev. 10:9f.). In the New Testament we have already come across the pure milk of the Word (1 Pet. 2:2);[26] and the Christian Middle Ages knew the theme of Jesus giving motherly suck to believers.[27] Clearly, then, there is potential for the renewed use of milk and honey in Christian ritual.[28]

Another liturgical theme that attaches to the power of the Word in creation is the blessing of seasonal fruits of the earth. There are traces of such blessings in the conclusion of the old Roman Canon of the Mass; the Eastern Orthodox churches have occasions for the blessing of corn, olives, and grapes; and even the churches of the Protestant north have celebrated "harvest festivals" since the nineteenth century. Set in a comprehensive Christian context, such as that suggested by Saint Irenaeus in passages already noted, these rites evoke and anticipate the "new heavens

25. Elisabeth Moltmann-Wendel, *A Land Flowing with Milk and Honey,* trans. John Bowden (New York: Crossroad, 1986), pp. 1f.

26. It must also be admitted that the apostle Paul, in a different usage, expects believers to move on from milk to solid food (1 Cor. 3:1-3; cf. Heb. 5:12-14).

27. See Caroline Walker Bynum, *Jesus as Mother: Studies in the Spirituality of the High Middle Ages* (Berkeley: University of California Press, 1982).

28. It is all the more to be regretted that, in a ceremony at a 1993 conference in Minneapolis on "Reimagining" that was in several respects controversial (as part of the Decade of the Churches in Solidarity with Women), milk and honey should have been employed as a *substitute* for the Eucharist (many participants holding that there was no need or room for atonement in the Christian faith).

and the new earth" of the "new creation" that has already been inaugurated in Christ.[29]

The time has, in fact, now come to attend to vision. For Christ the incarnate Word is also "the Image of the invisible God," and as believers look on him, they are being transformed "from glory into glory."

3. THE IMAGE OF THE INVISIBLE GOD

"The Word became flesh," says Saint John, "and we have beheld *(etheasametha)* his glory" (John 1:14): "No one has ever seen God; the only Son, who is in the bosom of the Father, he has made him known" (1:18). "For," says Saint Paul, "it is the God who said, 'Let light shine out of darkness,' who has shone in our hearts to give the light of the knowledge of the glory of God in the face of Christ" (2 Cor. 4:6); Christ, the apostle says, is "the image *(eikōn)* of God" (4:4), or again "the image of the invisible God" (Col. 1:15). Christ "reflects the glory of God," says the Letter to the Hebrews, "and bears the very stamp of his nature" (1:3).

In the Scriptures, light is a sign of the salutary presence of God: "In thy light do we see light" (Ps. 36:9); "The LORD is my light and my salvation" (Ps. 27:1); "Oh send out thy light and thy truth" (Ps. 43:3); "Thy word is a lamp to my feet and a light to my path" (Ps. 119:105); "Come, let us walk in the light of the LORD" (Isa. 2:5); "The people who walked in darkness have seen a great light" (Isa. 9:2; cf. Matt. 4:16); "Arise, shine, for your light has come, and the glory of the LORD has risen upon you" (Isa. 60:1). Taking the Christ child into his arms, the aged Simeon sings (Luke 2:29-32):

"Lord, now lettest thou thy servant depart in peace,
according to thy word;
for mine eyes have seen thy salvation
which thou hast prepared in the presence of all peoples,
a light for revelation to the Gentiles,
and for glory to thy people Israel."

29. See above, pp. 18-19, 37. For the theme of new creation in this connection, see A. Gignac, "I segni della nuova creazione e della speranza evangelica," in *Nelle vostre assemblee*, 2d ed., ed. D. Sartore and A. M. Triacca (Brescia: Queriniana, 1975), pp. 405-24.

In the Fourth Gospel, Jesus says, "I am the light of the world" (John 8:12), and in the very next chapter he recalls the saying as he heals the man born blind, who then in controversy testifies, "One thing I know, that though I was blind, now I see" (9:5-7, 25). Jesus asks him, "Do you believe in the Son of man?" and he answers, "And who is he, sir, that I may believe in him?" Jesus replies, "You have seen him, and it is he who speaks to you." The man said, "Lord, I believe," and he worshiped Him. Jesus makes the point: "For judgment I came into this world, that those who do not see may see, and that those who see may become blind" (John 9:35-39). Blind people are healed in the other Gospels also (Mark 8:22-26; 10:46-52 = Matt. 20:29-34 = Luke 18:35-43). Such healings are a sign of the dawning of the kingdom, as Jesus' answer to those who came from John the Baptist implies (Matt. 11:2-19 = Luke 7:18-35).

After his resurrection, Christ "was seen *(ōphthē)*" by his apostles, including Paul, and other disciples (1 Cor. 15:5-8; and, with other verbs of showing and sight, Mark 16:12, 14; Luke 24:31; John 20:20, 26-29; 21:1, 14). The "heavenly vision" to which Paul "was not disobedient" included being sent to the Gentiles — "to open their eyes, that they may turn from darkness to light and from the power of Satan to God, that they may receive forgiveness of sins and a place among those who are sanctified by faith in [Christ]," who by his resurrection from the dead was, as prophesied, now "proclaim[ing] light both to the people and to the Gentiles" (Acts 26:12-23).

During his earthly ministry, Jesus had established a parallel between *hearing* and *seeing* himself and his words and his deeds: "Blessed are your eyes, for they see, and your ears, for they hear. Truly, I say to you, many prophets and righteous men longed to see what you see, and did not see it, and to hear what you hear, and did not hear it" (Matt. 13:16f. = Luke 10:23f.; cf. Matt. 11:4 = Luke 7:22). The Eastern Orthodox churches in particular still maintain that parallel in a mode suited to the time between Christ's ascension and his return. Just as the written Gospels present in the church a verbal portrait of the incarnate, crucified, and risen Christ, so the icons of the church bear visual testimony to his living presence and continuing work.[30]

---

30. Introductions to the Orthodox understanding and practice of icons are to be found in Constantine D. Kalokyris, *The Essence of Orthodox Iconography,* trans. P. Chamberas (Brookline, Mass.: Holy Orthodox Press, 1985); Michel Quenot, *The Icon: Window on the Kingdom,* trans. a Carthusian Monk (Crestwood, N.Y.: St. Vladimir's Seminary Press,

In the month of August, which includes on the sixteenth the feast of the Holy Face, the Byzantine liturgy narrates the following story. King Abgar of Edessa, suffering from leprosy, sent his archivist to Christ asking him to come and heal him; if Christ refused, then Hannan, who was also a painter, should at least bring back a portrait. Christ had his mission to complete, and a portrait proved impossible "because of the indescribable glory of the Savior's face." But the Lord washed himself in water and left the imprint of his face on a linen towel, which he sent, with a letter, to Edessa. King Abgar was thereby cured from the worst of his illness. After Christ's ascension, Saint Thaddeus visited Edessa, as Christ had promised, and completed the healing, converting the king to Christianity. Abgar replaced an idol above the town gate with the holy image. Later on, the cloth was immured for protection, and the face left its imprint also on the covering tile. Both the cloth and the clay versions, the *mandulion* and *keramion* respectively, were eventually brought to Constantinople, but they disappeared during the Crusades. The icon "not made with human hands" had already become the prototype for many copies.[31] There is certainly, amid obvious nuances, a striking consistency in the iconic representation of Christ in the Orthodox tradition, where the painters follow strict rules and seek the inspiration of the Holy Spirit, "the divine Iconographer."[32]

Told in secular mode, the early history of Christian iconography is rather different. In the absence of artifacts from the first two centuries, it is usually held that the earliest church was not only aniconic in fact but iconophobic in principle: the second-century Apologists cashed in on the

---

1991); and, in more detail, Leonid Ouspensky, *Theology of the Icon*, 2 vols. (Crestwood, N.Y.: St. Vladimir's Seminary Press, 1978-92). These days there are many books that offer technically excellent photographic reproductions of icons. The following may be singled out: Leonid Ouspensky and Vladimir Lossky, *The Meaning of Icons*, trans. G. E. H. Palmer and G. Kadloubovsky (Crestwood, N.Y.: St. Vladimir's Seminary Press, 1982); Kurt Weitzmann and others, *The Icon* (London: Studio Editions, 1987); Mahmood Zibawi, *The Icon: Its Meaning and History* and *Eastern Christian Worlds* (Collegeville: Liturgical Press, 1993 and 1995).

31. The adjective *acheiropoiētos* ("not made with hands") seems virtually a Christian coinage; see Mark 14:58; 2 Cor. 5:1; Col. 2:11. Western equivalents to the story of Abgar are Veronica's veil, wherewith Christ's face had been wiped on his way to the cross, and the Shroud of Turin, which is said to bear the marks of his crucifixion and resurrection. In the traditions of both East and West, Saint Luke the evangelist is considered a painter, especially of the Virgin and Child.

32. See Paul Evdokimov, *L'art de l'icône: théologie de la beauté* (Paris: Desclée de Brouwer, 1972), in particular p. 13.

better kind of Greek and Roman philosophy that recognized the divine transcendence of matter, while Tertullian stuck to the prohibition of images in the second commandment (Exod. 20:4), observing that pagan images supplied the material occasion for idolatry (cf. Pss. 115:4-8; 135:15-18). When, around the beginning of the third century, the Christians started to adorn their catacombs with mural paintings and, a little later, their sarcophagi with sculpture, this development will have been a popular move in defiance of the theologians and pastors. That way of telling the story is not so different from the accounts given by the Byzantine iconoclasts in the eighth and ninth centuries,[33] by Calvin in the sixteenth,[34] and by liberal Protestants in the late nineteenth and early twentieth centuries.[35]

From the evidence of the catacombs it appears that early Christian art leaned not so much to naturalistic portraiture as to symbolic representation: the Good Shepherd is a common motif, and "stick figure" scenes from the Old Testament (understood typologically) and the Gospels point to the saving work of Christ, its application in the sacraments, and its expected completion in the end.[36] Extant evidence of "portraits" of Christ, in mosaic or in paint on wood, dates from the fourth and fifth centuries.[37] Liturgically and christologically, the question came to a head in the iconoclastic controversies of the eighth and ninth centuries. The iconodule

33. See Daniel J. Sahas, *Icon and Logos: Sources in Eighth-Century Iconoclasm* (Toronto: University of Toronto Press, 1986).

34. See Carlos M. N. Eire, *War against the Idols: The Reformation of Worship from Erasmus to Calvin* (Cambridge: Cambridge University Press, 1986).

35. Among secular historians, this account has been called into question by Paul Corby Finney, *The Invisible God: The Earliest Christians on Art* (New York: Oxford University Press, 1994). Finney emphasizes the *ad hominem* character of the Apologists' arguments and proposes that, far from being anti-iconic, early Christianity as a whole moved to images as soon as it had the material means for doing so. A weakness in Finney's thesis lies in its failure to pick up traces of the *dogmatic* exploration of the consequences of the incarnation for the attitudes of faith toward matter. That both iconic and iconoclastic streams should recur through Christian history suggests that the theological question is not a simple one.

36. A brief overview on the catacombs and their art is provided by James Stevenson, *The Catacombs: Rediscovered Monuments of Early Christianity* (London: Thames & Hudson, 1978); cf. Graydon F. Snyder, *Ante Pacem: Archaeological Evidence of Church Life before Constantine* (Macon, Ga.: Mercer University Press, 1985).

37. See, for example, F. van der Meer, *Early Christian Art*, trans. P. and F. Brown (Chicago: University of Chicago Press, 1967); Thomas F. Mathews, *The Clash of Gods: A Reinterpretation of Early Christian Art* (Princeton, N.J.: Princeton University Press, 1993).

position, represented theologically by such figures as Saint John of Damascus and then Saint Theodore the Studite, was that consecrated by the Seventh Ecumenical Council (Nicea 787): the veneration of icons was not idolatrous because, as Saint Basil the Great had argued in another context, "the honor offered to the icon is transferred to the prototype";[38] matter had been made a vehicle of salvation through the incarnation ("I do not worship matter," wrote Saint John of Damascus, "I worship the Creator of matter, who became matter for my sake, who willed to take his abode in matter, who worked out my salvation through matter");[39] and the unity of the divine Person of Christ allowed him to be represented in his human nature even though in his divinity he was "uncircumscribable."[40]

The Damascene also cited the pedagogical argument: "What the book is to the literate, the image is to the illiterate."[41] More than a century earlier, Gregory I of Rome had already declared that "in a picture, the illiterate are able to read";[42] and throughout the Middle Ages the notion of, say, carved stone portals or stained glass windows as the *biblia pauperum* obtained in the West.[43] The theologians at Charlemagne's court gave a cool reception to the more strongly "sacramental" account of icons made by the Seventh Ecumenical Council. But already during the Carolingian epoch a shift was taking place from an ornamented but still abstract cross as the sign of Christianity to a representation of the crucified Christ; that representation itself underwent a change of emphasis, for while the eighth century saw Christ triumphant on the cross, the ninth became bolder in the depiction of his suffering and death; yet ways were still found to suggest

38. John of Damascus, *First Apology against Those Who Attack the Divine Images*, 21; cf. Theodore the Studite, *First Refutation of the Iconoclasts*, 8. The text in Basil of Caesarea is *On the Holy Spirit*, 18 (Migne, *PG* 32:149). Translations of John and of Theodore, together with their second and third apologies and refutations respectively (which virtually repeat the arguments of the first), are found in *St. John of Damascus: On the Divine Images*, trans. David Anderson (Crestwood, N.Y.: St. Vladimir's Seminary Press, 1980), and *St. Theodore the Studite: On the Holy Icons*, trans. Catharine Roth (Crestwood, N.Y.: St. Vladimir's Seminary Press, 1981). These are the versions used here.

39. John of Damascus, *First Apology*, 16; Theodore the Studite, *First Refutation*, 7.

40. John of Damascus, *First Apology*, 4 and 8; Theodore the Studite, *First Refutation*, 2-4 and 12.

41. John of Damascus, *First Apology*, 17.

42. Gregory the Great, *Epistles* XI.13 (Migne, *PL* 77:1128-29).

43. See the classic work of Émile Mâle, *Religious Art in France of the Thirteenth Century*, trans. Dora Nussy (New York: Dutton, 1913), reprinted as *The Gothic Image* (New York: Harper & Row, 1958).

his role as both victim and victor, his identity as both human and divine.[44] As the Middle Ages went on, painted altarpieces in particular came to occupy a more important liturgical function, both affectively and effectively — the *Crucifixion* painted by Matthias Grünewald for the Antonine convent of Isenheim being a prime example.[45] Abusively, however, the image was turned from a venerated "visual sign" into a "sacred thing" in itself;[46] and that was what provoked the iconoclasm of the Reformation, particularly on the "Reformed" side.

In the ecumenical twentieth century, a remarkable recovery of the visual has taken place. The stimulus of Eastern Orthodoxy is obvious,[47] yet recognition must also be given to the flourishing of indigenous Christian art in Asian and African countries even in areas where missionary work had been largely in Protestant hands. So we meet Indonesian batiks, Chinese line drawings, African wood carvings. Samples can be found in Hans-Ruedi Weber's two anthologies on the nativity and the crucifixion,[48] or in the work of Masao Takenaka on Asian Christian art.[49] North American churches have taken to the use of banners in processions and in the sanctuary. Protestant writers, Lutheran and even Reformed, can now be discovered offering theologies of the image.[50]

44. See Marie-Christine Sepière, *L'image d'un Dieu souffrant. Aux origines du crucifix* (Paris: Éditions du Cerf, 1994).

45. See Barbara G. Lane, *The Altar and the Altarpiece: Sacramental Themes in Early Netherlandish Painting* (New York: Harper & Row, 1984); Andrée Hayum, *The Isenheim Altarpiece: God's Medicine and the Painter's Vision* (Princeton, N.J.: Princeton University Press, 1989).

46. The terminology is that of Jérôme Cottin, *Le regard et la Parole. Une théologie protestante de l'image* (Geneva: Labor et Fides, 1994).

47. On the Faith and Order side of official ecumenism, see Gennadios Limouris, ed., *Icons: Windows on Eternity: Theology and Spirituality in Colour* (Geneva: WCC Publications, 1990).

48. H. R. Weber, *Immanuel: The Coming of Jesus in Art and the Bible* (Geneva: WCC; Grand Rapids: Eerdmans, 1984) and *On a Friday Noon* (Geneva: WCC; Grand Rapids: Eerdmans, 1979).

49. Masao Takenaka, *Christian Art in Asia* (Tokyo: Kyo Bun Kwan, 1975); Masao Takenaka and Ron O'Grady, *The Bible through Asian Eyes* (Auckland, New Zealand: Pace, 1991).

50. For sympathetic history by Lutherans, note Jaroslav Pelikan, *Imago Dei: The Byzantine Apologia for Icons* (Princeton, N.J.: Princeton University Press, 1990), and Georg Kretschmar, "The Reformation and the Theology of Images," in Limouris, *Icons*, pp. 76-85. Coming from the Reformed side with its "congenital aversion to images," J. Cottin, in the work cited in note 46, detects elements in Luther's anthropology (the corporeity of

It remains true that the East took a more "ontological" route, and the West a more "explicative" route, in regard to images. In Orthodoxy, the icon becomes a vehicle of the exalted Christ's making himself present to his earthly church. Many in the West, especially among Protestants, would be happier to say, with the contemporary theologian Jérôme Cottin, that God is rather more indirectly "contemplated" in an experience where Christian iconography justifiably bears a kind of historical witness to the past events and present practice of God's relations with humankind.[51] That difference must be borne in mind as we now consider the salvific process where believers, "beholding the glory of the Lord," are changed from glory into glory (2 Cor. 3:18).

4. FROM GLORY INTO GLORY

In 2 Corinthians 3:18, the participle *katoptrizomenoi* has been taken either as "beholding" or as "reflecting."[52] In any case, the apostle's idea seems to be that those who contemplate the glory of the Lord also reflect it (as Moses did on coming down from the mountain, according to 2 Corinthians 3:7), for they are themselves transformed "into his image" *(tēn autēn eikona),* "from glory into glory." Redemption brings for believers, according to Colossians 3:10, restoration and renewal "after the image of the creator," in which they were made but from whose glory all mankind has fallen (cf. Rom. 3:23).

The achievement of likeness through contemplation is anthropologically a deep-rooted notion. In a Christian theological context, it must always be qualified in two directions. First: we can see God only if God

---

humankind) and Calvin's cosmology (the materiality of the world) that would allow a theologically responsible retrieval — such as he himself systematically undertakes — of the image. Other Reformed writers offering varied theological support for images include Alain Blancy, "Protestantism and the Seventh Ecumenical Council: Towards a Reformed Theology of the Icon," in Limouris, *Icons,* pp. 35-45, and (very cautiously) Marc Faessler, "L'image entre l'idole et l'icône: essai de réinterprétation de la critique calvinienne des images," in *Nicée II, 787-1987. Douze siècles d'images religieuses,* ed. F. Boespflug and N. Lossky (Paris: Éditions du Cerf, 1987), pp. 421-33.

51. Cottin, *Le regard et la Parole.*

52. See N. Hugedé, *La métaphore du miroir dans les épîtres de saint Paul* (Neuchâtel: Delachaux & Niestlé, 1957).

gives himself to be seen; but this we have in the Word made flesh, who said what he said and did what he did, and about whom Pontius Pilate wrote what he wrote. And second: faithful contemplation does not stay sheerly passive but contains a moment of active receptivity. According to Saint Augustine, the best service of God is to "imitate whom we worship."[53]

Saint Paul had already written: "Be imitators of me, as I am of Christ" (1 Cor. 11:1). By showing Christ in the company of those who have borne closest witness to him in their lives, the iconic practice of the Eastern Orthodox churches expresses the truth that growth into the likeness of Christ takes place within the communion of the saints. Successive generations are shown the transformative effect the contemplation and imitation of Christ had upon their predecessors in the faith. As Constantine Kalokyris interprets the style of Orthodox iconography,[54] the sensory organs of the saints — the eyes, the nose, the ears — are not represented according to biological, anatomical accuracy, but "each of them, having sensed and received the divine revelation, has now become an organ of the spirit and 'has been changed'"; each sensory organ has played its part in the way the saint has appropriated the grace of God and has in the process itself been sanctified. Thus "the eyes are painted large and animated" because they have been opened by study of God's Word to see the wonderful works of creation and redemption (Pss. 25:15; 119:18; 143:5; Luke 2:30). The ears are widened because they have been attentive to the commandments of the Lord and heard the mystery of the divine plan of salvation. The nose is elongated and narrow because it smells not the things of this world but rather "the scent of spiritual fragrance," "the fragrance of the Holy Trinity" (Didymus the Blind),[55] "the scent of incorruption" that Christ and the Holy Spirit emit (Irenaeus).[56] The mouth also is shaped small to denote that the saint has followed the Lord's commandment not to be "anxious about your life, what you shall eat or what you shall drink" (Matt. 6:25) and has sought rather the kingdom of God where the risen body will become a "spiritual wonder" that does not need the food of this earth (Cyril of Jerusalem).[57] The head is crowned with light, not as a merely

---

53. Augustine, *De civitate Dei* VIII.17.2 (Migne, *PL* 41:242).

54. Kalokyris, *The Essence of Orthodox Iconography,* chap. 2 (pp. 44-81).

55. Didymus the Blind, *On the Trinity* II.7.8 (Migne, *PG* 39:589).

56. Irenaeus, *Against the Heresies* I.4.1 (Migne, *PG* 7:480).

57. Cyril of Jerusalem, *Catecheses* XVIII.18 (Migne, *PG* 33:613).

external indicator of sainthood, but as "the radiating glory emitted from within the form of the represented saint," the head being "the center of the spirit, thought and understanding" and the yellow or golden halo becoming visually "the lighted space and the direct background in which the revered head is projected and emphasized" (Kalokyris). Sometimes the hands are disproportionately large as a sign of witness or blessing, while the feet are slender (cf. Rom. 10:15). The clothes will often suggest "the elegance and spiritual nobility of the figures," while the delicacy of the colors betokens modesty. Saint John of Damascus wrote: "The saints during their earthly lives were filled with the Holy Spirit, and when they fulfill their course, the grace of the Holy Spirit does not depart from their souls, or their bodies in the tombs, or from their likenesses and holy images, not by the nature of these things, but by grace and power"[58] — and it is the same Holy Spirit who is at work when, in contemplation and imitation of the Lord and in communion with all his saints, believers are being changed "from glory into glory" (cf. 2 Cor. 3:18).

According to Saint Irenaeus, "the glory of God is man alive" — and "the life of man is the vision of God."[59] The Old Testament may contain at least partial anticipations of the vision of God. At the giving of the covenant on Mount Sinai (Exod. 24:9-11),

> Moses and Aaron, Nadab, and Abihu, and seventy of the elders of Israel went up, and they saw the God of Israel; and there was under his feet as it were a pavement of sapphire stone, like the very heaven for clearness. And he did not lay his hand on the chief men of the people of Israel; they beheld God, and ate and drank.

Yet later on, the Lord said to Moses, "You cannot see my face; for man shall not see me and live"; and Moses saw the glory of the Lord only from behind (Exod. 33:17-23). Again, the prophet Isaiah "saw the Lord" in the temple, but the Lord was "high and lifted up" and "the house was filled with smoke" (Isa. 6:1-5). Under the New Testament, the glory of the Lord became visible in human form through the Word made flesh. Faithful eyes are privileged; but even with the mighty deeds of Christ, his transfiguration, and his resurrection, there remains an element of "enigma" in the revelation and the corresponding vision (*en ainigmati*, 1 Cor. 13:12). In

58. John of Damascus, *First Apology*, 19.
59. Irenaeus, *Against the Heresies* IV.20.7 (Migne, *PG* 7:1037).

the end, it will be "face to face" (13:12). The light of the heavenly city is the Lord God, and its lamp the Lamb (Rev. 21:22–22:5). And the prayer of the earthly church is meanwhile this:

> Finish then thy new creation,
> Pure and spotless let us be;
> Let us see thy great salvation,
> Perfectly restored in thee;
> Changed from glory into glory,
> Till in heaven we take our place,
> Till we cast our crowns before thee,
> Lost in wonder, love, and praise.[60]

And in the interval, the transformation which has begun to embrace us may be expected to manifest itself in visible works that will bring others also to glorify God and so complete the destiny for which humankind is intended: "Let your light so shine before men, that they may see your good works and give glory to your Father who is in heaven" (Matt. 5:16).

---

60. Charles Wesley, "Love Divine, All Loves Excelling," from *Hymns for Those that Have and Those that Seek Redemption* (London, 1747).

4

Scent and Touch

An Orthodox friend of mine, when he told his father that he intended to enter the priesthood, received the reply: "Why do you want to make smoke and kiss pictures?" The Orthodox writer Anthony Ugolnik joked that if the Orthodox Church distributed tracts, they would be of the "scratch and sniff" variety.[1] No ritual feature is so certain to raise Protestant hackles as the burning of incense. Anthropologically speaking, it may be the very strength of the sense of smell which renders its use so exhilarating and so threatening. Certainly its use occurs in the Scriptures, both literally and figuratively; and so even those of us belonging to traditions that fight shy of using this sense in the liturgy ought to be willing to consider whether it may not have a part to play in bringing home to us the Christ who "loved us and gave himself up for us, a fragrant offering and sacrifice to God" (Eph. 5:2), in such a way that we in turn become "the aroma of Christ" in the world (2 Cor. 2:14-16).

Smell is joined with touch in the practice of anointing. Again, unction occurs in the Scriptures, both literally and figuratively; and the use of oils, often scented by herbs and spices, is common in the history of Christian liturgy, whether in the rites surrounding water baptism, accompanying prayer for the sick, or composing ordination to the sacred ministry. Protestants also speak of being touched by Christ and by the

---

1. Anthony Ugolnik, *The Illuminating Icon* (Grand Rapids: Eerdmans, 1989), p. 80.

Spirit; and the laying on of hands is widely observed as a sign of divine blessing even in so-called nonliturgical traditions. In turn, our tactile gestures and actions become vehicles of our extended response to the self-gift of God in Christ as we seek (in a Roman phrase) to "imitate whom we handle."

The first half of this chapter will concentrate on the sense of smell, the second on the sense of touch.

1. A Fragrant Offering

John Henry Hopkins (1820-91), Episcopal rector of Christ's Church, Williamsport, Pennsylvania, wrote one of the most successful of modern carols in "We Three Kings of Orient Are":

The kings:
We three kings of Orient are;
Bearing gifts we traverse afar
Field and fountain, moor and mountain,
Following yonder star:

> [Refrain]
> *O star of wonder, star of night,*
> *Star with royal beauty bright,*
> *Westward leading, still proceeding,*
> *Guide us to thy perfect light.*

Melchior:
Born a King on Bethlehem plain,
Gold I bring, to crown him again —
King for ever, ceasing never,
Over us all to reign.

Caspar:
Frankincense to offer have I;
Incense owns a Deity nigh:
Prayer and praising, all men raising,
Worship him, God most high.

Balthasar:
Myrrh is mine; its bitter perfume
Breathes a life of gathering gloom;
Sorrowing, sighing, bleeding, dying,
Sealed in the stone-cold tomb.

All:
Glorious now, behold him arise,
King, and God, and sacrifice!
Heaven sings alleluya,
Alleluya the earth replies.

At his incarnation, for our sake and for our salvation, the Word entered upon a life that as the Son of God made man he would entirely surrender to the Father, even to the point of a redemptive death on the cross; and by his resurrection from the grave he would give us access to a share in his own regal dignity and condition. In the words of the ancient Te Deum:

Thou art the King of glory, O Christ.
Thou art the everlasting Son of the Father.
When thou tookest upon thee to deliver man,
thou didst humble thyself to be born of a Virgin.
When thou hadst overcome the sharpness of death,
thou didst open the kingdom of heaven to all believers.
Thou sittest at the right hand of God, in the glory of the Father.

In Christian liturgical usage, the use of incense may gratefully recall the one, all-sufficient sacrifice of Christ on Calvary; it may signify the offering of our prayers through our Great High Priest, and the faithful self-oblation of those who are accepted in the Beloved. The use of aromatic oils may gratefully recall what the ancient Irish hymn calls Christ's "bursting from the spicèd tomb";[2] it may signify the anointing with the Holy Spirit by which we become "Christians" and are made and kept as members of the body of Christ. All this needs some scriptural and historical explanation.

2. The phrase is from "St. Patrick's Breastplate," in the verse translation by Mrs. Cecil Frances Alexander.

Incense belonged to the pattern of worship instituted in the Penta-
teuch. The instructions and provisions for the liturgical life of Israel include
an altar of acacia wood, upon which fragrant incense was to be burned
every morning and evening, "a perpetual incense before the LORD
throughout your generations" (Exod. 30:1-8). A "holy anointing oil,"
perfumed with myrrh, cinnamon, cane, and cassia, was to be used for
consecrating the altar of incense as well as the other ritual places and
objects and the priests themselves (30:22-33); and the ritual incense was
to be blended from sweet spices, pure frankincense, and salt (30:34-38).
The materials were to be provided by the people's freewill offering (35:29),
and the craftsmen's work included plates and dishes for incense (37:16).
The altar of incense and the burning of incense figured also in various
rites of atonement (Exod. 30:10; Lev. 4:7; 16:12f.). Incense continued to
be used in Solomon's temple (1 Kings 7:50; 2 Kings 25:14; 1 Chron.
28:18; 2 Chron. 2:4; 4:22; 13:11; 24:14; 26:16-19).

The psalmist associated incense and prayer, without letting either be
a replacement of the other (Ps. 141:1f.):

> I call upon thee, O LORD; make haste to me!
>> Give ear to my voice, when I call to thee!
> Let my prayer be counted as incense before thee,
>> and the lifting up of my hands as an evening sacrifice!

When the prophet Isaiah had the Lord say, "Incense is an abomination to
me" (Isa. 1:13), he was not singling out this one feature of the ritual but
rather including it with all the feasts and sacrifices and prayers of a people
that did evil. What was condemned was *all* worship that was divorced
from purity and justice:

> "Wash yourselves; make yourselves clean;
>> remove the evil of your doings
>> from before my eyes;
> cease to do evil,
>> learn to do good;
> seek justice,
>> correct oppression;
> defend the fatherless,
>> plead for the widow." (1:16f.)

In the New Testament, the annunciation of the birth of Christ's forerunner was made to Zechariah the priest as he served at the altar of incense (Luke 1:10f.). Then Jesus himself is seen to have replaced the temple by his own body (John 2:19-22; cf. Matt. 12:6; Matt. 26:61 = Mark 14:58; Matt. 27:40 = Mark 15:29), and his death in particular is viewed as a sacrifice (Mark 10:45; Rom. 8:3; 1 Cor. 5:7; Eph. 2:13-16; Col. 1:22; 1 Tim. 2:5f.; Heb. 1:3; 7:27; 9:12-14, 26-28; 10:5-14; 13:11f.; 1 Pet. 1:19; 2:24). Most notably for the theme of this chapter, Ephesians 5:2 speaks of how "Christ loved us and gave himself up for us, a fragrant offering and sacrifice to God."

Through Christ, believers now "have access" to the Father (Eph. 2:18; cf. Heb. 4:14-16); and in the vision of Saint John in Revelation, incense both signifies the prayers of the saints and is mingled with them (Rev. 5:8; 8:3f.). The participation in his priesthood that Christ gives us as believers entails also what Saint Paul enjoins in Romans 12:1: "Present your bodies as a living sacrifice, holy and acceptable to God, which is your worship according to the Word *(logikē latreia)*" (cf. 1 Cor. 6:20); and this in turn includes the mutual service within the church which the apostle Paul records when he writes to the Philippians (4:18), "I am filled, having received from Epaphroditus the gifts you sent, a fragrant offering, a sacrifice acceptable and pleasing to God." The combination of prayer and practical Christian fellowship, the euchological and the ethical, is found also in Hebrews 13:15f.: "Through [Christ] then let us continually offer up a sacrifice of praise to God, that is, the fruit of lips that acknowledge his name. Do not neglect to do good and to share what you have, for such sacrifices are pleasing to God."

It is, above all, at the Eucharist that faithful participation in the sacrifice of Christ comes into focus. It is there that, in remembrance of Christ and in communion with him, the believing community gives thanks for Christ's redeeming work, receives again its benefits, and exercises mutual care among its members. So much is probably implied in Acts 2:42 ("And they devoted themselves to the apostles' teaching and fellowship, to the breaking of bread and the prayers") and, though in abused form, in Paul's description of the Lord's Supper at Corinth (1 Cor. 11:17-34). It is clearly the case in Justin Martyr's account of the Sunday assembly of the church in Rome around the middle of the second century, where the Scriptures are read and expounded, the people pray, the presider gives thanks over the bread and wine as Christ commanded, the consecrated elements are distributed (even to the absent members), and a collection is made for the help of orphans and widows, the sick and the needy, the imprisoned and temporary sojourners.[3] Concomitantly, the Christian eucharist was seen from very early times as the fulfillment of Malachi 1:11: "From the rising of the sun to its setting my name is great among the nations, and in every place incense is offered to my name, and a pure offering; for my name is great among the nations, says the LORD of hosts." The eucharistic application of the prophetic text is in fact made by the *Didache* (14:1-3), by Justin Martyr, Irenaeus, and Eusebius of Caesarea.[4] It would, then, hardly be surprising if incense came to be employed in connection with the Eucharist.

In fact, the matter is not so simple. The most complete study of "the use of incense in divine worship" roundly declares that "up to the time of Constantine the Great, or even later, there was no use of incense whatever in the public worship of the Church"; that "for the first five centuries of the Christian era" there was "a striking unanimity" among the Fathers against "any offering of incense as a sacrifice to God"; and that it was only gradually thereafter that a "change of opinion came over the Church" in regard to the "propriety" of such a practice.[5] Early opposition, it is said, was based on Christ's having replaced Jewish sacrifices, on "the philosophical argument that Almighty God, being an incorporeal spirit, could take no pleasure in a mere corporeal odor" (with Isaiah 1:13, so understood, being invoked in both cases), and on the association of incense with pagan rituals and especially with emperor worship. As we have seen in regard to icons, however, such an interpretation may require some nuancing, both historically and theologically.

In any case, the earliest literary evidence for the Christian use of incense, dating from the fourth century, occurs in connection with funerals, where the associations may have been not so much fumigatory, let alone apotropaic, but rather triumphal: the victorious were proceeding to glory; and we shall return later to the "odor of sanctity" attaching to

---

3. Justin Martyr, *First Apology,* 65-67 (Migne, *Patrologia Graeca* 6:428-32; hereafter cited as *PG*); see R. C. D. Jasper and G. J. Cuming, *Prayers of the Eucharist: Early and Reformed,* 3d ed. (New York: Pueblo, 1987), pp. 28-30.

4. Justin Martyr, *Dialogue with Trypho the Jew,* 41, cf. 116f. (Migne, *PG* 6:564, cf. 744-49); Irenaeus, *Against the Heresies* IV.17.5 (*PG* 7:1023-24); Eusebius of Caesarea, *Demonstration of the Gospel* I.10 (*PG* 22:92).

5. E. G. Cuthbert F. Atchley, *A History of the Use of Incense in Divine Worship* (London: Longmans, Green, 1909), here pp. 90, 117. Much of my historical information is derived from this work, despite its disorderly state.

Christians who are anointed members of Christ's body. By the sixth century we find, especially in the East, the "offering of incense" associated with liturgical prayers of propitiation and petitions for grace or the descent of the Holy Spirit. Attested a little later in the West, such usage lasted there for many centuries, although it is the Eastern eucharistic liturgies that remain more permanently and firmly marked by it. Clearly such "incense prayers" are problematic for those of us whose liturgical, and above all theological, context is Protestant. Less worrisome perhaps is the traditional Western Catholic use of incense, evidenced at least from the eighth century onward, at vespers (where it "doubtless was first suggested by the versicle and response before the canticle Magnificat: 'Let my prayer be set forth, O Lord, as incense in thy sight'") and at matins (where, as under the Old Law, it was the morning's "natural complement" to the evening, and where its association with the Benedictus canticle recalled Luke 1:5-23, 57-80).[6]

A further traditional liturgical use of incense, which in my estimation is the least problematic, is the honorific. The Seventh Ecumenical Council, that of Nicea II in 787, declared it proper to burn incense and lights, in a "veneration of honor," before icons as before "the precious and life-giving cross" and the book of the Gospels.[7] Similar honorific censing came to be shown also to the altar-table, the bread and wine, the ministers, and indeed the entire congregation. This is intelligible as honor shown to Christ, since all those objects and persons may be taken, in various ways, as signs, vehicles, or instances of the active presence of our Lord and Savior.

At this point we move quite easily into the notion of Christians as the bearers of "the aroma of Christ." To sum up what has so far been said about incense as recalling the "fragrant offering" of Christ's sacrifice, and to prepare for what will be said about the aromatic effects of Christ's grace to Christians, we may quote Saint Thomas Aquinas on the reverential and grace-signifying purposes of the use of incense at the Eucharist (noting that the medieval schoolman was not above acknowledging the need for fumigation):

> We use incense, not as commanded by a ceremonial precept of the Law,
> but as prescribed by the Church; accordingly we do not use it in the

6. Atchley, *Use of Incense*, p. 152.

7. See Daniel J. Sahas, *Icon and Logos: Sources in Eighth-Century Iconoclasm* (Toronto: University of Toronto Press, 1986), p. 179.

same fashion as it was ordered under the Old Law. It has reference to two things: first to the reverence due to this sacrament [the Eucharist], i.e. in order by its good odor to remove any disagreeable smell that may be about the place; secondly, it serves to show the effect of grace, wherewith Christ was filled as with a good odor, according to Genesis 27:27, "Behold, the odor of my son is like the odor of a ripe field"; and from Christ it spreads to the faithful by the work of his ministers, according to 2 Corinthians 2:14, "He manifesteth the odor of his knowledge by us in every place"; and therefore when the altar, which represents Christ, has been incensed on every side, then all are incensed in their proper order.[8]

2. The Aroma of Christ

In the Gospel stories, the anointing of Christ's own body is associated with his burial, and hence with his resurrection. When, during dinner at the house of Simon the leper in Bethany, just before Jesus' impending passion and death, a woman came up to him with "an alabaster flask of very expensive ointment" and poured it on his head, Jesus acknowledged the "beautiful thing" she had done to him and said: "In pouring this ointment on my body she has done it to prepare me for burial"; and he prophesied that "wherever this gospel is preached in the whole world, what she has done will be told in memory of her" (Matt. 26:6-13; Mark 14:3-9; cf. John 12:1-8; Luke 7:36-38). On the first Easter Sunday morning, Mary Magdalene, Mary the mother of James, and Salome, having "bought spices, so that they might go and anoint," found to their surprise the stone rolled back and the tomb void of his body (Mark 16:1-8; Luke 24:1-11; cf. Matt. 28:1-10) — and what the Eastern Orthodox liturgical tradition calls "the myrrh-bearing women *(hai murophorai)*" became the first carriers of the gospel, even to the apostles (Matt. 28:7-10; Luke 24:8-11; cf. Mark 16:7f.; John 20:18).

Responding in faith to the gospel, Christians "have been anointed by the Holy One" (1 John 2:20, 27). The same Holy Spirit, accompanying the Word from all eternity, has remained with the incarnate Christ, dead, buried,

---

8. Thomas Aquinas, *Summa Theologiae* III.83.5 ad 2 (cited from *St. Thomas Aquinas: Summa Theologica,* trans. the Fathers of the English Dominican Province [New York: Benziger, 1947], 2:2521).

and risen (Luke 1:35; Matt. 3:16 = Mark 1:10 = Luke 3:22; Luke 4:1, 14, 18; John 1:32-34; Heb. 9:14; Rom. 8:11), and at Christ's exaltation has now been poured out upon the followers of Christ (Luke 24:49; John 14:16f., 26; 15:26; 16:13-15; 20:22; Acts 1:8; 2:33; Rom. 5:5). The Syriac *Teaching of the Apostles* affirms that "a sweet odor, strange to the world" accompanied the outpouring of the Holy Spirit at Pentecost.[9] However that may be, the apostle Paul can write that Christians, having by their baptism died with Christ and been buried with him and raised to newness of life in him (Rom. 6:1-4) and been sealed with the Holy Spirit (2 Cor. 1:21f.; Eph. 1:13f.), are by their very presence "the aroma of Christ" in the world, a fragrance of life to those who are being saved, and by the same token a fragrance of death to those who are perishing (2 Cor. 2:14-16):

> But thanks be to God, who in Christ always leads us in triumph, and through us spreads the fragrance of the knowledge of him everywhere. For we are the aroma of Christ to God among those who are being saved and among those who are perishing, to one a fragrance from death to death, to the other a fragrance from life to life.

And shortly afterward in the same epistle, in a passage we have already noted, the apostle tells how spoken testimony to Christ is a vehicle for the extension of God's grace, so that more and more people may be added to the eucharistic chorus (2 Cor. 4:13-15).[10]

There are stories from the early centuries of the church that tell of the sweet smell of the saints.[11] Thus the account from the church at Smyrna concerning the martyrdom of Saint Polycarp in the year 155 or 156 reports that "the fire encompassed as by a circle the body of the martyr. And he appeared within not like flesh which is burnt, but as bread that is baked, or as gold and silver glowing in a furnace. Moreover, we perceived such a sweet odor [coming from the pyre], as if frankincense or some such precious spices had been smoking there."[12] The dead body of Saint Simon Stylites was said by his disciple Anthony to have exhaled a sweet fragrance.[13] Saint Gregory

---

9. *Syriac Documents Attributed to the First Three Centuries,* trans. B. P. Pratten, in The Ante-Nicene Christian Library, vol. 20, part 2 (Edinburgh: T. & T. Clark, 1871), p. 37.

10. See above, pp. 30-31.

11. See Atchley, *Use of Incense,* pp. 108-14.

12. *Martyrdom of Polycarp,* 15 (Migne, *PG* 5:1040-41).

13. Joannes Bollandus, *Acta Sanctorum,* ed. J. Carnandet (Paris: Victor Palmé, 1863ff.), 1(1863):268 (for January 5).

of Tours is particularly rich in recounting the odor of sanctity: when, for example, the tomb of bishop Valerius of Saint-Lizier de Conserans was opened, such a sweet smell arose that "no one could doubt that there lay a friend of God"; and when the aid of Saint Martin of Tours was invoked during a storm at sea, a balsamic scent covered the whole ship, and the waves became calm.[14] The relics of Saint Germain of Auxerre, it is said, gave off some fifty years after death a fragrance of lilies and roses.[15] The Venerable Bede records the visions of a Northumbrian man, where paradise was described as "a vast and delightful field, full of fragrant flowers," and from the kingdom of heaven itself there came forth "so wonderful a fragrance that the other, which I had before thought most delightful, then seemed to me but very insipid."[16] An Anglo-Saxon poem based on Lactantius's "Carmen de Phoenice" paints paradise thus:

> Beauteous is all the plain
> with delights blessed,
> with the sweetest of earth's odors. . . .
> There a holy fragrance
> rests o'er the pleasant land.[17]

Returning to earth, we find oils, often aromatic, used in various Christian rituals. Thus already the early church order identified as the *Apostolic Tradition* of Hippolytus prescribes a twofold anointing after baptism that has persisted in the Roman rite to this day. First, a presbyter anoints the newly baptized with the oil of thanksgiving and says, "I anoint you with holy oil in the name of Jesus Christ." Then the neophytes are brought from the baptistery into the full assembly, and the bishop lays hands on them and invokes the Holy Spirit (as having just been the agent of regeneration or as about to fill the recipients with grace), and "then, pouring the oil of thanksgiving from his hand and placing it on their head, he shall say: I anoint you with holy oil in God the Father almighty and

14. See, respectively, Gregory of Tours, *Liber de gloria confessorum*, 84 (Migne, *Patrologia Latina* 71:892; hereafter cited as *PL*) and *De miraculis sancti Martini* I.9 (*PL* 71:922-23).

15. Bollandus, *Acta Sanctorum* 34 (1868):275 (for July 31).

16. Bede, *Historia Ecclesiastica* V.12 (Migne, *PL* 95:249-50).

17. Translation from Benjamin Thorpe, *Codex Exoniensis: A Collection of Anglo-Saxon Poetry from a Manuscript in the Library of the Dean and Chapter of Exeter* (London: Society of Antiquaries of London, 1842).

Christ Jesus and the Holy Spirit."[18] When the initiation rites became split into "baptism" and "confirmation," the first Roman postbaptismal anointing stayed with baptism and was given a strongly christological interpretation, while the second postbaptismal anointing went with the imposition of episcopal hands to make confirmation, pneumatologically understood — however theologically awkward the disjunction between Christ and the Spirit. In the Orthodox East, water baptism and the anointing with chrism remained ritually together, so that there was less risk of divorcing Christ and the Spirit. Thus Saint Cyril of Jerusalem expounded the ritual and theological connection in the following way:

> Just as Christ was truly crucified, buried, and raised again, and you are considered worthy to be crucified, buried, and raised with him in likeness by baptism, so too in the matter of anointing, Christ was "anointed with the spiritual oil of gladness" because he is the author of spiritual joy [Ps. 45:6f.; cf. Acts 10:38]; and you have been anointed with chrism because you have become fellows and sharers of Christ. But be sure not to regard the chrism merely as ointment. Just as the bread of the eucharist after the invocation of the Holy Spirit is no longer just bread but the body of Christ, so the holy chrism after the invocation is no longer ordinary ointment but Christ's grace, which through the presence of the Holy Spirit instills his divinity into us. It is applied to your forehead and organs of sense with a symbolic meaning; the body is anointed with visible ointment, and the soul is sanctified by the holy, hidden Spirit.[19]

In the current Roman Catholic rite for the consecration of oils on Maundy Thursday, the new prayer over the chrism that will be used to anoint the baptized and the confirmed runs in large part thus:

> By his suffering, dying, and rising to life
> Christ saved the human race.

18. Geoffrey J. Cuming, *Hippolytus: A Text for Students* (Bramcote, Nottingham: Grove Books, 1976), p. 20.

19. Cyril of Jerusalem, *Mystagogical Catecheses* III.2-3 (Migne, *PG* 33:1089-92); translation from Edward Yarnold, *The Awe-Inspiring Rites of Initiation: Baptismal Homilies of the Fourth Century* (Slough, Buckinghamshire: St. Paul Publications, 1972), pp. 80f. The significance of the anointing of the various organs has already been detailed (see above, pp. 16-18).

He sent your Spirit to fill the Church
with every gift needed to complete your saving work.
From that time forward,
through the sign of holy chrism,
you dispense your life and love to men.
By anointing them with the Spirit,
you strengthen all who have been reborn in baptism.
Through that anointing
you transform them into the likeness of Christ your Son
and give them a share in his royal, priestly, and prophetic work.
And so, Father, by the power of your love,
make this mixture of oil and perfume
a sign and source of your blessing.
Pour out the gifts of your Holy Spirit
on our brothers and sisters who will be anointed with it.
Let the splendor of holiness shine on the world
from every place and thing
signed with this oil.
Above all, Father, we pray
that through this sign of your anointing
you will grant increase to your Church
until it reaches the eternal glory
where you, Father, will be all in all,
together with Christ your Son,
in the unity of the Holy Spirit,
for ever and ever. Amen.[20]

"Anointing with oil in the name of the Lord" is prescribed by James 5:13-15 together with prayers by the elders of the church over the sick person (cf. Mark 6:13). The practice of anointing the sick has a checkered history, especially in the West (where it was turned into a penitential rite before death); but it has been revived in more recent times, even in some Protestant churches that had abandoned it altogether.[21] The current Roman prayer for the blessing of the oil of the sick reads as follows:

20. *The Roman Missal: The Sacramentary,* trans. International Commission on English in the Liturgy (New York: Catholic Book Publishing Co., 1974), pp. 1020f.
21. See Élie Mélia, "The Sacrament of the Anointing of the Sick: Its Historical Development and Current Practice," in *Temple of the Holy Spirit: Sickness and Death of the*

Lord God, loving Father,
you bring healing to the sick
through your Son Jesus Christ.
Hear us as we pray to you in faith,
and send the Holy Spirit, man's Helper and Friend,
upon this oil, which nature has provided
to serve the needs of men.
May your blessing
come upon all who are anointed with this oil,
that they may be freed from pain and illness
and made well again in body, mind, and soul.
Father, may this oil be blessed for our use
in the name of our Lord Jesus Christ,
who lives and reigns with you for ever and ever. Amen.[22]

Anointing is a relative latecomer to the rites of ordination. It seems to be a Gallican innovation at the time of Charlemagne, when Old Testament typologies previously associated with the royal and priestly status of all the baptized in Christ came to be particularly applied to civil rulers and to the ministerial *sacerdotium*. For our theme, an interesting prayer of accompaniment is one that was taken from the Missale Francorum into the later composite Romano-German rite and so spread throughout the West: "May these hands be consecrated and hallowed by this unction and our blessing, so that whatever they bless may be blessed, and whatever they hallow may be hallowed."[23]

Whether in chrismation or in ministry to the sick or in the rites of ordination, anointing is associated with the imposition of hands, and that brings us to the sense of touch, which will occupy the rest of this chapter. But a brief extra note needs perhaps to be inserted meanwhile. Lest all

---

Christian in the Liturgy, trans. M. J. O'Connell, Twenty-First Liturgical Conference Saint-Serge (New York: Pueblo, 1983), pp. 127-60; and, for ecumenical breadth, Karen Westerfield Tucker, "Christian Rituals Surrounding Sickness," in *Life Cycles in Jewish and Christian Worship,* ed. P. F. Bradshaw and L. A. Hoffman (Notre Dame, Ind.: University of Notre Dame Press, forthcoming).

22. *The Roman Missal: The Sacramentary* (1974), p. 1017. For current Roman Catholic pastoral practice and its historical background, see Charles W. Gusmer, *And You Visited Me: Sacramental Ministry to the Sick and Dying* (New York: Pueblo, 1984).

23. See Paul F. Bradshaw, *Ordination Rites of the Ancient Churches of East and West* (New York: Pueblo, 1990), pp. 18f., 227, 241, 242.

this talk of incense and aromatic oils prove too much for some of my fellow Protestants, let it be noted that our nostrils also are sometimes engaged by the worship assembly. The flowers that are placed on our altar-tables and around our sanctuaries continue a practice that goes back at least to the fourth century.[24] Easter lilies perfume an entire building. The scent of pine has been admitted to our churches with the Christmas tree. Imported palm branches may retain just a trace of their natural odor on Passion Sunday, and their burning at the start of next year's Lent brings a pungency to the air at the ancient practice of the imposition of penitential ashes which has caught on in our churches over the past few years. A freshly baked loaf of bread will improve the smell of any Eucharist. And failing that, there is always the reek of coffee at the fellowship hour.

3. The Hand of God

According to Luke 11:20, Jesus confuted his accusers in the Beelzebul controversy with the argument that "if it is by the finger of God that I cast out demons, then the kingdom of God has come upon you" — or, in Matthew's version (12:28), "if it is by the Spirit of God. . . ." Saint Irenaeus thought of the Word and the Spirit as the two "hands" of God in his work toward the creation.[25] It was by a mighty hand and an outstretched arm that God had delivered Israel from Egypt (Exod. 3:19f.; 7:5; 13:3, 9, 16; Deut. 6:21; 7:8, 19; 9:26; 11:2; 26:8; Pss. 98:1; 136:12). Certainly the incarnate Son made salutary use of his hands and exercised a touch of healing and blessing.

Take, for example, the story in Mark 7:31-37 of Jesus healing the deaf-mute:

> They brought to [Jesus] a man who was deaf and had an impediment in his speech; and they besought him to lay his hand upon him. And

---

24. See Atchley, *Use of Incense*, p. v.

25. The figure occurs frequently in books III-V of *Against the Heresies*, almost always in connection with God's "molding" of humankind (cf. Gen. 1:26f.; 2:7; Job 10:8f.; Ps. 119:73). When "hand" is used in the singular, the reference is always to the Son, as notably in Saint Irenaeus's mention of Jesus' healing of the man born blind in John 9 (*Against the Heresies* V.15.2; Migne, *PG* 7:1165). See Jacques Fantino, *La Théologie d'Irénée. Lecture des Écritures en réponse à l'exégèse gnostique* (Paris: Éditions du Cerf, 1994), pp. 306-9.

taking him aside from the multitude privately, he put his fingers into his ears, and he spat and touched his tongue; and looking up to heaven, he sighed, and said to him, "Ephphatha," that is, "Be opened." And his ears were opened, his tongue was released, and he spoke plainly. And he charged them to tell no one; but the more he charged them, the more zealously they proclaimed it. And they were astonished beyond measure, saying, "He has done all things well; he even makes the deaf hear and the dumb speak."

That healing act of Christ inspired, in the Roman rites of initiation, the ceremony of the *"ephphatha,"* also known as "the opening of the ears *(apertio aurium),"* whereby the candidates for baptism were readied for the hearing of the gospel.[26] It also helped to inspire a stanza of Charles Wesley's "O for a Thousand Tongues to Sing":

> Hear him, ye deaf; his praise, ye dumb,
> Your loosened tongues employ;
> Ye blind, behold your Saviour come,
> And leap, ye lame, for joy.[27]

In the Greek of Mark 7:37a, the echo to Genesis 1:31 (LXX) resounds: "He has done all things well" recalls "God saw everything that he had made, and behold, it was very good" and thus suggests that Christ is in fact the creative Word made flesh.

Again, the story in the Fourth Gospel of Jesus healing the man born blind runs thus: "[Jesus] spat on the ground and made clay of the spittle and anointed the man's eyes with the clay, saying to him, 'Go, wash in the pool of Siloam' (which means Sent). So he went and washed and came back seeing" (John 9:6f.). In fact, several cases of cures by Jesus involve the use of his healing touch: he touched the leper (Matt. 8:3 = Mark 1:41 = Luke 5:13), he took by the hand both Peter's mother-in-law (Matt. 8:15 = Mark 1:31) and Jairus's daughter (Matt. 9:25 = Mark 5:41 = Luke 8:54), he touched the eyes of various other blind people (Matt. 9:29; 20:34).

---

26. For the somewhat complicated history of this ceremony, see Alois Stenzel, *Die Taufe. Eine genetische Erklärung der Taufliturgie* (Innsbruck: Rauch, 1958), pp. 64-67, 164-66, 190-93.

27. From "Glory to God, and Praise and Love," which was published in John and Charles Wesley, *Hymns and Sacred Poems* (London, 1740).

Indeed, it sufficed for a hemorrhaging woman to touch "the fringe of his garment" in order to be healed (Matt. 9:20f. = Mark 5:27f. = Luke 8:44).

In the course of his earthly ministry, people brought children to Jesus, "that he might lay his hands on them and pray" (Matt. 19:13; cf. Mark 10:13; Luke 18:15); and "he took them in his arms and blessed them, laying his hands upon them" (Mark 10:16; cf. Matt. 19:15). As Jesus was about to ascend to the Father, he led his disciples out as far as Bethany, and "lifting up his hands he blessed them" (Luke 24:50).

As ministerial gestures, both the imposition and the raising of hands in blessing are well known in Christian ritual practice. The laying on of hands characteristically occurs in confirmation, in the healing of the sick, and in ordination.

The rite of "confirmation" in the West has a distinct history ever since the temporal separation of the bishop's imposition of hands and anointing from the water baptism.[28] The most constant theme of the prayer that accompanies the episcopal gesture — whether of a general extension of the hand over all the candidates or an individual hand-laying on each — is the sevenfold gift of the Holy Spirit (derived from Isaiah 11:2), a growth in grace needed either for strengthening in the fight against sin or for the proclamation to others of the same salvation as one has oneself received (and the latter notion may have contributed to confirmation's becoming an occasion for the personal profession of faith on the part of one who had received baptism as an infant).[29] In either case, the Holy Spirit comes at the prayer of the Lord Jesus Christ, in whom we "have strength for everything" and "are more than conquerors" (Phil. 4:13; Rom. 8:37; cf. Col. 1:11; 2 Thess. 3:3), and who appoints us as his witnesses and ambassadors in the world (Acts 1:8; 2 Cor. 5:20).

Imposition of hands has been a part of Christian ministry to the sick.[30] According to Mark 16:18, Jesus promised that believers "will lay their hands

28. See, for example, Gerard Austin, *Anointing with the Spirit: The Rite of Confirmation* (New York: Pueblo, 1985).

29. The notion of confirmation as "strengthening for the fight" goes back to a much-quoted sermon for Pentecost from fifth-century Gaul, now ascribed to Faustus of Riez (Migne, *PL,* Supplementum 3 [Paris: Garnier, 1963], 615-17; see L. A. van Buchem, *L'homélie pseudo-eusébienne de pentecôte* [Nijmegen: Janssen, 1967]); that of "preaching to others," to a phrase developed from the Carolingian Alcuin of York by his pupil Rabanus Maurus (see his *De clericorum institutione* I.30; Migne, *PL* 107:314).

30. See again, Tucker, "Christian Rituals Surrounding Sickness."

on the sick, and they will recover." The instruction in James 5:14f. that "the elders of the church" should "pray over" the sick has been taken to imply the imposition of hands,[31] although ritually the gesture appears sometimes to have been subsumed under the anointing that the same passage authorizes. The gesture may be implied in the fourth-century Egyptian prayer of Sarapion that the "Lord God of mercies" would "stretch out [a] hand and grant that all the sick may be healed."[32] Most Eastern rites of ordination typically include among the rights and duties of the priest and bishop the laying of hands upon the sick for their healing.[33] Luther thought the "elders" mentioned in James 5:14 need not be clergy but might be senior laypeople.[34] In contemporary times, even some Protestant churches with an aversion to oil have increasingly resumed the laying of hands on the sick with prayer, recognizing also (as the church in the early centuries certainly did) that laypersons may be endowed with the gift of healing.

Imposition of hands is attested as part of appointment to ministry in the New Testament, especially for preaching and teaching (Acts 13:1-5; 1 Tim. 4:13-16; 2 Tim. 1:6-14). The action accompanies the oldest extant prayer for the ordination of a bishop, which is found in the so-called *Apostolic Tradition* of Hippolytus and has greatly influenced some modern revisions of the rite. The prayer itself asks God the Father to "pour forth now . . . the sovereign Spirit, whom you gave to your beloved Son Jesus Christ, which he gave to your holy apostles who established the Church in every place as your sanctuary, to the unceasing glory and praise of your name"; the gift will enable the bishop to feed the flock and to lead God's people in its priestly service.[35]

The ascending Lord's action of lifting his hands in blessing upon his disciples rests on a history reaching back at least to Aaron (Lev. 9:22;

---

31. So, for example, Origen, *Homilies on Leviticus* II.4 (Migne, *PG* 12:419).

32. Prayer 30, in *The Sacramentary of Sarapion of Thmuis: A Text for Students*, ed. and trans. R. J. S. Barrett-Lennard (Bramcote, Nottingham: Grove Books, 1993), p. 19.

33. See the prayers in Bradshaw, *Ordination Rites:* Armenian (pp. 130f.), East Syrian (pp. 161, 164), Georgian (pp. 171, 172); cf. the less precise Coptic (pp. 146, 153) and Jacobite (pp. 181, 184).

34. *D. Martin Luthers Werke* (Weimar: Böhlau, 1883ff.), 6 (1888):569, 26-36.

35. Translation basically from Cuming, *Hippolytus: A Text for Students*, p. 9. The translation of the phrase *principalis Spiritus* is mine. For a summary statement on the variable place of the imposition of the hands in ordination rites (granted that it is "almost universally attested as the principal ritual gesture of ordination"), see Bradshaw, *Ordination Rites*, pp. 33f.; cf. pp. 44-46, 59f., 72f.

cf. Num. 6:22-27). The use of a solemn trinitarian blessing, familiar in the Anglican and related traditions, as a dismissal at the end of the Eucharist may well have some unfortunate origins in a medieval gesture of compensation to noncommunicants.[36] In any case, a similar blessing became a customary conclusion in Protestantism to the main Sunday service (whether a "service of the word" or the Lord's Supper), with Lutheran and Calvinist practice favoring the Aaronic formulary. Jesus' own parting benediction was fulfilled in the descent of the Holy Spirit at Pentecost; and that thought should determine all liturgical uses of the gesture and prayer.

4. IMITATE WHAT YOU HANDLE

The solidity of Jesus' flesh, even when transformed by the resurrection, was such that he could invite his startled disciples in Jerusalem: "See my hands and my feet, that it is I myself; handle me, and see; for a spirit has not flesh and bones as you see that I have." And the story continues: "And while they still disbelieved for joy, and wondered, he said to them, 'Have you anything here to eat?' They gave him a piece of broiled fish, and he took it and ate before them" (Luke 24:36-43). A week later, he invited doubting Thomas: "Put your finger here, and see my hands; and put out your hand, and place it in my side; do not be faithless, but believing." And Thomas confessed, "My Lord and my God!" (John 20:24-28). If Mary Magdalene had earlier provoked the risen Lord's *"Noli me tangere"* (which became a favorite scene in both Eastern iconography and Western art), modern exegetes tend less toward "Touch me not" than "Do not hold on to me" — which may better match the ground given by Christ: "For I have not yet ascended to the Father" (John 20:17).

When Saint John, at the opening of his first epistle, speaks of what he has not only seen and heard but "touched with our hands" concerning the word of life (1 John 1:1-3), the reference is apparently both to "the Word made flesh" *and* (since it is a matter of transmission to his addressees) the audible, visible, and tangible means by which the exalted Lord con-

36. See A. G. Martimort, *L'Église en prière* (Paris: Desclée, 1961), pp. 422-24; cf. A. G. Martimort and others, *The Church at Prayer,* trans. M. J. O'Connell, new ed. (Collegeville: Liturgical Press, 1986), 2:115f.

tinues to convey himself to his followers.[37] It is above all at the Lord's Supper that Christ "gives himself into our hands," and thence into our mouths, and through them into the very marrow of our being — though never into our pockets. In the words of George Herbert:

> The greatest shepherd of the fold
> Us did make, for us was sold.
> He our foes in pieces brake;
> Him we touch, and him we take.[38]

At their ordination, Roman Catholic priests are told, "Imitamini quod tractatis." Looking forward to their presidency at the Lord's Table and to their entire pastoral ministry, they receive the following charge:

> Know what you are doing. *Imitate what you handle.* In as much as you celebrate the mystery of the Lord's death and resurrection, endeavor to mortify all sin in your members, and to walk in newness of life.[39]

The notion of "imitating" in daily life what is done in the liturgy is by no means confined to the ministerial priesthood. Several prayers at Mass during the Easter season in particular carry the idea through for the entire assembly of the faithful. Thus it is prayed on Easter Monday that the baptized may "keep in their lives to the sacrament they have received in faith"; on the Friday in the first week of Easter, that "we may imitate and achieve what we celebrate and profess"; on the Second Sunday of Easter, that the paschal sacrament "may live for ever in our hearts and minds"; and on the final Saturday of the season, that "we who have celebrated the Easter ceremonies may hold fast to them in life and conduct."[40]

That baptism, and the faith that it signifies, engages in a spiritual

---

37. See above, pp. 12-13.

38. From George Herbert, *The Temple* (Cambridge, 1633).

39. From the Roman Pontifical of 1968: *De ordinatione presbyterorum,* 14, where the references to the resurrection are new additions. The official English-language translation loses much by saying, "Imitate the mystery you celebrate"; see *The Rites of the Catholic Church,* trans. International Commission on English in the Liturgy, vol. 2 (New York: Pueblo, 1980), p. 63. The "imitate what you handle" goes back as far as Durandus of Mende in the thirteenth century.

40. My translations from the *Missale Romanum* of Paul VI; somewhat freer versions are found in *The Roman Missal: The Sacramentary* (1974).

way our entire bodily existence is well expressed in the total immersion practiced by the Orthodox and by the Baptists. Baptism is the sacramental basis of what the Mennonite theologian James McClendon calls "body ethics"[41] and also of what we may correspondingly designate "body piety." The piety shows itself in the informal signing of one's body with the sign of the cross, in what 1 Timothy 2:8 calls "lifting holy hands" in prayer (a gesture stretching from the *orans* pictures in the catacombs to modern Pentecostalism), in penitential or submissive kneeling, in reverential genuflections, in the ascetical practices suggested by the apostle Paul's athletic imagery (1 Cor. 9:24-27; 1 Tim. 6:6-16; 2 Tim. 4:7f.). All this, and a matching ethical behavior, is appropriate to those whose bodies are "members of Christ" and "temples of the Holy Spirit" (1 Cor. 6:9-20; 2 Cor. 6:14–7:1). Our Lord is both Savior and Judge: "For we must all appear before the judgment seat of Christ, so that each one may receive good or evil, according to what he has done in the body" (2 Cor. 5:10).

A gesture which expresses and reinforces the communal character of the life in Christ is the kiss of peace. Found already as the "holy kiss" in the letters of the apostle Paul (Rom. 16:16; 1 Cor. 16:20; 2 Cor. 13:12; 1 Thess. 5:26; cf. 1 Pet. 5:14), the ritual exchange came to be seen as the sign of that reconciliation among brothers and sisters that the Lord said should precede the offering of a gift at the altar (Matt. 5:23f.; cf. *Didache* 14), and so it figures in ancient rites, between the prayers of the faithful and the presentation of the bread and wine; in Rome and North Africa, it shifted to a point just before Communion, attracted there perhaps by the fifth petition of the Lord's Prayer said at that juncture. The beginning of the gesture's restoration to Protestant rites appears to have occurred with the influential *Order for the Lord's Supper* of the newly united Church of South India (1950), where it was borrowed from a culturally adapted form that had been preserved among the Thomas Christians.[42]

Body language passes into what Orthodox Christians have taken to calling "the liturgy after the Liturgy" when we come to the traditional corporeal works of mercy. In Galatians 6:10, the apostle Paul exhorted the Christians to "do good to all . . . , and especially to those who are of the household of faith." Christ's parable of the Last Judgment in Matthew

---

41. James W. McClendon, *Ethics: Systematic Theology I* (Nashville: Abingdon, 1986), pp. 78-109, cf. 255-59.

42. See T. S. Garrett, *Worship in the Church of South India,* rev. ed. (London: Lutterworth Press, 1965), pp. 34f.

25:31-46 probably concerned the destiny of the nations according to their treatment of Christ's disciples and messengers;[43] but over the centuries, Christians themselves have been moved by it to practice compassion toward their necessitous sisters and brothers in the faith. Charles Wesley detects service to the common Lord in the help thus given to fellow members of his body:

> The Master of all
> For our service doth call,
> And deigns to approve
> With smiles of acceptance our labour of love.
>
> His burden who bear,
> We alone can declare
> How easy his yoke,
> While to love and good works we each other provoke,
> By word and by deed,
> The bodies in need,
> The souls to relieve,
> And freely as Jesus hath given to give.
>
> Then let us attend
> Our heavenly Friend
> In his members distressed,
> By want, or affliction, or sickness oppressed;
> The prisoner relieve,
> The stranger receive,
> Supply all their wants,
> And spend and be spent in assisting his saints.[44]

The parable has further provoked works of mercy even toward the hungry and the thirsty, the stranger and the naked, the sick and the imprisoned,

---

43. See Jindrich Máek, "Mit wem identifiziert sich Jesus (Matt. 25:31-46)?" in *Christ and Spirit in the New Testament,* ed. B. Lindars and S. S. Smalley (Cambridge: Cambridge University Press, 1973), pp. 15-25.

44. *A Collection of Hymns for the Use of the People called Methodists* (1780), no. 482, in *The Works of John Wesley,* vol. 7, ed. F. Hildebrandt and O. A. Beckerlegge (Oxford: Clarendon Press, 1983; Nashville: Abingdon, 1989), p. 669.

whatever their allegiance or lack of it. In our day, Mother Teresa of Calcutta is but the most conspicuous among a long line who have been seen as witnesses to Christ in this way — even to the point of being "spoken against" (cf. Luke 2:34).

With the practice of ministry to and through the members of his ecclesial body we are brought back to the earthly body of Christ: through that body he exercised his power to heal and to bless; through the nailing of that body to the cross he gave himself for our redemption as a fragrant offering to God; through the resurrection of that anointed body he opened up new life and the very kingdom of heaven to all believers. The aroma of Christ is now spread in the world by those to and through whom he makes himself very palpably present in water and oil, in bread and wine, and the words and gestures that accompany them.

We have now run the gamut of the bodily *senses* — hearing, vision, taste, smell, and touch — as the channels by which we receive and respond to the Word *made flesh.* The time has come to concentrate again on the meaning of the communication: what is the *sense* of *the Word* made flesh? The fifth and last of these chapters takes advantage of some twentieth-century studies in language to deal once more with that perennial question.

5

Speech, Song, Silence, Scripture

The density of God's Word, it was the argument of the first chapter, reached its most solid form in the incarnation of Christ for our salvation: his life, his teachings and his deeds, his death and his resurrection. The next three chapters showed how all five human senses play their part in the revelation of the gospel and its reception, the response to the gospel and its further transmission as Christ continues his active presence in modes suited to the interval before the final advent of God's kingdom. The point was to take with full seriousness the materiality of God's earthly creation, of the constitution of humankind, of God's redemptive self-engagement with the world, and of the ultimate condition in which God's purpose and human salvation will both be achieved. The emphasis on corporeality, however, should in no way detract from spirituality. "God is spirit" (John 4:24),[1] and the value of the human body resides precisely in its being the organic expression of the soul. That is why we have sought to bring out the training of the senses by and for their proper use, which is to serve "the chief end of man," namely, to "glorify God and enjoy him for ever."

Set in the perspective of this human vocation to personal communion with God, the density of the Word made flesh therefore detracts in no way from its own rationality and intelligibility nor yet abandons its rootage in the transcendent mystery of God. The present chapter will seek

---

1. See G. Wainwright, "The Holy Spirit," in *The Cambridge Companion to Christian Doctrine,* ed. Colin Gunton (Cambridge: Cambridge University Press, forthcoming).

to show this through a theological examination of speech, its stretching in song, its suspension in silence, and finally its standard in the sacred Scriptures. We shall end up affirming a biblical hermeneutic that the eighth-century English scholar, the Venerable Bede, entertainingly described in terms of cuisine which implicitly or explicitly engage all our physical senses: as sayings and events plainly told, the Scripture gives us food cooked on an open griddle; frequent turning over as in a frying pan is needed in order to comprehend Scripture's meaning for faith and conduct in respect of Christ, the church, and the ways of individuals; we need to search in the oven to lay hold in Scripture of what we hope to see in the future.[2]

1. The Intelligibility of Language

In the twentieth century, a great deal of intellectual attention has been devoted to language, in many fields of reflection, science, and endeavor. The so-called linguistic turn has brought out the thoroughgoing linguisticality of human existence. The study of semiotics reckons with our exceedingly complex, subtle, and pervasive systems of communication that comprise words, pictures, symbols, gestures, actions, objects, even institutions. By means of these signs, people and communities explore reality, describe reality, interpret reality, and fashion reality; by these same means, we express and form our thoughts, our emotions, and our values; and by them again, we communicate across time and space in ways which both build and convey traditions, as well as both allowing and reflecting social relations in the present. In the broad sense of the term, we are constantly being addressed by "a word," are constantly taking in "a word," and are constantly uttering "a word." The question is always: *which* word?

It is Christian teaching that humankind is made "in the image of God" (Gen. 1:26f.). Language is involved in all three main strands in the traditional interpretation of that phrase. First, we are made for personal communion with God, who addresses us and to whom we may respond; communion with God, as the whole of Scripture attests, is "dialogical."

2. Bede, *In Samuelem* II.2 (Migne, *Patrologia Latina* 91:562; hereafter cited as *PL*); cf. Peter Hunter Blair, *The World of Bede* (Cambridge: Cambridge University Press, 1990), p. 300.

Second, we are made to be stewards of God's earthly creation, and Adam's naming of the animals is a token of that (cf. Gen. 2:19f.). Third, we are made for society with one another (Gen. 2:21-25), and speech is integral to our social constitution (cf. Gen. 11:1). Accordingly, human use of language is properly governed by the vocation with which God addresses us, by the purpose God has in store for us, and by the need to pass from the calling to the achievement. It should serve to tell, extend, and complete the story that runs from Eden through Calvary to the New Jerusalem. The prime Agent in that comprehensive story is the creative Word of God, who became incarnate for our salvation, and who will continue to receive the adoration of the heavenly company and delight us with his presence. In this divine Word, all human speech and action finds its judgment and the chance of redemption.

Within the general "linguistic turn" of the twentieth century, a particular part was played by "the philosophy of language," and more particularly yet by "linguistic analysis." After the self-destruction of the "logical positivists" (whose own axiom met neither of its own criteria for a meaningful statement; namely, that it must either be analytic, that is, contain the predicate already in the subject, or else refer to a state of affairs that could in principle be verified by empirical or natural-scientific procedures), a more flexible approach to linguistic analysis nevertheless performed the useful function of setting a watch against nonsense. Christian thinkers and speakers should be grateful for this, and we have nothing to fear from it. For here we may draw on that theme of order and purpose which is associated with the Greek *logos* but which is far from lacking in the Scriptures of Israel. It is precisely the orderliness of the created world which allows it to be investigated; and it is precisely the intuition and discovery of purpose which feeds human history and personal existence. Christians believe of Christ that all things were made "through him" and "for him," and "in him all things hold together" (Col. 1:16f.). True "rationality" belongs to the divine Word. In that Word, all things "make sense," a sense which has so far been chiefly revealed to us in the incarnate Christ — his life and his story — and which will be fully disclosed in God's good time. This faith we enjoy, and this gospel we proclaim, in the face of all that presently frustrates happiness and in the face of all ideologies that preach ultimate absurdity.

Another lesson of linguistic philosophy is that the meaning of a word or a sentence or any unit of language is to be found in its use. In the broadest framework, some archaeologists of language have looked for its origins in signals (of warning or summons) or in technology (ideas and words as mental analogues of material tools). The theologian Wolfhart Pannenberg has argued — historically, ethologically, and philosophically — in favor of "festal play" or "cult" as the decisive context for the characteristically human procedure whereby "word" is constituted as "symbol," i.e., as that by which "the absent object becomes present." By a long route, and with many safeguards, Pannenberg gets from there to the Christian understanding of "Jesus as being the revelation of the divine Logos and thus himself the Word of God."[3] Our point here is simply to alert believers to the practical and theological fact that, for us, the *primary use* of language is communication — or communion — between God and the community of faith that gathers in the name of Jesus; that is where its *meaning* is to be found. This makes of the worship assembly and its liturgy the "source and summit" of Christian thinking, speech, and life.[4]

Within many of the various broad areas of linguistic use (or "language games," to extend a notion of Ludwig Wittgenstein),[5] there recurs a feature denominated "performative language," whereby a word does what it says. It is described, among other things, in a book by J. L. Austin whose title reflects beautifully the "density of the *dabar*": *How to Do Things with Words*.[6] Liturgists and sacramental theologians are familiar with the feature "I absolve thee," for example, or (in a composite word-act employing also water and a gesture) "I baptize thee . . ." Theologically, the efficacy of such a speech-act requires that the speaker be authorized to perform it and that it be performed "with the intention of doing what the church does." Performed outside an accepted context of meaning, the act would be void. That points us to a much more comprehensive way in which the divine Word is "performative." George Lindbeck speaks thus of the Scriptures: "For those who are steeped in them, no world is more real than the ones they create. A scriptural world

3. Wolfhart Pannenberg, *Anthropology in Theological Perspective*, trans. M. J. O'Connell (Philadelphia: Westminster, 1985), pp. 315-96.

4. The notion of "source and summit" comes from the Second Vatican Council's constitution on the sacred liturgy, *Sacrosanctum Concilium*, 10.

5. An introduction to Wittgenstein's thought by way of his biography is provided by Ray Monk, *Ludwig Wittgenstein: The Duty of Genius* (New York: Free Press, 1990). Herbert H. Clark talks of "arenas of language use" in a book under that title (Chicago: University of Chicago Press, 1992).

6. J. L. Austin, *How to Do Things with Words* (Cambridge, Mass.: Harvard University Press, 1962).

is thus able to absorb the universe. It supplies the interpretive framework within which believers seek to live their lives and understand reality. . . . Scripture creates its own domain of meaning and . . . the task of interpretation is to extend this over the whole of reality."[7] The Bible is able to accomplish this, not in its own right, but because it bears testimony to the Word who finally became flesh as Jesus Christ and who continues his active presence through the Scriptures and the various practices of the church which they shape and inform. Thus, when the gospel is preached, "whoever hears you hears me" (cf. Luke 10:16). Whoever the ecclesiastical minister of baptism, "it is Christ who baptizes."[8] His presidency signified by the minister who presides in his name, the Lord gives himself in the bread and wine of his Table. At each new gathering of his people, the Word speaks and acts in a context of meaning which was established in the course of his incarnate life and fate, has been maintained in the Tradition of the church, and is refreshed by each of his self-communications. Thus the particular "performative words" of the liturgy depend on the Word made flesh and on his continuing address to a faithful community.

2. Ecstatic Reason

"What is received," says Saint Thomas Aquinas, "is received after the manner of the receiver."[9] The revelation of God that we receive through our senses does not, however, leave us unchanged. While the transformation will become fully evident only at the general resurrection, one manifestation of it occurs already in our thought and our speech through what may be called, borrowing a phrase from Paul Tillich, "ecstatic reason."[10]

---

7. George A. Lindbeck, *The Nature of Doctrine: Religion and Theology in a Postliberal Age* (Philadelphia: Westminister, 1984), p. 117. I will not enter into discussion with Lindbeck's willingness to extend this principle (at least phenomenologically) to the "canonical writings" of religious communities other than Christian.

8. *Hic [Christus] est, qui baptizat:* Augustine, *In Joannis Evangelium* VI.7 (Migne, *PL* 35:1428).

9. See above p. 15.

10. Paul Tillich, *Systematic Theology* (Chicago: Chicago University Press, 1951), 1:60.

For all the prophecies and expectations of a messianic intervention by God, it could not have been guessed beforehand, by human creatures and especially not by fallen humankind, that the second person of the Trinity would, for our salvation, *take flesh* as Jesus of Nazareth and, moreover, *die.* What initially appeared as foolishness and a stumbling block could, however, after the event and only after the event, be appreciated as the wisdom of God who, in his very "foolishness," is "wiser than men" (1 Cor. 1:18-25); so that Christ Jesus can be confessed as "our wisdom, our righteousness and sanctification and redemption" (1 Cor. 1:30). It is, above all, the incarnation, passion, and death of Christ that have provoked and drawn out believers to "ecstatic reason."

It is possible that glossolalia, or speaking with "the tongues of angels" (1 Cor. 13:1), is an exercise of ecstatic reason. I shall look rather at the use of verbal paradox to express deeper truth. Such use is found in the Greek and Latin fathers and hymnographers, in Luther with his insistence on the *sub contrario,* in the English metaphysical poets of the seventeenth century, and (in the liturgical tradition which I know best) in the hymns of the Wesleys. It is, perhaps, the hymnic tradition which best allows the entire worshiping community to appropriate the use of ecstatic reason; our thought and our speech are there stretched in song.

Take, then, Charles Wesley. As a British Methodist I was raised on the *Methodist Hymn Book* of 1933, of whose 984 hymns almost 300 were Wesleyan; for amid all the ecumenical expansion of the twentieth century we had retained at the core of our *lex orandi* many of the texts from the classic *Collection of Hymns for the Use of the People called Methodists* of 1780 and other Wesleyan sources. As a child, I sat in short trousers on the prickly cushions of the hard pews in the Yorkshire village chapel and whiled away many a sermon time by reading through the hymnbook — and gratefully rose to join in the singing of texts I came to know by heart. At Christmas we were able to sing:

> Glory be to God in high,
> And peace on earth descend:
> God comes down, He bows the sky,
> And shows himself our friend:
> God the invisible appears,
> God, the blest, the great I AM
> Sójourns in this vale of tears,
> And Jesus is His name.

Him the angels all adored,
Their Maker and their King;
Tidings of their humbled Lord
They now to mortals bring.
Emptied of His majesty,
Of his dazzling glories shorn,
Being's source begins to be,
And God Himself is born!

Just in that last couplet I absorbed in reverse order, before ever directly hearing of them, both the Council of Ephesus (431) and Paul Tillich.[11] Or there is the more tender expression of the wonder of the incarnation by way of Mary "the God-bearer":

Who gave all things to be,
What a wonder to see
Him born of His creature and nursed on her knee![12]

And, come Passiontide and Good Friday, there was an embarrassment of riches to choose from. "Thou Shepherd of Israel, and Mine" took us to "a place" that turned out to be Calvary:

Ah! show me that happiest place,
The place of Thy people's abode,
Where saints in an ecstasy gaze,
And hang on a crucified God;
Thy love for a sinner declare,
Thy passion and death on the tree;
My spirit to Calvary bear,
To suffer and triumph with Thee.[13]

11. *The Methodist Hymn Book* (London: Methodist Conference Office, 1933), no. 134; originally published in Charles Wesley's *Hymns for the Nativity of our Lord* (London, 1745, but without indication of author, publisher, or date).

12. Unfortunately this text did not make it into the hymnbook. It occurs in Charles Wesley's *Hymns for the Use of Families* (Bristol, 1767). J. A. Kay uses the stanza as part of a composite Christmas hymn in his *Wesley's Prayers and Praises* (London: Epworth Press, 1958), p. 103.

13. *The Methodist Hymn Book*, no. 457; originally in Charles Wesley's *Short Hymns on Select Passages of the Holy Scriptures* (Bristol, 1762).

And so we learned the "crucified God" of Gregory Nazianzen, Martin Luther, and Jürgen Moltmann.[14]

Then there was "God of Unexampled Grace," where ecstasy and paradox unite in the second and third stanzas:

> God of unexampled grace,
> Redeemer of mankind,
> Matter of eternal praise
> We in Thy passion find:
> Still our choicest strains we bring,
> Still the joyful theme pursue,
> Thee the Friend of sinners sing,
> Whose love is ever new.

> Endless scenes of wonder rise
> From that mysterious tree,
> Crucified before our eyes,
> Where we our Maker see:
> Jesus, Lord, what hast Thou done?
> Publish we the death divine,
> Stop, and gaze, and fall, and own
> Was never love like Thine!

> Never love nor sorrow was
> Like that my Saviour showed:
> See Him stretched on yonder Cross,
> And crushed beneath our load!
> Now discern the Deity,
> Now His heavenly birth declare!
> Faith cries out: 'Tis He, 'tis He,
> My God, that suffers there![15]

14. Gregory Nazianzen speaks of *theos stauroumenos,* "a God hanging on a cross," in *Orations* XLV.29 (Migne, *Patrologia Graeca* 36:661; hereafter cited as *PG*); Luther, of *crucifixus et absconditus deus,* "the crucified and hidden God" (*Luthers Werke* [Weimar: Böhlau, 1883ff.], 1[1883]:614); Moltmann, of *der gekreuzigte Gott* (*The Crucified God,* trans. R. A. Wilson and J. Bowden [New York: Harper & Row, 1974]).

15. *The Methodist Hymn Book,* no. 191; originally in John and Charles Wesley's *Hymns on the Lord's Supper* (Bristol, 1745).

Or, as a final example, my village of farmers and coal miners could sing a hymn that echoes both the affectivity of a "crucified love" (as in Ignatius of Antioch and in Origen) and the bold ontology of the Syriac acclamation, "One of the Trinity has suffered":

O Love divine! what hast Thou done?
The immortal God hath died for me!
The Father's co-eternal Son
Bore all my sins upon the tree;
The immortal God for me hath died!
My Lord, my Love is crucified.[16]

Singing is a liturgical action in which the body works to raise the spirit toward God. Nor need the expression of ecstatic reason be limited to the vocal. While serving in West Africa during the 1960s and 1970s, my wife and I would occasionally attend Sunday Mass in a Roman Catholic parish, and the open-air service was known to our children as "the singing and dancing church." To the accompaniment of African instruments, the entrance, offertory, and communion processions would make their way to the altar with rhythmic sways and shuffles. As lovers know, bodily movement can accentuate the experience of transcendence rather than diminish it.

There is, of course, a risk in being "carried away." Saint Augustine, music lover that he was, worried lest even singing, let alone instruments or dance, might by its delights obscure rather than enhance the sense of the biblical words.[17] Ecstatic reason, in its movement of transcendence,

---

16. *The Methodist Hymn Book,* no. 186; originally in John and Charles Wesley's *Hymns and Sacred Poems* (Bristol, 1742). Ignatius's "My love was crucified" (*Letter to the Romans,* 7:2 [Migne, *PG* 5:693]) is taken in a christological sense by Origen, in the prologue to his Commentary on the Song of Songs (Migne, *PG* 13:70). At the turn of the sixth century, the West Syrian patriarch Peter the Fuller interpolated a striking phrase into the liturgical Trishagion: "Holy God, Holy and Mighty, Holy and Immortal, *crucified for us,* have mercy on us." Although this provoked a Byzantine charge of theopaschitism, it is perfectly in line (provided the hymn is interpreted christologically) with a neo-Chalcedonian stress on the unity of Christ's divine Person in the duality of his natures, as John Meyendorff approvingly argues in his *Christ in Eastern Christian Thought* (Crestwood, N.Y.: St. Vladimir's Seminary Press, 1975), pp. 69-89 ("God Suffered in the Flesh").

17. Augustine, *Confessions* X.33.49f. (Migne, *PL* 32:799-800); see James McKinnon, *Music in Early Christian Literature* (Cambridge: Cambridge University Press, 1987), pp. 154f.

should not lose the shape of Christ. If believers are enabled to enter into the ultimate mystery of God, it is only by way of the free and gratuitous self-communication of God that has reached us in the Word made flesh and the Spirit who comes at the prayer of the exalted Lord.

3. INEXHAUSTIBLE MYSTERY

The Word belongs to the inner life of the triune God: the Logos, to use the terminology of the early Christian Apologists, is immanent *(endiathētos)* before being uttered *(prophorikos)*. In being uttered toward the world, the Word "proceeds from the Silence *(apo sigēs),"* says Saint Ignatius of Antioch, and "whoever possesses in truth the word of Jesus can hear even its silence *(hēsychia)."*[18] Accordingly, the modern Russian Orthodox theologian Vladimir Lossky wrote of "a margin of silence" accompanying the "words of revelation" attested in Scripture, and this margin of silence is Tradition in its pure form, which is nothing less than "the life of the Holy Spirit in the Church, communicating to each member of the Body of Christ the faculty of hearing, of receiving, of knowing the Truth in the Light which belongs to it."[19] And so, in turn, the English theologian Andrew Louth can speak of Tradition, on the human side, as "the tacit dimension of the life of the Christian"; it is the "personal knowledge" (to borrow from Michael Polanyi) that is built, maintained, integrated, and perpetuated through habitual participation in the liturgical and ethical practices of the church.[20]

There is, therefore, appropriately a dimension of silence surrounding the Christian liturgy. While always present for "whoever has ears to hear," the silence becomes more evident at particular points. Aided perhaps by the French carol tune "Picardy," English-speaking churches both Catholic and Protestant have in the twentieth century accepted into use G. Moul-

18. Ignatius of Antioch, *Letter to the Magnesians,* 8:2 (Migne, *PG* 5:969; but, with later scholarship, taking the reading without the negative *ouk*); *Letter to the Ephesians,* 15:2 (*PG* 5:657).

19. Vladimir Lossky, *In the Image and Likeness of God,* ed. J. H. Erikson and T. E. Bird (Crestwood, N.Y.: St. Vladimir's Seminary Press, 1974), pp. 141-68 ("Tradition and Traditions"); quotations from pp. 150f., 152.

20. Andrew Louth, *Discerning the Mystery: An Essay on the Nature of Theology* (Oxford: Clarendon Press, 1983), pp. 73-95 ("Tradition and the Tacit"); the quotation is from p. 86. Louth had drawn theological implications from Polanyi on pp. 59-66.

trie's translation of the Cherubic Hymn that is sung at the great entrance with the bread and wine in the Eastern liturgy of Saint James:

> Let all mortal flesh keep silence, and with fear and trembling stand;
> Ponder nothing earthly-minded, for with blessing in his hand
> Christ our God to earth descendeth, our full homage to demand.
>
> King of kings, yet born of Mary, as of old on earth he stood,
> Lord of lords, in human vesture — in the body and the blood —
> He will give to all the faithful his own self for heavenly food.
>
> Rank on rank the host of heaven spreads its vanguard on the way,
> As the Light of light descendeth from the realms of endless day,
> That the powers of hell may vanish as the darkness clears away.
>
> At his feet the six-winged seraph; cherubim with sleepless eye
> Veil their faces to the Presence, as with ceaseless voice they cry —
> Alleluia, alleluia, alleluia, Lord most high![21]

More prosaically, the linguist David Crystal comments thus on silence in the liturgy:

> The use of silence becomes meaningful and distinctive in liturgical events, in a way that is not found elsewhere. Periods of silence are encountered during the act of Consecration, following communion and at other climactic points. Here the limitations of the verbal mode are intuitively felt, and the only alternative to silence is to underline the significance of the moment by other means, such as the sounding of a bell, the use of incense or the playing of music. In conversation, by contrast, lapsing into silence is inadvertent and discomfiting (in our own culture, at least); on the radio it is a state of affairs to be avoided at all costs; in a court of law silence from a witness may be interpreted as contempt. But in liturgy silence is positive and creative.[22]

21. Moultrie's version dates from the second edition of Orby Shipley's *Lyra Eucharistica* (London, 1864). The Cherubic Hymn *(Sigēsato pasa sarx)* can be found in F. E. Brightman, *Liturgies Eastern and Western* (Oxford: Clarendon Press, 1896), pp. 41f.

22. D. Crystal, "Liturgical Language in a Sociolinguistic Perspective," in *Language and the Worship of the Church,* ed. David Jasper and R. C. D. Jasper (New York: St. Martin's Press, 1990), pp. 120-46; the quotation occurs on p. 137.

Thus the divine Word proceeds from Silence and is received in silence — but is not thereby reduced to silence. The Eastern Orthodox *hesychasts* — the practitioners of silence or stillness — remain founded on "the Jesus prayer," even if it be condensed (or, historically speaking, returned) from "Lord Jesus Christ, Son of God, have mercy on me" into the single name "Jesus." Bishop Kallistos Ware writes thus:

> Those brought up in the tradition of the Jesus Prayer are never allowed for one moment to forget the Incarnate Christ. . . . Orthodox believe that the power of God is present in the Name of Jesus, so that the invocation of this Divine Name acts "as an effective sign of God's action, as a sort of sacrament." "The Name of Jesus, present in the human heart, communicates to it the power of deification. . . . Shining through the heart, the Light of the Name of Jesus illuminates all the universe."[23]

As Christians enter into the mystery of God, and progress further and further into the salvation the Orthodox call "deification" or "divinization" (though the distinction between Creator and creature will never be lost), our speech may be suspended in silence; but it will not be a vacuous or an irrational silence. How could it be, since we owe our salvation to the divine Logos who became incarnate for our sake and, according to the teaching of the church, retains his humanity in perpetuity? It will be what the Dutch Reformed theologian K. H. Miskotte called a "filled silence."[24] If there is a silence in heaven (cf. Rev. 8:1), it will echo with the "new song" (cf. Rev. 5:9; 14:3), the praises of the Lord God and of the Lamb; and the marriage feast of the Lamb will doubtless include a "symposium" in which "with sober intoxication" the guests will converse with one another and their Host as the company deepens the "communio sanctorum" in the enjoyment of God.[25]

God is "always greater," and so there will always be more to discover. But God will always remain the God whose being and character and story with the world are told in the Scriptures. Therefore we return again, and finally, to their witness.

23. Timothy Ware, *The Orthodox Church* (Harmondsworth, Middlesex: Penguin Books, 1993), pp. 74f., 312f.

24. K. H. Miskotte, *Gevulde stilte* (Kampen: Kok, 1974).

25. On the eschatologically constitutive character of the praise of God and the messianic banquet, see G. Wainwright, "The Church as a Worshiping Community," in *Pro Ecclesia* 3 (1994): 56-67. "Sober intoxication" is a patristic expression for what might be called, reversing the phrase I have been employing, "rational ecstasy."

4. SENSES OF THE WORD

The standard for Christian speech — and action — resides in the Scriptures which bear primary and permanent testimony to the Word by which God addresses his world and which became incarnate as Jesus Christ, who spoke, acted, died, and was raised, and continues to present himself to his followers in the Holy Spirit. There is a traditional pattern of scriptural interpretation which respects the character of the divine Word as I have displayed it in these chapters: a Word that engages with the materiality of the earthly creation, the concreteness of human history, and the solidity of human flesh; a Word that has its own rationality, offers itself intelligibly to persons made in God's image, and invites their faithful reception and response; a Word that expresses itself also in deeds and calls for their imitation in matching conduct; a Word that attracts redeemed people into a present and future participation and communion in the life of God. I am referring to that patristic and medieval practice of the Scriptures which recognizes their "fourfold sense."[26]

In some accounts of the senses of Scripture, a distinction is made between the literal and the spiritual senses, whereby the former is the meaning intended by the original human author of a text and the latter covers the (further) meaning or meanings which by later events it transpires (also) to have — and which were intended by its divine Author all along. With some basis in 2 Corinthians 3, this approach was primarily employed to allow a Christian reading of the Old Testament, although it could also justify the search for a deeper meaning in New Testament texts. What is of value in it can be included in the fourfold hermeneutical schema that I am about to expound.

A particularly interesting version of the fourfold sense of Scripture is laid out in a verse that is variously attributed to Nicholas of Lyra or Augustine of Denmark, and which I will immediately explain:

Littera gesta docet,
quid credas allegoria,
moralis quid agas,
quo tendas anagogia.

26. See Henri de Lubac, *Exégèse médiévale. Les quatre sens de l'Écriture*, 4 vols. (Paris: Aubier-Montaigne, 1959-64); J. S. Preus, *From Shadow to Promise: Old Testament Interpretation from Augustine to the Young Luther* (Cambridge, Mass.: Harvard/Belknap, 1969).

91

The letter teaches what happened.
Allegory teaches what you shall believe.
The moral sense, what you shall do.
Anagogy, where you shall aim.

This provides a grid for the reading of the *whole* of Scripture, though of course passages will vary in their susceptibility to being taken in one or more of the various senses — partly dependent upon the original genre and intention of the passage (thus, for example, the *telling* of a parable will be a historical event, but the *purpose* of the parable will not be to report events but to convey doctrinal truth, summon to ethical action, or orient lives toward God and his kingdom, or all of those things). With that understanding, let us look at each of the four senses of Scripture and see its appropriateness to what we have developed concerning the incarnation of the Word for the salvation of its own rational and embodied creatures who are called to a destiny of communion with God.

First, "the letter teaches what happened." From my point of view, there is a certain awkwardness about this formulation, for I would not wish, by categorizing historical events under "the letter" in a reductive sense, to rob them of their *inherent* spiritual quality. With that proviso, I take it that the basic and unsupersedable sense of Scripture resides in the reporting — and conveyance through continuing rehearsal of the story — of the *gesta Dei,* the "mighty deeds" by which God "brought us out of darkness into his marvelous light" (cf. 1 Pet. 2:9), the "glorious might" by which God "delivered us from the dominion of darkness and transferred us to the kingdom of his beloved Son, in whom we have redemption, the forgiveness of sins" (cf. Col. 1:11-14). In that sense, a "historical" reading of the Scriptures is indispensable; and historical investigation — even "critical" investigation — of the Scriptures can be helpful, provided that it is not undertaken according to criteria which, on philosophical or ideological grounds, exclude the very notion of a God who acts in human history to the very point of taking flesh as Jesus of Nazareth, whom Christians confess to be the living Lord.

The *consequences* of the *gesta Dei* (and therefore the *purposes,* as we may discern them after the event, of God's actions in history) then entitle and require us to look for the faith, love, and hope that characterize the Christian appropriation of God's self-communication and self-gift — and therefore to read the Scriptures (which testify to God's presence and actions in history) for their doctrinal, ethical, and eschatological sense. These are what were called, in an earlier terminology, the allegorical, the tropological, and the anagogical senses of the Scriptures.

Second, then, "allegory teaches us what to believe." Allegory, says Saint Augustine, is broadly a "mode of speech in which one thing is understood from another"; and he cites as an example 1 Thessalonians 5:6-8 and, more pertinently for our purposes, Galatians 4:22-31, where the apostle finds "an allegory" in the Hagar and Sarah of the book of Genesis: "these women" — and their respective children — "are two covenants."[27] As this latter example illustrates, the primary employment of an allegorical approach was to allow a Christian reading of the Old Testament (along the lines indicated earlier in reference to the so-called literal and spiritual senses): it was a means of finding Christ and the church in the texts. That, in fact, is a good principle to apply to the New Testament texts also. And so "the allegorical sense" came to cover the object, content, and locus of faith — "what you shall believe" as a member of the church. In the church, we read Scripture for the guidance and nourishment of faith — what to "believe in the heart" and "confess with the lips" — in response to the incarnate Word, who remains "near" to his body (cf. Rom. 10:8f.).

This second, or doctrinal, sense of the Scriptures is respected when "the Sacred Scriptures" are taken as, in the words of Pope John Paul II, "the highest authority in matters of faith."[28] For doctrinal purposes, the Scriptures are to be read "according to the analogy of faith." That is to say, the key to this reading of the Scriptures is to be found in the complex but coherent pattern of truth that the early Christian centuries knew as the "rule of faith" and which found a concise expression in the ancient ecumenical creeds.[29] This is not to impose an external test on the Scriptures because the rule of faith itself contains in a nutshell their story, whether such instruments as the creeds be considered, historically speaking, as

27. Augustine, *De Trinitate* XV.9.15 (Migne, *PL* 42:1068-69).

28. John Paul II, encyclical letter of May 25, 1995, *Ut Unum Sint,* par. 79. For the current ecumenical potential of reading the Scriptures in a fourfold sense, see G. Wainwright, "Towards an Ecumenical Hermeneutic: How Can All Christians Read the Scriptures Together?" in *Gregorianum* 76 (1995): 639-62.

29. See H. E. W. Turner, *The Pattern of Christian Truth: A Study in the Relations between Orthodoxy and Heresy in the Early Church* (London: Mowbray, 1954). The 1992 Roman Catholic "universal catechism" handily defines the "analogy of faith," from a systematic point of view, as "the coherence of the truths of faith among themselves and within the whole plan of Revelation" (*Catechism of the Catholic Church* [Mahwah, N.J.: Paulist Press, 1994], p. 33, par. 114).

directly distilled from the Scriptures or as the products of a parallel (but really interactive) development. Thus the Anglican Articles of Religion can say both that "Holy Scripture containeth all things necessary to salvation, so that whatsoever is not read therein, nor may be proved thereby, is not to be required of any man that it should be believed as an article of the Faith, or be thought requisite or necessary to salvation" (article 6) and that the creeds "ought thoroughly to be received and believed, for they may be proved by most certain warrants of holy Scriptures" (article 8). All the teaching of the church is, therefore, properly governed by Scripture; and so Pope John Paul can properly say, in turn, that "Sacred Tradition" is "indispensable to the interpretation of the Word of God."[30]

The third sense of Scripture was denominated "tropological" because it made "figurative" application to the soul and its virtues; substantially, it was "moral explanation pertaining to the cleansing of life and to practical instruction."[31] If the allegorical sense has to do with faith, the tropological has to do with love. We are not to be hearers, or even speakers, of the Word only, but also doers (cf. James 1:22): hearing *(akouē)* must issue in obedience *(hup-akouē);* calling Jesus "Lord" must be matched by "doing the will of his Father who is in heaven" (cf. Matt. 7:21). We look to Scripture in order to discern "the mind of Christ" (1 Cor. 2:16) or "the law of Christ" (Gal. 6:2) and have ourselves and our conduct shaped by them (cf. Rom. 12:1f.; Phil. 2:5).

Such reading of the Scriptures again affects the entire Christian community and the individual members within it. As part of its work on "The Apostolic Tradition," the Joint Commission between the Roman Catholic Church and the World Methodist Council sought in its Singapore Report of 1991 to discern together a "pattern of Christian community"; here is a fragment from this ecumenical effort to read the Scriptures in their moral sense, which shows also the significance of Christian obedience for a witness to the Word before the world:

Whenever the Word of God is truly heard, the Church shapes its life in due obedience; the pattern thus brought into being becomes in turn a means of showing forth the Word. As individuals are healed and remade in Christ, so also are the relationships within which their life is

30. *Ut Unum Sint,* par. 79.
31. That phrase comes from John Cassian, *Collationes* XIV.8 (Migne, *PL* 49:962-65), where he introduces the very terms of "allegoria," "tropologia," and "anagoge."

brought to fulfilment. When, for example, the community of Christians at Philippi was told to have the mind of Christ, who emptied himself and took the form of a servant, this was not just an instruction to private individuals, but an exhortation for the benefit of their common life. Further still, it was not just for their own health and happiness as a community, but for a making known the Word to the world: it was a setting forth of the Word through an effective embodiment of the servanthood of the Incarnate One.[32]

A similar paradigm can be found in 1 Corinthians, where the apostle sets before us the permanent need to "discern the body" (cf. 11:29) by making the proper connection between the body of Christ that has been given for us (11:24) and the body of Christ that should be built up (12:4-31), not destroyed (11:18-22, 30-34). Given the communal character of the church across time and space, the moral and pastoral strands in ecclesial Tradition are vital to the reading of Scripture in this third sense for "what to do."

The fourth sense of Scripture is the anagogical. "Where to go," the designation suggests, is "onward and upward." The mode is hope. The church reads the Scriptures in order to orient itself toward God and his kingdom. The anagogical reading of Scripture is concerned with present mystical aspirations and future eschatological expectations. In Christ we already have the privilege of access to God in prayer as "Abba! Father!" (Rom. 8:15; Gal. 4:6); but, given our own imperfection and the incompleteness of God's kingdom in the world, much of our prayer still has to consist in petition for ourselves and intercession for others, with the Holy Spirit helping us in our weakness (Rom. 8:18-27). When the church gathers at the Lord's Table, we are summoned by the Sursum Corda to "lift up our hearts," and we may already join with the whole company of heaven in singing "Holy, holy, holy"; but we still await the return of our Savior (Phil. 3:20), and, in proclaiming the Lord's death until he comes (1 Cor. 11:26), we receive him under bread and wine, not yet seeing him as he is (1 John 3:2).

The liturgy is a vital strand in the Tradition of the church.[33] The

32. *The Apostolic Tradition* (Lake Junaluska, N.C.: World Methodist Council, 1991), p. 26, par. 50.

33. Elsewhere I have argued that Tradition finds its origin, continuance, and goal in worship; see G. Wainwright, "Tradition as a Liturgical Act," in *The Quadrilog: Tradition and the Future of Ecumenism: Studies in Honor of George H. Tavard* (Collegeville: Liturgical Press, 1994), pp. 129-46.

church offers thanks and prayers to God and looks forward to the day when all will be pure doxology and the complete enjoyment of God; and therefore the worship assembly constitutes an appropriate, indeed the primary, hermeneutical context and continuum for the understanding and application of Scriptures whose composition, arrangement, selection, and transmission were themselves to a considerable extent governed by liturgical factors.[34] As the Scriptures are read, expounded, and "performed" in and by the community gathered in the name of Jesus and in the power of the Spirit,[35] the goal of God's revelation and self-gift is glimpsed: the Word, who became flesh and redeemed us, is heard, seen, touched, and tasted by an anointed body called to be and to spread the fragrance of Christ in the world until such time as all who shall become part of it are joined in a perfect fellowship of praise and delight. "To crown all," says John Wesley at the close of his sermon on "The New Creation,"

> there will be a deep, an intimate, an uninterrupted union with God; a constant communion with the Father and his Son, through the Spirit; a continual enjoyment of the Three-One God, and of all the creatures in him.[36]

Amen.

---

34. See Geoffrey Wainwright, *Doxology: The Praise of God in Worship, Doctrine, and Life* (New York: Oxford University Press, 1980), pp. 149-81 ("Scripture").

35. For the notion of Christian practice — focused in the celebration of the Eucharist — as an enacted interpretation of the biblical text, see Nicholas Lash, *Theology on the Way to Emmaus* (London: SCM Press, 1986), pp. 37-46 ("Performing the Scriptures").

36. Sermon 64, in *The Works of John Wesley*, vol. 2, ed. A. C. Outler (Nashville: Abingdon, 1985), p. 510.

PART II

THE THREEFOLD OFFICE

Join All the Glorious Names

1. Join all the glorious names, of wisdom, love, and
2. Great prophet of my God, my tongue would bless thy
3. Jesus, my great high priest, offered his blood and
4. Our dear almighty Lord, our conqueror and our

power that ever mortals knew, that
name; by thee the joyful news of
died; my guilty conscience seeks no
king, thy sceptre and thy sword, thy

an - gels ever bore. All are too mean to
our sal - va - tion came; of hell sub - dued and
sac - ri - fice be - side: his power - ful blood did
reign - ing grace we sing. Thine is the power; be -

speak his worth, too mean to set my Sav - ior forth.
peace with heaven, the joy - ful news of sins for - given.
once a - tone, and now it pleads be - fore the throne.
hold, we meet thy will - ing bond - men at thy feet.

AUTHOR: Watts. From *Hymns and Spiritual Songs*, 1709, in 12 stanzas of 6 lines, here abbreviated to st. 1, 4, 8, 10 of the original. Alterations here are: st. 4, from first person singular to first person plural, line 5 and 6, from "Behold I sit, in willing bonds beneath thy feet," to "Behold we meet, thy willing bondmen at thy feet."

TUNE: *Arthur's Seat*, 6.6.6.6.8.8.

6

The Threefold Office in Retrospect

"What force has the name Christ?" asks Calvin in the Geneva Catechism, and he gives the answer: "By this epithet his office is best expressed; for it signifies that he is anointed by his Father to be king, priest, and prophet."[1] Jesus, the Son upon whom the divine Spirit rests, thereby appears as the holder of a *munus triplex,* a threefold office, in which the royal, priestly, and prophetic functions among the people of God have been united under a single Head for the work of salvation. In the final edition of the *Institutes,* Calvin presents his fullest exposition of the Redeemer's work under the titles of Prophet, King, and Priest.[2] From that time on, the notion of Christ's threefold office has occupied a privileged place in Reformed catechetics and dogmatics. It is there that we shall look first, before going on to explore its ecumenical range and promise.

1. The French original of the Catechism of the Church of Geneva dates from 1542, and the Latin version from 1545. The latter is cited here from the English translation in *Calvin: Theological Treatises,* ed. J. K. S. Reid (Philadelphia: Westminster, 1954), in particular p. 95.

2. The 1559 edition is quoted here and hereafter from the two-volume English translation in *Calvin: Institutes of the Christian Religion,* ed. John T. McNeill and Ford Lewis Battles (Philadelphia: Westminster, 1960). The key passage occurs in book 2, chap. 15 (in the translation, vol. 1, pp. 494-503). For the location of this text in Calvin's total opus and a systematic evaluation of the doctrine as Calvin presents it, see Klauspeter Blaser, *Calvins Lehre von den Ämtern Christi,* Theologische Studien 105 (Zurich: EVZ-Verlag, 1970).

I. THE REFORMED TRADITION

The general good fortune of the *munus triplex* in the Reformed tradition may in part be explained by its pedagogical convenience, but it has seemed also to allow a theologically comprehensive account of the redemption. The confluence of sound doctrine and practical application is illustrated by the Heidelberg Catechism. Question 31 runs thus:

> *Why is he called Christ, that is, Anointed?*
> Because he is ordained of God the Father, and anointed with the Holy Ghost, to be our chief Prophet and Teacher, who fully reveals to us the secret counsel and will of God concerning our redemption; and our only High Priest, who by the one sacrifice of his body has redeemed us, and ever lives to make intercession for us with the Father; and our eternal King, who governs us by his Word and Spirit, and defends and preserves us in the redemption obtained for us.[3]

The Westminster Shorter Catechism sets its own accents within the same structure and introduces some nuances that will recur in our own discussion. In displaying Christ as the Mediator of the covenant of grace under the New Testament, questions 23-26 read as follows:

> *What offices doth Christ execute as our Redeemer?*
> Christ, as our Redeemer, executeth the offices of a Prophet, of a Priest, and of a King, both in his estate of humiliation and exaltation.

> *How doth Christ execute the office of a Prophet?*
> Christ executeth the office of a Prophet, in revealing to us by his Word and his Spirit, the will of God for our salvation.

> *How doth Christ execute the office of a Priest?*
> Christ executeth the office of a Priest, in his once offering up of himself a sacrifice to satisfy divine justice, and reconcile us to God, and in making continual intercession for us.

3. *The Creeds of Christendom*, ed. Philip Schaff and David S. Schaff, reprinted from the 6th ed. (Grand Rapids: Baker, 1990), here vol. 3, pp. 317f.

How doth Christ execute the office of a King?
Christ executeth the office of a King, in subduing us to himself, in ruling and defending us, and in restraining and conquering all his and our enemies.[4]

Having been much employed in the Reformed Orthodoxy of the seventeenth century but then losing some of its vigor in the eighteenth century,[5] the notion of the *munus triplex* recovered a prominent place in the most important schools of theology later in the Reformed tradition. In his "doctrine of the faith," Friedrich Schleiermacher takes the threefold office as the necessary and sufficient description of "the achievements of Christ in the corporate life founded by him," appropriate to the divine rule newly brought by Christ in both continuity and difference with God's kingdom in Israel. In the framework of redemption as Christ's "assuming believers into the power of his God-consciousness," and of reconciliation as Christ's "assuming believers into the fellowship of his unclouded blessedness," Schleiermacher sets the three theses that "the prophetic office of Christ consists in teaching, prophesying, and working miracles"; that "the priestly office of Christ includes his perfect fulfilment of the law (i.e. his active obedience), his atoning death (i.e. his passive obedience), and his intercession with the Father for believers"; and that "the kingly office of Christ consists in the fact that everything which the community of believers requires for its well-being continually proceeds from him."[6] In his influential textbook of "Reformed Dogmatics" (1861), Heinrich Heppe notes that, in the order of divine intention, the royal office comes first of the three, as the goal of Christ's mediation was to bring many to eternal glory under his rule.[7] In his *Systematic Theology* (1871), the Princetonian Charles Hodge insisted upon the perfect execution, by the one Person in

4. *The Creeds of Christendom* (Schaff and Schaff), 3:680f.
5. See A. Krauss, "Das Mittlerwerk nach dem Schema des munus triplex," *Jahrbücher für deutsche Theologie* 17 (1872): 599-655.
6. Friedrich Schleiermacher, *Der christliche Glaube nach den Grundsätzen der evangelischen Kirche*, 2d ed. (Berlin: Reimer, 1830), pars. 101-5; English translation, *The Christian Faith*, ed. H. R. Mackintosh and J. S. Stewart (Edinburgh: T. & T. Clark, 1928), in particular pp. 425-75.
7. Heinrich Heppe, *Reformed Dogmatics Set Out and Illustrated from the Sources*, trans. G. T. Thomson (London: Allen & Unwin, 1950), in particular pp. 452-87. Heppe's prime witness for the point mentioned was J. H. Heidegger's *Corpus theologiae christianae* (Zurich, 1700).

his two natures, of all the three offices diversely adumbrated by "the ancient prophets, priests, and kings" and needed for a salvation that "includes all that a prophet, priest, and king in the highest sense of those terms can do."[8]

In the twentieth century, Emil Brunner in his "Dogmatics" employs the threefold office as part of his "inductive," "Pauline," and "salvation-historical" procedure to treat the work of Christ — revelation, atonement, and the establishment of divine sovereignty, all interlocked — before arriving at his person.[9] Keen to keep together the person and work of Christ the Mediator, Karl Barth employs in volume IV of his *Church Dogmatics* a tripartite structure, in which he sees "Jesus Christ, the Lord as Servant" corresponding to the *munus sacerdotale,* "Jesus Christ, the Servant as Lord" corresponding to the *munus regium,* and "Jesus Christ the Witness" or even "the Guarantor" corresponding to the *munus propheticum;* and he intends by the latter to rescue the prophetic office from its modern representation of "Jesus as the supreme teacher and example of perfect divine and human love" to its proper role of affirming that "he who is himself the material content of the atonement, the mediator of it, stands security with man as well as God that it is our atonement, he himself being the form of it as well as the content."[10]

Providing a clear and appropriate structure for expounding the work of the Savior, even while being itself affected by the theological frame in which it is set by different authors, the notion of Christ's threefold office has a secure place in the inherited Reformed tradition. Part of the purpose of these chapters is to explore its ecumenical promise. This requires first of all a retrospect upon its presence in the particularities of the separated traditions as well as in the earlier and continuing Tradition insofar as

---

8. Charles Hodge, *Systematic Theology* (New York: Scribner, 1929), 2:459-609 (in particular pp. 460f.).

9. Emil Brunner, *The Christian Doctrine of Creation and Redemption,* trans. O. Wyon (London: Lutterworth Press, 1952), pp. 271-321.

10. Karl Barth, *Kirchliche Dogmatik* IV/1, sec. 58.4; see *Church Dogmatics* IV/1, trans. G. W. Bromiley (Edinburgh: T. & T. Clark, 1956), particularly pp. 128-38. Karin Bornkamm has argued that the purpose of Barth's new insistence on Christ's prophetic office was to strengthen the contemporary church in its missionary task of proclaiming the gospel by letting Christ appear in the present as the effective guarantor of the reconciliation included in his priestly and royal work: "Die reformatorische Lehre vom Amt Christi und ihre Umformung durch Karl Barth," in *Zeitschrift für Theologie und Kirche,* Beiheft 6, ed. E. Jüngel (Tübingen: Mohr, 1986), pp. 1-32.

Christians were once united in the one church of Jesus Christ and to the extent that they have remained so.

2. The Ecumenical Range

Calvin was not the first sixteenth-century writer to take up the notion of Christ's threefold office: there are scattered anticipations of his more developed use. Already in his *Commentary on the Second Psalm* (1522), Erasmus speaks of the senseless raging of the prince(s) and peoples of this world against the Lord and his Anointed when in fact Christ has come, full of grace, for the salvation of all nations: "the prophet of prophets," the "priest who has given himself as victim to purge all the sins of those who believe in him," the "ruler to whom all power has been given" and who "kindly offers peace" before returning as judge; "by his teaching he has dispelled our darkness," "by his death he has reconciled us to God," and "by his leadership *(ductu)* he has opened up the way to eternal life."[11] Then, in 1530, Andreas Osiander had written to the Diet of Augsburg on the subject of false teachers who seek righteousness and holiness through meritorious works and ways of life rather than finding them in Jesus Christ alone:

> We must understand this [the title "Christ"] of his office, since he is Christ, that is, Master, King, and High Priest. For as Christ means anointed, and only prophets, kings, and priests were anointed, so one sees that all three offices apply to him: the prophet's office, for he only is our Teacher and Master (Matthew 23:8-10); the king's power, for he rules forever in the house of Jacob (Luke 1:32f.); and the priest's office, for he is a priest forever according to the order of Melchizedek (Psalm 110:4). That is now his office, that he may be our wisdom, righteousness, sanctification, and redemption, as Paul testifies (1 Corinthians 1:30).[12]

11. Erasmus, *Commentarius in Psalmum II,* cited from *Opera omnia Desiderii Erasmi Roterodami,* vol. 5/2 (Amsterdam: North-Holland, 1985), pp. 110-12.

12. "Rechtfertigungsschrift von Andreas Osiander zum Reichstag von Augsburg 1530"; cited from Wilhelm Gussmann, *Quellen und Forschungen zur Geschichte des Augsburgischen Glaubensbekenntnisses* I/1 (Leipzig and Berlin: Teubner, 1911), p. 302.

Probably the most direct inspiration for Calvin's use, however, came from Strasbourg, where he himself spent time in the 1530s. Already in the late 1520s, Martin Bucer was there writing in his commentaries on the Gospels that

> Christ was anointed, so that he might be our king *(rex)*, teacher *(doctor)*, and priest *(sacerdos)* for ever. He will govern us, lest we lack any good thing or be oppressed by any ill; he will teach us the whole truth; and he will reconcile us to the Father eternally.

And again:

> Just as they used to anoint kings, priests and prophets to institute them in their offices, so now Christ is king of kings *(rex regum)*, highest priest *(summus sacerdos)*, and chief of the prophets *(prophetarum caput)*. He does not rule in the manner of an external empire; he does not sacrifice with brute beasts; he does not teach and admonish only with an external voice. Rather, by the Holy Spirit he directs minds and wills in the way of eternal salvation; by the Spirit he offered himself as an expiatory sacrifice for us, so that we too might become an acceptable offering to God; and by the same Spirit he teaches and admonishes, in order that those destined for his kingdom may be made righteous, holy and blessed in all things.[13]

While the pairing of royal and priestly offices had been a commonplace in the Middle Ages, it has been suggested by George Williams that "the conceptualization of Christ as Prophet, Priest, and King in Strasbourg and also elsewhere among Protestants" was connected with "the contemporary enhancement of the status of the university-trained teacher *(magister/Meister/Lehrer)* among them": the new pastor-teachers were claiming an authority coordinate with the civil magistracy, were relativizing the sacerdotal view of ecclesiastical ministry, and at the same time were countering Christocratically the pretension of some radical separatists to a direct authority from the Holy Spirit.

After Calvin's time, the *munus triplex* was taken up into Lutheran

---

13. Quoted from the combined version of Bucer's commentaries on the first three Gospels and on John: M. Bucer, *In sacra quatuor evangelia, Enarrationes* (Basel, 1536), pp. 9 and 606. For the location of Bucer's use of the threefold office in the social and political context of Strasbourg, see George H. Williams, *The Radical Reformation*, 3d ed. (Kirksville, Mo.: Sixteenth Century, 1992), pp. 372-77.

Orthodoxy as well as into Reformed Orthodoxy, but such a coincidence was too good to last, and the Lutherans, with their endemic suspicion that nothing good can come out of Geneva, eventually let it drop.[14] As late as Wolfhart Pannenberg's *Grundzüge der Christologie* we find a sharp critique of the appropriateness and adequacy of the threefold office as a description of Christ's work.[15] Pannenberg's main argument is that the *munus triplex,* when used in a temporally undifferentiated way, does not mesh very well with another, more chronological schema, that of the two "states" of Christ: the state of humiliation and the state of exaltation.[16] That is an important matter, for at stake is the unity of Christ's person; and I shall therefore return to the question later, with at least an indirect response to Pannenberg's criticism. On the other hand, the Lutheran Helmut Thielicke makes systematic use of the threefold office of Christ in his dogmatics, *Der evangelische Glaube.*[17] His grounds are similar to those of the Reformed Emil Brunner, centering on the fact that we have access to the person of Christ only through his work. Nevertheless, Thielicke offers no sustained justification for the adoption precisely of the threefold formula beyond a rather schematic repetition of the traditional point that Jesus was the unique fulfillment — and correction — of the three offices to which the bearers were anointed in Israel: prophet, priest, and king.

Looking from Geneva not toward Wittenberg but rather in the other direction, toward Rome, we find Calvin advancing a polemical reason for his treatment of the threefold office of Christ:

> In order that faith may find a firm basis for salvation in Christ, and thus rest in him, this principle must be laid down: the office enjoined upon Christ by the Father consists of three parts. For he was given to

14. See Krauss, "Das Mittlerwerk," especially pp. 621, 627-35. According to Krauss, Lutheranism remained "foreign soil" for the threefold office; Lutheran interest focused more narrowly on the *person* of Christ and on justification.

15. Wolfhart Pannenberg, *Jesus — God and Man,* trans. L. L. Wilkins and D. A. Priebe (Philadelphia: Westminster, 1968), in particular pp. 212-25. Perhaps the first Lutheran polemic against the threefold office is found in J. A. Ernesti, *De officio Christi triplici* (1773); see Krauss, "Das Mittlerwerk," p. 630.

16. As cited earlier, the Westminster Catechism typically affirms the threefold office of Christ in both his "estate of humiliation" (from birth to death and descent into hell) and his "estate of exaltation" (from resurrection to return).

17. Helmut Thielicke, *The Evangelical Faith,* trans. G. W. Bromiley, 3 vols. (Grand Rapids: Eerdmans, 1974-82), in particular 2 (1977): 342-452.

be prophet, king, and priest. Yet it would be of little value to know these names without understanding their purpose and use. The papists use these names, too, but coldly and rather ineffectually, since they do not know what each of these titles contains.[18]

Might Calvin have been content with the exposition of the threefold office of Christ given in the Roman Catechism for Parish Priests of 1566, even while doubtless differing from Rome on the location of the church toward which Christ exercised this ministry? The Roman Catechism explains in this way "what the name Christ means, and the several reasons it is appropriate to our Jesus." When "Jesus Christ our Savior came into the world," he took up all three offices from the Old Testament and fulfilled them, discharging them not by an earthly unction but by being anointed by his heavenly Father with the Holy Spirit:

> Jesus Christ was the supreme Prophet and Teacher, from whom we have learned the will of God, and by whom the world has been taught the knowledge of the heavenly Father. . . .
>
> Christ was also a Priest, not indeed of the same order as were the priests of the tribe of Levi in the Old Law, but of that of which the prophet David sang: "Thou art a priest for ever according to the order of Melchizedek" [Ps. 110:4]. This subject the apostle fully and accurately develops in his epistle to the Hebrews [chaps. 5–7].
>
> Christ not only as God, but also as man and partaker of our nature, we likewise acknowledge to be a King. Of him the angel testified, "He shall reign in the house of Jacob for ever; and of his kingdom there shall be no end" [Luke 1:33]. This kingdom of Christ is spiritual and eternal, begun on earth but perfected in heaven. He discharges by his admirable providence the duties of King towards his Church, governing and protecting her against the open violence and hidden designs of her enemies, legislating for her and imparting to her not only holiness and righteousness, but also power and strength to persevere. . . . To him God delivered the government of the whole world, and to this sovereignty of his, which has already begun, all things shall be made fully and entirely subject on the day of judgment.[19]

18. Calvin, *Institutes* II.15.1 (ET, 1:494).

19. Roman Catechism, I.2.7; version based on the successive English-language editions of *The Catechism of the Council of Trent, promulgated by command of Pope Pius the Fifth,* trans.

On the ecumenical front, the Roman Catholic Church at the Second Vatican Council made frequent and (shall we say?) warmer and more effective use of the *munus triplex* of Christ as that in which, by their baptism, Christians are given derivative participation and find their mission in the world described, with the ordained ministry having the task of building up the whole body in the exercise of its offices. The historical route by which Vatican II came to that position has its own twists and turns, and not all of it was positively ecumenical (as will be seen in a moment); but the council has created a favorable climate for a differentiated understanding of the *munus triplex* in an ecumenically helpful way.[20] The idea will be kept alive by the 1992 universal *Catechism of the Catholic Church:*

> Jesus fulfilled the messianic hope of Israel in his threefold office of priest, prophet, and king. . . . Jesus Christ is the one whom the Father anointed with the Holy Spirit and established as priest, prophet, and king. The whole People of God participates in these three offices of Christ and bears the responsibilities for mission and service that flow from them. . . . In the Church, Christ has entrusted to the apostles and their successors the office of teaching, sanctifying, and governing in his name and by his power.[21]

My own ecclesiastical allegiance is neither Reformed nor Lutheran nor Roman Catholic, but Methodist. John Wesley did not make sustained systematic use of the *munus triplex*. Yet John Deschner's interpretation of Wesley's christology uses it as a major structuring factor.[22] Although the threefold formula occurs only ten times in Wesley's writings, the substance of the three offices is heavily present in Wesley. One of the formal occurrences falls in his open "Letter to a Roman Catholic," where Wesley

---

J. Donovan (Baltimore: F. Lucas, after 1829), pp. 34f.; *Catechism of the Council of Trent for Parish Priests,* ed. J. A. McHugh and C. J. Callan (New York: Wagner, ca. 1923), pp. 35f.; *The Roman Catechism,* ed. R. I. Bradley and E. Kevane (Boston: St. Paul Editions, 1985), pp. 39f.

20. See especially *Lumen Gentium,* 9-13; 20-21 and 25-27; 31 and 34-36; *Ad Gentes,* 15; *Apostolicam Actuositatem,* 2; 10; *Presbyterium Ordinis,* 1 and 4-6.

21. *Catechism of the Catholic Church* (Mahwah, N.J.: Paulist Press, 1994), pars. 436, 783-86, 871-73 (pp. 109f., 207f., 231).

22. John Deschner, *Wesley's Christology: An Interpretation* (Dallas: Southern Methodist University Press, 1960).

expounds the faith of "a true Protestant" by way of an expansion on the Nicene Creed.[23] At the beginning of the second article he exegetes the name Jesus Christ:

> I believe that Jesus of Nazareth was the Savior of the world, the Messiah so long foretold; that, being anointed by the Holy Ghost, he was a Prophet, revealing to us the whole will of God; that he was a Priest, who gave himself a sacrifice for sin, and still makes intercession for transgressors; that he is a King, who has all power in heaven and in earth, and will reign till he has subdued all things to himself.

Wesley would have been aware that a similar use was not only a commonplace of Protestant catechisms but figured also, as we saw, in the Roman Catechism commissioned by the Council of Trent.[24] Wesley's most interesting use of the *munus triplex,* however, is to show the correspondence between Christ's threefold office and our need as fallen humanity. In the *Explanatory Notes upon the New Testament,* he writes at Matthew 1:16:

> The word Christ in Greek, and Messiah in Hebrew, signify "Anointed"; and imply the prophetic, priestly, and royal characters which were to meet in the Messiah. Among the Jews, anointing was the ceremony whereby prophets, priests, and kings were initiated into those offices. And if we look into ourselves, we shall find a want of Christ in all these respects. We are by nature at a distance from God, alienated from him, and incapable of a free access to him. Hence we want a Mediator, and Intercessor; in a word, a Christ in his priestly office. This regards our state with respect to God. And with respect to ourselves, we find a total darkness, blindness, ignorance of God and the things of God. Now here we want Christ in his prophetic office, to enlighten our minds, and teach us the whole will of God. We find also within us a strange misrule of appetites and passions. For these we want Christ in his royal character, to reign in our hearts, and subdue all things to himself.[25]

23. "Letter to a Roman Catholic," in *The Works of the Rev. John Wesley,* ed. Thomas Jackson (London: Wesleyan Conference Office, 1872), 10:80-86.

24. See above, n. 19.

25. John Wesley, *Explanatory Notes upon the New Testament* (London: Epworth Press, 1976), p. 16. The first edition dates from 1754.

In what follows I shall not limit myself, either historically or theologically, to passages or reflections where the three offices of Christ occur precisely as a triad. Rather, I shall avail myself of the freedom taken by earlier expositors to consider the substance and consequences of Christ's work as Prophet, Priest, and King, in distinction if necessary. And I shall try in the end to show that what finally holds the notion of the *munus triplex* together is neither simply familiar traditional usage (for the Tradition is quite uneven in the matter) nor even the semantic connection through the anointing which Christ, and Christians in him, receive from the Holy Spirit. Rather, the systematic integrity of the notion resides in its entire suitability for the doxological and dogmatic description of the Savior and his work, and (derivatively) of the existence of his church before God and in the world.

3. FIVE HISTORIC USES

Before the systematic exposition, however, a little more history is necessary. For to see the uses to which the triad of prophet, priest, and king has been put in the Christian Tradition will provide certain elements among which to make systematic connections. Five uses of the triad may be distinguished in the past. Roughly speaking, the first two predominate in the patristic period; the third received a new emphasis in the Reformation; and the remaining two date largely from the nineteenth century. At this point I will prescind from the Scriptures, first because the triad as such can be found only indirectly there, and second because I wish to use the Scriptures rather to fund the exposition of the three offices in their distinction. The five uses may be styled (1) the christological, (2) the baptismal, (3) the soteriological, (4) the ministerial, and (5) the ecclesiological. Naturally, there is overlap among them.[26]

26. Valuable historical sketches, covering different parts of the range of the Tradition, are found in John F. Jansen, *Calvin's Doctrine of the Work of Christ* (London: James Clarke, 1956); and L. Schick, *Das dreifache Amt Christi und der Kirche. Zur Entstehung und Entwicklung der Trilogien* (Frankfurt am Main: Peter Lang, 1982).

The Christological Use

Here the emphasis falls on the identity and dignity of Jesus Christ.[27] While the titles certainly imply function, the attention centers on the person who fulfills the offices. A second-century precursor in this usage is Justin Martyr, who wrote in his *Dialogue with Trypho the Jew:* Jesus "received from the Father the titles of King and Christ and Priest and Messenger and" (somewhat vaguely) "whatever other such titles as he holds or held."[28] The first firm uses of the triad are found in Eusebius of Caesarea well into the fourth century. Both in his *Ecclesiastical History* and in his *Demonstration of the Gospel* he intends to show how Jesus Christ is the fulfillment of the Old Testament, and indeed of all religions. Like many of his successors, Eusebius takes his departure from the title Christ, the Anointed. So in the third chapter of the first book of the *Ecclesiastical History* Eusebius writes:

> All these [priests, kings, and prophets of Israel] have reference to the true Christ, the divine and heavenly Word, the only High Priest of the universe, the only King of all creation, and of prophets the Father's sole supreme Prophet. Of all who in former times were anointed with chrism as a type, whether of priests or kings or prophets, no one until now received such power of divine virtue as our Savior and Lord Jesus demonstrates, who is the only and true Christ.[29]

Next comes Saint John Chrysostom, later in the century, who commented thus on the name of Jesus Christ and his genealogy at Matthew 1:1:

> Christ was to have three dignities: King, Prophet, Priest. . . . Abraham was prophet and priest (cf. Genesis 15:9; 20:7). . . . David was king

27. George Stroup speaks of Christ's "narrative identity" in connection with the three titles. The historical emphasis is fine, provided it is not set in opposition to, but rather seen as grounded in, his ontological identity. See George W. Stroup, *Jesus Christ for Today* (Philadelphia: Westminster, 1982), pp. 88-106.

28. Justin Martyr, *Dialogue with Trypho the Jew,* 86 (Migne, *Patrologia Graeca* 6:681; hereafter cited as *PG*). Justin has a tendency to pile up the names (see, e.g., chaps. 34, 61, and 126).

29. *Historia Ecclesiastica* I.3 (Migne, *PG* 20:72). Similar passages are found in the *Demonstratio Evangelica* IV.15 (*PG* 22:289-305) and VIII. intro. (*PG* 22:368).

and prophet, but not priest. Thus [Jesus] is called the son of both, that the threefold dignity of his two forefathers might be recognized by hereditary right in Christ.[30]

Another preacher, Peter Chrysologus, fifth-century bishop of Ravenna, spoke thus in sermon 59:

> He was called Christ by anointing, because the unction, which in former times had been given to kings, prophets, and priests as a type, was now poured out as the fulness of the divine Spirit into this one person, the King of kings, Priest of priests, Prophet of prophets.[31]

Without himself developing the threefold schema, Thomas Aquinas will later argue that Christ not only received the perfection of all graces but also correspondingly became the source of all graces for others:

> Other men have certain graces distributed among them, but Christ, as being the Head of all, has the perfection of all graces. Wherefore, as to others, one is a lawgiver, another is a priest, another is a king; but all these concur in Christ as the fount of all grace.[32]

With the notion of Christ as the source of all graces for others, we are already at the second use of the triad — in connection, this time, with restored humanity. Because baptism is the sign of our restoration, by grace through faith, to the image of God, this second use may be called the baptismal use.

---

30. At least, Thomas Aquinas, in the "Golden Chain" on Matthew, attributes this passage to Chrysostom (*Sancti Thomae Aquinatis Opera Omnia,* reprint of the Parma edition of 1852-73 [New York: Musurgia Publishers, 1948-49], 11:6). In Migne's *PG,* the passage occurs in an "unfinished work on Matthew" of "uncertain authorship" (*PG* 56:613). The text comes close to a passage in the second authentic *Homily on Matthew* of John Chrysostom, although our triad is not found there (*PG* 57:27).

31. Peter Chrysologus, *Sermo* 59 (Migne, *Patrologia Latina* 52:363).

32. Thomas Aquinas, *Summa Theologiae* III.22.1 (cited from *St. Thomas Aquinas: Summa Theologica,* trans. the Fathers of the English Dominican Province [New York: Benziger, 1947], 2:2142).

The Baptismal Use

A witness here again is Saint John Chrysostom. He is preaching on 2 Corinthians 1:21f.: "It is God who establishes us with you in Christ and has anointed us all; he has put his seal upon us and given us his Spirit in our hearts as a guarantee." The preacher comments:

What does that mean, "He has anointed and sealed us"? He has given us the Spirit, by whom he has done both things, making us at once prophets, priests, and kings, for these three kinds were in former times anointed. We, however, have not received just one dignity, but all three at once, and that in a superior way. We taste the kingdom; we become priests, offering our bodies as a sacrifice, for it says "Present your members as living sacrifices, acceptable to God" [cf. Rom. 12:1]; moreover, we are made prophets, for "what eye has not seen, nor ear heard, this has been revealed to us" [cf. 1 Cor. 2:9].[33]

It is in fact the royal dignity of Christians that John Chrysostom most develops: Their kingship does not consist in wearing regal clothes and insignia; they do not rule over armies. Their kingship consists in ruling over untoward thoughts; in being crowned with God's mercy, grace, and glory (cf. Pss. 5:12; 8:5; 103:4; Prov. 1:9). This kingship is worth more than that of secular rulers.[34]

To that characterization of kingship we shall return. Meanwhile we note that the threefold dignity of Christians came to sacramental expression, for Chrysostom, in the anointing they received at their baptism. Several early prayers for the consecration of the holy oils use the threefold formula. This goes back to the blessing "when someone brings oil" in the ancient church order identified as the *Apostolic Tradition* of Hippolytus (chap. 5):

As Thou sanctifiest this oil, so grant to those who use and receive and enjoy it health and strength, just as Thou didst in former times to the kings, priests and prophets whom Thou didst anoint.

Ritually, oils were employed for the baptismal anointing. Somewhat exotically, the fourth-century Persian poet Aphraates reflects this when he

---

33. John Chrysostom, *Third Homily on Second Corinthians* (Migne, *PG* 61:411).
34. John Chrysostom, *Third Homily* (*PG* 61:411-12).

pictures the working of Christ as reopening Paradise and making its olive tree accessible again:

> But for whoever seeks peace, the gate [of Paradise] has been opened again; darkness has flown from the minds of many, and the light of understanding has dawned; and the fruits of the bright olive-tree have grown, in which is found the sign of the mystery of life [that is, baptism], by which Christians are perfected into priests and kings and prophets.[35]

In our times, the Russian-American Orthodox theologian Alexander Schmemann has found in the Byzantine liturgy of baptism an expression of the threefold office as the ground of an authentic Christian spirituality. To have "put on" Christ in baptism is explicated by the vesting in a white garment or "shining robe," which takes up the linen ephod of King David (2 Sam. 6:14), the sacerdotal vestments of Aaron and his sons (Exod. 28), and the mantle of the prophet Elijah (2 Kings 2:14). One is thus prepared to receive by chrismation "the Holy Spirit, the very Spirit of Christ, the very gifts of Christ the Anointed — the King, the Priest and the Prophet." Redeemed and restored by Christ, we resume the original dignity and calling of humankind: to rule the earth as its benefactor and thus be free to enjoy it rather than exploit it; to sanctify the world by offering it to God rather than consuming it for ourselves; to discern the will of God and convey it to the world instead of seeking to possess the world in the absence of God.[36]

Lest there be any suspicion that effects are being attributed to a sacrament by some kind of "mechanical" or "automatic" operation, it will be well to state that what is here, and in the appropriate section of the next three chapters, being placed under the head of baptism, is being affirmed of baptism precisely as it is the basic sacrament of faith. And so question 32 of the Heidelberg Catechism may be cited as a parallel:

> *But why art thou called a Christian?*
> Because by faith I am a member of Christ, and thus a partaker of his anointing; in order that I also may confess his name, may present myself a living sacrifice of thankfulness to him, and may with free

35. Aphraates, *Demonstratio XXIII*, 3 (*Patrologia Syriaca* I/2 [Paris: Firmin-Didot, 1907], 9-10).

36. Alexander Schmemann, *Of Water and the Spirit: A Liturgical Study of Baptism* (Crestwood, N.Y.: St. Vladimir's Seminary Press, 1974), pp. 71-108.

conscience fight against sin and the devil in this life, and hereafter, in eternity, reign with him over all creatures.[37]

The royal, priestly, and prophetic dignity of Christians depends on the work of Christ into whom they are, by the Spirit, incorporated. With that, we come to the third use of the *munus triplex,* the soteriological.

The Soteriological Use

As already indicated at the start, the sixteenth-century Reformation brought the threefold office of Christ into a new prominence. Emphasis was placed again on the work of Christ, by virtue of which human beings could be admitted to the salvation for which they were made. Calvin, in particular, made the *munus triplex* the principal instrument for his systematic exposition of the work of the "Son of God, Redeemer of the world": "To know the purpose for which Christ was sent by the Father, and what he conferred upon us, we must look above all at three things in him: the prophetic office, kingship, and priesthood."[38] The soteriological purpose of the threefold office itself, and of Calvin's treatment of it, is explicit: "that faith may find a firm basis for salvation in Christ, and thus rest in him." As the fountainhead of modern use of the *munus triplex,* Calvin's thought will be drawn on in the chapters which deal with the three offices in distinction. Staying close to Calvin will both serve as a reminder that the three offices belong together in an integrated understanding and help to maintain the desired soteriological concentration. In this last connection, Calvin will also assist in upholding the primacy of Christ in the fourth and fifth uses of the *munus triplex,* the ministerial and the ecclesiological, which have chiefly been developed in Roman Catholicism of the past two centuries.

The Ministerial Use

The fourth use of the threefold office was developed by Roman Catholic canonists in the early decades of the nineteenth century.[39] Ironically, it

37. *The Creeds of Christendom* (Schaff and Schaff), 3:318.
38. Calvin, *Institutes* II.15.1 (ET, 1:494).
39. See Schick, *Das dreifache Amt,* pp. 103-8.

came as a reaction to some outgrowths of the Reformed and other Protestant traditions. The ancient and medieval Roman rites for ordination did not mention our triad as such, but the envisaged ministerial duties certainly included sanctifying and the offering of sacrifices, ruling and leading the people, and preaching and teaching.[40] The nineteenth-century canonists grant to the hierarchy — and notably the bishops, under the pope — the threefold ministry of *magisterium, ministerium, regimen.* That is: doctrinal teaching; sacrificing and sanctifying priesthood; and government with jurisdiction. Whereas the earlier Catholic tradition had emphasized the dual function of priesthood and rule (canonically, the *potestas ordinis* and the *potestas jurisdictionis*), it appears that the Protestant stress on "the Word" called forth a new and distinct emphasis on the *magisterium,* the hierarchy's "teaching office."

These beginnings in controversial theology give sufficient warning that discussion of the fourth use of the threefold office will be delicate, but it would be a pity to forgo its ecumenical potential as the churches seek convergence in understanding and practice of the ordained ministry. It will need to be kept in close relationship to the fifth use of the *munus triplex,* which looks to the corporate dignity and functions of the entire people of God in Christ.

The Ecclesiological Use

Again, the modern beginnings are controversial. The key motif was the conception of the Tübingen Catholic theologians in the early nineteenth century, and particularly J. A. Möhler, of the church as the "extension of the Incarnation." As the *Christus prolongatus,* the church as a whole (meaning, strictly, the Roman Catholic Church) shared the prophetic, priestly, and royal character of its Head.[41]

Somewhat less massively but certainly still (or already) in a very Catholic vision, the train of thought is displayed in the majestic prose of John Henry Newman's Easter sermon of 1840, while he was yet an Anglican, on "The Three Offices of Christ."[42] Newman shows first the

40. Schick, *Das dreifache Amt,* pp. 80-83.
41. Schick, *Das dreifache Amt,* pp. 111f.
42. Quotations here and hereafter will be taken from John Henry Newman, *Sermons Bearing on Subjects of the Day* (London: Longmans, Green, new impression 1909), pp.

threefold office of Christ himself (and again it is interesting to note the nuances introduced by particular authors into their basic descriptions of the three offices performed by Christ):

> Christ exercised his prophetical office in teaching, and in foretelling the future — in his sermon on the mount, in his parables, in his prophecy of the destruction of Jerusalem. He performed the priest's service when he died on the cross, as a sacrifice; and when he consecrated the bread and the cup to be a feast upon that sacrifice; and now that he intercedes for us at the right hand of God. And he showed himself as a conqueror, and a king, in rising from the dead, in ascending into heaven, in sending down the Spirit of grace, in converting the nations, and in forming his Church to receive and to rule them.[43]

Then Newman goes on to show how Christ "left behind . . . a ministerial order, who are his representatives and instruments":

> And they, though earthen vessels, show forth according to their measure these three characteristics — the prophetical, priestly, and regal, combining in themselves qualities and functions which, except under the Gospel, are almost incompatible the one with the other. He consecrated his Apostles to suffer, when he said, "Ye shall indeed drink of my cup, and be baptized with my baptism"; to teach, when he said, "The Comforter, which is the Holy Ghost, He shall teach you all things"; and to rule, when he said to them, "I appoint unto you a kingdom, as my Father appointed unto me; that ye may eat and drink at my table in my kingdom, and sit on thrones, judging the twelve tribes of Israel."[44]

Finally, Newman applies the three offices to the whole church, though not without some acknowledgment of a diversity of gifts:

52-62. Newman was familiar with the threefold office of Christ from such varied sources within Anglicanism as the learned bishops Joseph Hall, John Pearson, and George Horne, the episcopal philosopher Joseph Butler, and the Evangelicals Thomas Scott and Charles Simeon; see H. D. Weidner's introduction to his edition of *The "Via Media" of the Anglican Church by John Henry Newman* (Oxford: Clarendon Press, 1990), pp. xlix-lviii.

43. Newman, "The Three Offices of Christ," *Sermons,* p. 53.

44. Newman, "The Three Offices of Christ," *Sermons,* p. 55.

Nay, all Christ's followers in some sense bear all three offices, as Scripture is not slow to declare. In one place it is said, that Christ has "made us kings and priests unto God and his Father"; in another, "Ye have an unction from the Holy One, and ye know all things." Knowledge, power, endurance, are the three privileges of the Christian Church: endurance, as represented in the confessor and monk; wisdom, in the doctor and teacher; power, in the bishop and pastor.[45]

Pope Pius XII would develop the "Body of Christ" ecclesiology in his encyclicals *Mystici Corporis* (1943) and *Mediator Dei* (1947); but he was reluctant to apply our triad to the entire church, restricting it rather to the hierarchy who had been instituted in their triple office of *magisterium, ministerium,* and *regimen* by Christ's special commission to the apostles. The Second Vatican Council maintained the special position of the hierarchy but was courageous enough to return also to the threefold dignity of the faithful baptized in their communal and corporate quality that would be expressed by the postbaptismal anointing in the revised rites of initiation:

> God, the Father of our Lord Jesus Christ, . . . now anoints you with the chrism of salvation. As Christ was anointed Priest, Prophet, and King, so may you live always as a member of his body, sharing everlasting life.[46]

On the whole, the documents of Vatican II see the bishops and presbyters, in their special *munus triplex,* as ministering in and to the entire church for the better prosecution of its prophetic, priestly, and royal ministry before God and toward the world. Here is a theme to set in relation to the Reformation notion of the church as a "royal priesthood" with a prophetic duty of declaring "the wonderful deeds of him who called you out of darkness into his marvelous light" (cf. 1 Pet. 2:1-10).

After this retrospect to show the ecumenical base and potential of the *munus triplex* and the various uses of the notion that will guide systematic reflection on each office, the first chapter of this part may now be closed by three considerations that will further explain the substance, sequence, and purpose of what follows.

---

45. Newman, "The Three Offices of Christ," *Sermons,* pp. 55f.
46. *The Rites of the Catholic Church,* trans. International Commission on English in the Liturgy, vol. 1 (New York: Pueblo, 1976), pp. 148, 208.

4. SUBSTANCE, SEQUENCE, AND PURPOSE

Substantially, every mention of the threefold office, or of one particular office, explicitly or implicitly contains a reference to the Holy Spirit. Thus there is no pneumatological "use" listed for the *munus triplex* for the simple reason that the Holy Spirit is the Father's gift by which Christ himself, Christians, and the church and its ministers are all anointed. The threefold office is christocentric but it is not christomonist. It is set within a fully trinitarian frame. This means also that a "Spirit-christology" should not be seen as an alternative to an "incarnation of the Word." That these two are compatible and complementary is demonstrated in the christological tome of the German Catholic bishop-theologian Walter Kasper, to which we shall refer later for an illuminating interpretation of the *munus triplex;* and it is explicitly argued in the later work of the younger American Catholic Ralph Del Colle, *Christ and the Spirit.*[47]

Structurally, the order in which the three offices will be treated needs explanation. In some earlier texts, prophet is tacked on as a third after the originally more familiar pair of king and priest. Calvin indeed went through that stage as the *Institutes* developed from edition to edition. For his own sound theological reasons, Karl Barth deliberately reverted to the order of *munus sacerdotale, munus regium, munus propheticum* in his re-working of the *munus triplex.* We remain, however, most accustomed to prophet, priest, and king, which has predominated in the Reformed tradition, resonating through English-speaking Christendom thanks to a line in John Newton's hymn "How Sweet the Name of Jesus Sounds."[48] Prophet, priest, and king *could* be taken in a "chronological" order, corresponding to a succession of Christ's "state of humiliation" and "state of exaltation": prophecy may describe his earthly teaching ministry; on the cross he became priest and victim; kingship came with the resurrection and ascension. W. Pannenberg finds it the least unacceptable: prophet is not too bad a category for the pre-Easter Jesus; admittedly, a sacrificial cross poses difficulties; but Jesus certainly became the "kingly messiah," according to Pannenberg, only by the resurrection. At stake, however, is the unity of

47. Walter Kasper, *Jesus the Christ,* trans. V. Green (New York: Paulist Press, 1976); Ralph Del Colle, *Christ and the Spirit: Spirit-Christology in Trinitarian Perspective* (New York: Oxford University Press, 1994).

48. The hymn was entitled "The Name of Jesus: Canticles 1:3" in the *Olney Hymns* (London, 1779).

Christ's person, as it always must be on the adoptionist, "Antiochene" side of things. Even Pannenberg's "from below" methodology has to make room for a "retroactive" effect of the resurrection on the earthly ministry — and eventually indeed for the incarnation of an "eternal" Word. I prefer to place an "Alexandrian" insistence on the unity of Christ's person throughout, which grounds an "exchange of properties *(communicatio idiomatum)*" between his two natures, human and divine, at all stages, and which is the profound intention of the Westminster Catechism's answer that Christ executes all three offices "both in his estate of humiliation and exaltation." In my book *Doxology* I showed how the church's liturgical experience of Christ as "object of worship," "mediator in worship," and "pattern for worship" matched (and funded) the dogmatic definition of Chalcedon concerning the one person and two natures.[49] I want now to do the same for "prophet, priest, and king"; and for reasons that I hope will become clear by the end, that can be suitably (though not exclusively) done by following precisely the now familiar sequence of prophet, priest, and king.

As to the various purposes of this book as a whole (and of this half in particular), I am overridingly concerned with the active appreciation and further transmission of classic Christianity. The greatest need of our North American mainline Protestant churches is for a reappropriation of evangelical, catholic, orthodox Christianity. My first procedure in what follows will be to allow the Scriptures and the great Tradition to speak as clearly and as directly as possible. Intelligent reception and vital communication require, however, that we face questions of contemporary interpretation amid the cultural circumstances of our time. A culture may contain, or in our case retain, certain positive elements that the churches can welcome and find helpful in their own life and tasks; a culture may also be warped by sin in such ways that it needs drastic correction in the light of God's will and work; in any case, our cultures will provide us at least in part with languages and conceptualities with which we in the Christian Tradition, with its inherited language and conceptuality, will have to engage if the gospel is to be proclaimed to our contemporaries and applied in our time and place. In each chapter, therefore, on the "prophetic," the "priestly," and the "royal" offices respectively, I will toward the end at least hint at some hermeneutical issues. I will try, in each case,

49. Geoffrey Wainwright, *Doxology: The Praise of God in Worship, Doctrine, and Life* (New York: Oxford University Press, 1980), in particular pp. 45-86.

to discern the human questions and needs that are being addressed as well as the problems and possibilities inherent in the traditional categories of prophet, priest, and king, as we seek to allow Christ as Savior to address the human condition. It will not be forgotten that answers may challenge and transform the initial presuppositions of the questioners.

Both the rediscovery of historic Christianity and the attempt to communicate the gospel are best undertaken ecumenically. An ecumenical approach will provide our best chance to draw on the threefold office for what W. A. Visser 't Hooft, the Dutch Reformed theologian and first general secretary of the World Council of Churches, called its potential for a "pastoral dogmatics."[50] As a reminder, this introductory chapter can be concluded by one more quotation from Cardinal Newman. Not that I shall develop the message, the questions, and the answers in quite the same way, but Newman delineates some perennial features of the human condition to which the gospel of Christ — Priest, King, Prophet (that is Newman's order) — is addressed:

> Let it be observed, that these three offices seem to contain in them the three principal conditions of mankind; for one large class of men, or aspect of mankind, is that of sufferers — such as slaves, the oppressed, the poor, the sick, the bereaved, the troubled in mind; another is, of those who work and toil, who are full of business and engagements, whether for themselves or others; and a third is that of the studious, learned, and wise. Endurance, active life, thought — these are the three perhaps principal states in which men find themselves. Christ undertook them all. . . . And therefore in like manner did he unite in himself, and renew, and gives us back in him, the principal lots or states in which we find ourselves — suffering, that we might know how to suffer; labouring, that we might know how to labour; and teaching, that we might know how to teach.[51]

50. W. A. Visser 't Hooft, *The Kingship of Christ* (New York: Harper, 1948), pp. 15f.

51. Newman, "The Three Offices of Christ," *Sermons*, p. 54.

7

The Prophetic Office

As Jesus stood on Mount Tabor conversing with Moses, the prophet of Mount Sinai, and Elijah, the prophet of Mount Carmel, his face shone like the sun and his garments became white as light, and the voice of the Father resounded from the cloud, "This is my beloved Son. Listen to him!" The revelation of God was now taking place by the One through whom all things were made. Those summoned to listen were Peter, James, and John, the disciples of the Master and the eyewitnesses of his life, who, after the "exodus he was to accomplish at Jerusalem" (Luke 9:31), would be part of the Spirit-filled apostolic band that was charged to bear testimony to him to the ends of the earth, inviting others to accept baptism into his body. The prophetic office, in all its uses, conveys the word and work of God to the world.

1. THE CHRISTOLOGICAL USE

Let us begin, as Calvin began in the relevant chapter of the final edition of the *Institutes*, with Jesus reading one sabbath from the scroll of Isaiah in the synagogue at Nazareth (Luke 4:16-21):

> "The Spirit of the Lord is upon me,
> because he has anointed me to preach good news to the poor.
> He has sent me to proclaim release to the captives

and recovering of sight to the blind,
to set at liberty those who are oppressed,
to proclaim the acceptable year of the Lord."

"We see," Calvin comments, that Christ "was anointed by the Spirit to be herald and witness of the Father's grace."[1]

To take up two proverbs that Jesus will use in a rather ironic way, we have in this early incident at Nazareth a "prophet in his own country" (Luke 4:24), "a prophet," however, who must not "perish away from Jerusalem" (Luke 13:33). At Nazareth there takes place the inauguration of a ministry that the populace, almost willy-nilly, will recognize as "prophetic." Jesus appeared as a wandering rabbi (Matt. 4:23; 9:35; Mark 1:39; 6:6; Luke 4:15, 44), yet the people "were astonished at his teaching, for he taught them as one who had authority, and not as their scribes" (Matt. 7:28f.; Mark 1:22; cf. Luke 4:31). The category of rabbi was not sufficient, then. So the Son of Man was popularly said to be Elijah, Jeremiah, or one of the old-time prophets come back (Matt. 16:13f.; Mark 8:27f.; Luke 9:18f.). Perhaps he was even "the prophet like Moses," who would announce the kingdom of God (cf. Acts 3:22; 7:37; Deut. 18:15). Yet not even that description would suffice. According to Matthew 11:7-15, Jesus himself identifies rather John the Baptist as "a prophet, and more than a prophet," the "Elijah who is to come"; John is he of whom it is written "Behold, I send my messenger before thy face, who shall prepare thy way before thee" (cf. Luke 7:24-28). The Gospels make clear that Jesus is the mightier one, for whom the Baptist is a forerunner (Matt. 3:1-17; Mark 1:1-11; Luke 3:1-21; John 1:19-34).

Liberal Protestants liked to classify Jesus as a prophet. That at least helped us all to recover the genuine humanity of Jesus. But the category must not be used reductionistically, as happened with the Harnackians and threatened to happen with the Dominican Edward Schillebeeckx even when he prefixed the adjective *eschatological:* Jesus "the eschatological prophet."[2] Hints as to Jesus' unique status are to be found in his own recorded teaching. He interiorizes, radicalizes, even (at least on the surface)

---

1. John Calvin, *Institutes* II.15.2 (English translation: *Calvin: Institutes of the Christian Religion,* ed. John T. McNeill and Ford Lewis Battles, 2 vols. [Philadelphia: Westminster, 1960], 1:496; hereafter cited as ET).

2. Edward Schillebeeckx, *Jesus: An Experiment in Christology,* trans. Hubert Hoskins (New York: Crossroad, 1981).

contradicts the Law of Moses, hitherto identified as direct divine revelation. Whereas the prophets say, "Thus says the LORD," Jesus says, "I say unto you" — prefaced indeed by the peculiar use of "Amen," which makes of his words a personal asseveration of the divine truth (*'emeth)*. The implications of this are confessed when the Fourth Gospel declares, "The Word became flesh and dwelt among us. . . . The law was given through Moses; grace and truth came through Jesus Christ. No one has ever seen God; the only Son, who is in the bosom of the Father, he has made him known" (John 1:14, 17f.). Or with the Letter to the Hebrews (1:1-3a):

> In many and various ways God spoke of old to our fathers by the prophets; but in these last days he has spoken to us by a Son, whom he appointed the heir of all things, through whom also he created the world. He reflects the glory of God and bears the very stamp of his nature, upholding the universe by his word of power.

After his servants the prophets, God sent his beloved Son (Matt. 21:33-46; Mark 12:1-12; Luke 20:9-19).

Jesus climaxes the prophetic line by being himself the very *dabar* of God. In Hebrew, *dabar* means not only word, but also action and event. Jesus is the word, act, event of God made flesh. He is the personal address of God to humanity, coming to manifold expression in his individual sayings (Newman took as the text for his sermon on "The Three Offices of Christ" Psalm 45:2: "Full of grace are thy lips"), his significant deeds (healing, forgiving, eating with sinners), and the events of his life and death.

Yet this unsurpassable uniqueness of Jesus as the Word made flesh is in some way inclusive; and there we come to the second use of the prophetic office: Christians as prophets.

2. THE BAPTISMAL USE

Let us begin again with Calvin. As we heard, Calvin says that Jesus received the Spirit's anointing as a prophet, and then goes on:

> And that not in the common way — for he is distinguished from other teachers with a similar office. On the other hand, we must note this: he

received anointing, not only for himself that he might carry out the office of teaching, but for his whole body that the power of the Spirit might be present in the continuing preaching of the Gospel. . . . This anointing was diffused from the Head to the members, as Joel had foretold: "Your sons shall prophesy and your daughters shall see visions."[3]

Far from wanting to keep the prophetic office to himself, Moses already had expressed the desire "that all the LORD's people were prophets, that the LORD would put his Spirit upon them!" (Num. 11:29). At the first Christian Pentecost, that is what happened; and that it was meant to continue is illustrated by what happened when the disciples at Ephesus were baptized in the name of the Lord Jesus (Acts 19:5-7): "And when Paul had laid his hands upon them, the Holy Spirit came on them; and they spoke with tongues and prophesied."

The content of prophecy by Christians is governed by the gospel received and by the faith correspondingly professed. As the church developed in the early centuries its liturgical practices for admission into membership of the body, there occurred in the weeks before baptism a ceremonial "opening of the ears" for the hearing of the gospel and a dual rite of the "tradition" and "rendition" of the creed, whereby the faith of the community was made over to the candidates and they made it their own. And now what is "believed in the heart" is also to be "confessed with the lips" (cf. Rom. 10:8-10). "By the Holy Spirit," Christians are enabled to say "Jesus is Lord" (1 Cor. 12:3).

In a sense, Christians, like Jesus himself, have transcended the category of prophet, for they no longer *need* the prophetic message. What the prophets had to tell them, they have now been given: "Let the word of Christ dwell in you richly" (Col. 3:16). Remember how John Chrysostom cited 1 Corinthians 2:9 in this connection:

> "What no eye has seen, nor ear heard,
> nor the heart of man conceived,
> what God has prepared for those who love him,"
> God has revealed to us through the Spirit.

Baptized by the Spirit into Christ, we have as Christians been initiated into the eschatological mystery of God. Or to put it in the more sober

3. Calvin, *Institutes* II.15.2 (ET, 1:496).

terms with which Calvinists will be more comfortable: As sharers in the new covenant, we no longer need anyone to teach us the law, for God himself has written the law on our hearts by his Spirit, in fulfillment of the promise of Jeremiah 31:31-34:

> Behold, the days are coming, says the LORD, when I will make a new covenant with the house of Israel and the house of Judah, not like the covenant which I made with their fathers when I took them by the hand to bring them out of the land of Egypt, my covenant which they broke, though I was their husband, says the LORD. But this is the covenant which I will make with the house of Israel after those days, says the LORD: I will put my law within them, and I will write it upon their hearts; and I will be their God, and they shall be my people. And no longer shall each man teach his neighbor and each his brother, saying, "Know the LORD," for they shall all know me, from the least of them to the greatest, says the LORD; for I will forgive their iniquity, and I will remember their sin no more.

The "third use of the law," on which Calvinists traditionally and rightly insist, is an interiorized law. It is the *lex Christi:* Christ lives in us by his Spirit, so that we may walk by the Spirit and bring forth the Spirit's fruit (Gal. 5:16-26; cf. 2:20). That spiritual conduct is part of our testimony before the world.

If Christians have become more than prophets, it is thanks to the saving work of Christ; and so we come to the soteriological office of Christ as Prophet.

3. THE SOTERIOLOGICAL USE

Calvin makes clear the New Testament affirmation that it is in Christ that the saving truth of God is to be found:

> The perfect doctrine he has brought has made an end to all prophecies. All those, then, who, not content with the gospel, patch it with something extraneous to it, detract from Christ's authority. The voice that thundered from heaven, "This is my beloved Son: Hear him," exalted him by a singular privilege beyond the rank of all others. . . . Paul says

125

that he was given to us as our wisdom [1 Cor. 1:30], and in another place, "In him are hid all the treasures of knowledge and understanding" [Col. 2:3]. That is, outside Christ there is nothing worth knowing, and all who by faith perceive what he is like have grasped the whole immensity of heavenly benefits. For this reason, Paul writes in another passage: "I decided to know nothing precious except Jesus Christ and him crucified" [1 Cor. 2:2]. This is very true, because it is not lawful to go beyond the simplicity of the gospel. And the prophetic dignity in Christ leads us to know that in the sum of doctrine as he has given it to us all parts of perfect wisdom are contained.[4]

What Christ has revealed is the character of God and the mystery of God, the saving purpose of the loving God who invites his fallen human creatures back to share in his life.

By his very coming into the world, and then by his teaching and his conduct, Christ discloses, first, the character of God. As Jesus tells Zacchaeus, "The Son of man came to seek and to save the lost" (Luke 19:10). In a parable, he speaks of the owner searching for a straying sheep until he finds it, and the joy in heaven over the sinner who repents (Luke 15:3-7; cf. Matt. 18:12-14); and the rescue of a sheep from the pit on a sabbath is the basis of an *a fortiori* justification for Jesus' healing of a man on the sabbath day (Matt. 12:10-13). Jesus graciously enters into table fellowship with sinners (Matt. 9:10-13; Mark 2:15-17; Luke 5:29-32) — and invites them to repentance (Luke 5:32). God's mercy toward the humble penitent is declared in the parable of the Pharisee and the tax collector who went up into the temple to pray (Luke 18:9-14), and Jesus himself exercises divine authority to forgive the sins of the paralytic (Mark 2:3-12; Matt. 9:2-8; Luke 5:18-26). The Beatitudes of Jesus (Matt. 5:3-10) express both the character of God and the character of those who will share the life of his kingdom (we recall Saint Augustine's dictum that the best worship is to "imitate the One you worship [*imitari quem colis*]"):[5]

"Blessed are the poor in spirit, for theirs is the kingdom of heaven. Blessed are those who mourn, for they shall be comforted.

4. Calvin, *Institutes* II.15.2 (ET, 1:496).

5. Augustine, *De civitate Dei* VIII.17.2 (quoted by John Wesley in Sermon 29, "Upon Our Lord's Sermon on the Mount, IX," in *The Works of John Wesley*, vol. 1 [Nashville: Abingdon, 1984], p. 635).

Blessed are the meek, for they shall inherit the earth.
Blessed are those who hunger and thirst for righteousness, for they
   shall be satisfied.
Blessed are the merciful, for they shall obtain mercy.
Blessed are the pure in heart, for they shall see God.
Blessed are the peacemakers, for they shall be called sons of God.
Blessed are those who are persecuted for righteousness' sake, for
   theirs is the kingdom of heaven."

And, in evidence of the dawning kingdom, Jesus sent John the Baptist's
disciples back to him in prison to report on "the deeds of the Christ"
(Matt. 11:2-6; cf. Luke 7:18-23):

"Go and tell John what you hear and see: the blind receive their sight
and the lame walk, lepers are cleansed and the deaf hear, and the dead
are raised up, and the poor have good news preached to them."

God's character, then, is matched by his good purpose for
humankind. That is what the Pauline writings call the "mystery" of God
which has now been revealed in Jesus Christ (Rom. 16:25-27; 1 Cor.
2:7-10; Eph. 1:9f.; 3:1-21; Col. 1:24–2:3; 1 Tim. 3:16). The "unsearchable
riches of Christ" (Eph. 3:8), "the hope of glory" (Col. 1:27), comprise the
plan of God to give a share in what he "has prepared for those who love
him" (1 Cor. 2:9) not only to Israel but also to the Gentiles. According
to Ephesians 3:4-6, this is

the mystery of Christ, which was not made known to the sons of men
in other generations as it has now been revealed to his holy apostles and
prophets by the Spirit; that is, how the Gentiles are fellow heirs, members
of the same body, and partakers of the promise in Christ Jesus through
the gospel.

Hence the gospel is to be "made known to all nations," "to bring about
the obedience of faith" (Rom. 16:25f.). For God's "purpose," "set forth in
Christ as a plan for the fulness of time," is no less than universal in scope:
to "unite all things in him, things in heaven and things on earth" (Eph.
1:9f.).

Thus Peter preaches in Acts 4: "There is salvation in no one else, for
there is no other name under heaven . . . by which we must be saved"

(v. 12). That is why believers in him are given his name: Christ makes Christians. According to the First Letter of Saint John (2:20-27):

> You have been anointed by the Holy One, and you all know. . . . Let what you heard from the beginning abide in you. If what you heard from the beginning abides in you, then you abide in the Son and in the Father. And this is what he has promised us, eternal life. . . . The anointing which you received from him abides in you, and you have no need that any one should teach you; as his anointing teaches you about everything, and is true, and is no lie, just as it has taught you, abide in him.

And that is why we, in turn, are obliged to testify to the gospel truth, the whole gospel truth, and nothing but the gospel truth. One of the themes associated with the rite of confirmation in the medieval West was that of a "strengthening by the Holy Spirit for preaching to others the same gift as one has received in baptism."[6]

We shall consider soon the prophetic mission of the church before the world. But if Christians themselves have no further need of prophets, what room is there for a prophetic ministry in the church? We come, nevertheless, to the fourth use of the prophetic office.

4. THE MINISTERIAL USE

The New Testament church did include recognizable people who were, in some sense, "prophets." The Acts of the Apostles mentions certain ones by name: Agabus and others (11:27-30); Barnabas, Simeon Niger, Lucius of Cyrene, Manaen, and Saul (13:1-3); and the four daughters of Philip the evangelist (21:8f.). Paul lists prophets among the special ministries (1 Cor. 12:28), even while telling the Corinthians: "Earnestly desire the spiritual gifts, especially that you may prophesy. . . . I want you *all* to speak in tongues, but even more to prophesy" (1 Cor. 14:1-5, emphasis added; cf. vv. 29-33, 39f.). Similarly, teachers are mentioned as a special

---

6. "Ut roboretur per Spiritum Sanctum ad praedicandum aliis idem donum quod ipse in baptismate consecutus est." This classic expression comes from Rabanus Maurus (A.D. ca. 780-856), *De clericorum institutione* I.30 (Migne, *Patrologia Latina* 107:314).

ministry, to which not all are admitted (1 Cor. 12:28; Eph. 4:11; James 3:1) — while Hebrews 5:12 holds out another ideal: "Though by this time you ought to be teachers, you need some one to teach you again the first principles of God's word."

There, surely, lies at least one clue to ministerial office in the church. In principle, the basic dignities and functions of the church's life are open to all Christians; but in the present state of imperfection, special ministries are needed to remind, to guide, to encourage, and (where necessary) to correct; and as, with the delay of Christ's return, generation succeeds generation, these ministries have served the continuing transmission of the gospel, "the faith which was once for all delivered to the saints" (Jude 3). It is hard to know how precisely the primitive church distinguished between "teachers" and "prophets." Perhaps the teachers transmitted the received gospel, while the prophets interpreted it in each new situation. Certainly these two tasks appear to impose themselves; and through much of church history they have been concentrated upon the "ministers of the word." Yet the ideal of a prophetic people which knows the Lord at first hand means that there can be no unqualified distinction, let alone separation, between a "church of the teachers" and a "church of the taught," *ecclesia docens* and *ecclesia discens*. To the "magisterium" of the church all faithful Christians belong: the "reception," whether positive or negative, given by the people as a whole to the special ministers' proclamation of the gospel and discernment of the faith is an indispensable part of the quite complex operation of preserving the truth as it is in Jesus.

These matters have been controversial in Christian history, and even divisive, but some ecumenical progress is under way. An example may be taken from the international dialogue between the Roman Catholic Church and the World Methodist Council. In its statement on revelation and faith, entitled *The Word of Life*, the Joint Commission writes thus of "discernment by the people of God":

> According to Scripture, the discernment of God's will is the task of the whole people of God. The admonition to prove and to approve *(doki-mazein)* what is good in the eyes of God is a major theme within the letters of the Apostles (cf. Rom. 12:2; Eph. 5:10, 17; Phil. 1:9f.; 1 Thess. 5:21; 1 John 4:1f.). Paul prays for the Church in Philippi, "that your love may abound more and more, with knowledge and all discernment, so that you may approve what is excellent, and may be pure and blameless for the day of Christ, filled with the fruits of righteousness

which come through Jesus Christ, to the glory and praise of God" (Phil. 1:9f.). The people of God in their daily life have "to learn what is pleasing to the Lord" (Eph. 5:10) and what will meet the needs of their neighbours. In this discernment God's love is the leading power, and the needs of the community of the believers and the sufferings of the people around them are pointers to the right direction. Such active openness in love to the very truth which is Jesus, and to the disinherited people of their times, drove many of the saints in our two communions to new forms of piety and service in the world. By this kind of discernment Wesley taught that it was not enough that masters should treat their slaves justly and fairly, but that it was God's will that slavery be abolished.[7]

At times, "prophetic voices of warning and admonition have arisen," as both "shepherds and flock have gone astray." Some of these prophetic voices "were readily listened to, and some not." The difficulty of "weighing" or "discerning" these words "should not diminish the challenge to listen to prophetic voices." At times, "the Church needs a formal decision about whether some doctrines are right or wrong, or which actions are appropriate to the needs of the time as well as to the calling of the Church." The Methodist-Catholic Commission declares that "it is the common belief of our churches that there are those who are authorised to speak for the Church as a whole and who, after having carefully listened to Scripture and Tradition and the experience of believers trying to live out the Gospel, and after a reasonable and prayerful discussion, may say, 'It has seemed good to the Holy Spirit and to us' (Acts 15:28a; cf. 1 Cor. 7:40b)."[8] Who properly constitutes those teaching organs remains, of course, subject to ecumenical investigation.

Meanwhile, there is an ongoing and perennial ministry of preaching and teaching in the Christian communities. Season by season, catechumens are instructed in preparation for membership in the church. Sunday by Sunday in the principal gathering for worship, the Scriptures are read and expounded. Day in and day out, children are taught in Christian schools and families. Study groups meet regularly,

7. Joint Commission between the Roman Catholic Church and the World Methodist Council, *The Word of Life* (Lake Junaluska, N.C.: World Methodist Council, 1996), par. 63.

8. Joint Commission, *The Word of Life,* pars. 64-67.

in which laypeople help and encourage each other in exploring their faith and life together. In theological faculties and seminaries, ordinands and others preparing to teach receive an education in the various disciplines of Bible, history, dogmatics, and church practice. The aim of it all is the upbuilding of the whole people of God. All of it should lead, to revert to the language of the Catholic-Methodist Commission, "to a growing interdependence and mutual recognition of those who exercise pastoral authority within the Church, those who offer prophetic vision, and all those who, by their response to revelation and their inspiration through the creative love of God, participate in active tradition of the Gospel and compassionate discernment of the will of God for his Church and the world."[9]

That brings us finally to the fifth use of the prophetic office, concerning the church as a whole as it fulfills its mission in the world.

5. The Ecclesiological Use

As themselves "more than prophets," Christians form a prophetic body in the world. The church bears a prophetic mission in the world. It inherits the commission given to the apostles by the Christ who has all authority in heaven and on earth (Matt. 28:16-20):

> "Go therefore and *make disciples* of all nations, baptizing them in the name of the Father and of the Son and of the Holy Spirit, *teaching* them to observe all that I have commanded you. . . ." (emphasis added)

The church's prophetic mission is nothing more and nothing less than discipling people to Christ: nothing more spectacular, exotic, novel, relevant; nothing less than offering them eternal salvation in Christ.

"And lo," the risen Lord continued, "I am with you always, to the close of the age." The church can fulfill its prophetic mission only when Christ is present to it. The Christian band cannot be dispersed without the compensating rhythm of gathering. When the gospel is announced Sunday by Sunday in the liturgical assembly, we stand to hail the Word made flesh, present anew in the Spirit:

9. Joint Commission, *The Word of Life*, par. 72.

Glory to you, Lord Christ.
Praise to you, Lord Christ.

If he is not there, then neither have we a message for the world; and those who hear *us* do not then hear *him* (cf. Luke 10:16), but only *our* "wisdom," which is no better than the rest of the world's.

The church, however, lives from the faith that Christ is present in the midst of those gathered together in his name (Matt. 18:20) and accompanies them on their mission (Matt. 28:20). In one way or another, it is in fact traditional teaching and experience that Christ is ahead of his messengers. Not only is Christ present as the Father's universal agent in creation and preservation (John 1:1-3; 1 Cor. 8:6; Col. 1:15-17; Heb. 1:2f.), but as Logos he is also particularly present among humankind as the source of wisdom and law, wherever these are found preparing for the advent of the gospel of redemption. For the Word who was made flesh as Jesus Christ is the "light that enlightens every man" (John 1:9, cf. 14), and what Justin Martyr said about the good Greeks who lived "according to the Logos" before the incarnation of Christ[10] can subsequently be applied to people living before the proclamation of the gospel reaches them. And if, according to Justin Martyr, Christ himself was the fulfillment of the promise of "an eternal law and a new covenant for the whole world,"[11] then Christ may be considered present in a promissory capacity to those who, before receiving the gospel, are analogous to Saint Paul's Gentiles who, without the particular revelation, to some degree at least know and even do the law (Rom. 2). Thus the messengers of Christ find themselves anticipated by the One who sends them, not in such a way as to render their mission unnecessary but rather to make it awaited.

As Jesus Christ expressed the revelation of God by words and signs and actions, so the church's missionary proclamation of Christ takes place in a variety of forms. The apostle Paul reminded the church at Thessalonica that "our gospel came to you not only in word, but also in power and in the Holy Spirit" (1 Thess. 1:5). The Holy Spirit empowers many expressions of the gospel, through storytelling and preaching, through sacrament and gesture, through drama and film, through hospitals and healing,

---

10. Justin Martyr, *First Apology,* 46 (Migne, *Patrologia Graeca* 6:397; hereafter cited as *PG*).

11. Justin Martyr, *Dialogue with Trypho the Jew,* 43 (Migne, *PG* 6:568); cf. chaps. 11, 51, 122.

through schools and orphanages, through agriculture and feeding the hungry. In all these ways the church can in Christ's name set up signs of God's coming kingdom, whose reality will transcend them all.

Christ, after all, remains a Prophet in the sense that he himself is the future of the world; and the task of the church, under his direction, is to help the world see its own best future.

6. The Contemporary Hermeneutic

The foregoing has provided, I think, a fair scriptural and traditional description of the prophetic office exercised by Christ, and in which Christians are given a share. What now about contemporary interpretation? What is the human condition being addressed by this office, what human question is being offered an answer? And what are the problems and possibilities for letting this answer be heard?

The fundamental question being addressed by the prophetic office is the question of *knowledge* — or, in a more existential modern formulation, the question of *meaning.* The explosion of knowledge characteristic of the modern world does not seem to have been accompanied by a corresponding increase in wisdom. Our *scientia* is not matched by our *sapientia,* to borrow Saint Augustine's terms for this distinction.[12] Space telescopes can penetrate toward the edges of the universe, but we are not sure what we are about on planet earth. Life is yielding the secrets of its physical structure to the biochemists, but that does not particularly help us in the moral decision as to when a human life begins and ends. Psychology can uncover some mental processes, but it leaves open the questions of responsibility and freedom. Among Western intellectuals, an ultimate nihilism may remain for the moment the dominant fashion, but there is also a modest revival of interest in teleology.

The question of the *meaning* — of the universe as such, of the world, of human history, of individual lives — is given to us with our very existence in the midst of, and as part of, these realities. In religious, and particularly in biblical, terms it is the question of the will and purpose of

12. On this theme, see Heiko A. Oberman, *Contra vanam curiositatem. Ein Kapitel der Theologie zwischen Seelenwinckel und Weltall,* Theologische Studien 113 (Zurich: Theologischer Verlag, 1974).

God, of God's project for creation. That is a question which poses itself ever afresh to us as the circumstances of the world, of history, and of our own lives change. Christians believe that the answer has in principle already been given in Jesus Christ, but it is an answer that has continually to be reappropriated and indeed "worked out" by ourselves right up to the final advent of Christ to establish the definitive kingdom of God, for we are *part of* the answer to our own question, and "it does not yet appear what we shall be" (1 John 3:2).

How does our putting of our own question look in the North American churches today? Many Christians, both learned and not, live under the pressures of radical doubt which has, since Descartes, become the fundamental epistemological principle of the modern West. It affects them over a whole range of issues, from the value of prayer through the uncertainty of any "quest for the historical Jesus" to their lack of orientation in ethical matters. Other Christians, of various stripes, claim to have all the answers, yet they remain ignorant of the extraneous ideological factors that have contributed to their interpretation of the gospel and the faith; and they appear epistemologically unworried by the fact that *their* "answers" are not received by the whole church. Needed is the recovery of what Bishop Lesslie Newbigin has called a "proper confidence" that both recognizes the fiduciary character of all human knowledge and trusts the God of the biblical story, fully aware that "the affirmation that the One by whom and through whom and for whom all creation exists is to be identified with a man who was crucified and rose bodily from the dead cannot possibly be accommodated within any plausibility structure except one of which it is the cornerstone."[13]

Our problems, of course, are not simply epistemological in an intellectualist sense. When one has reached, however tentatively or however firmly, an interpretation of God's will and purpose in a particular set of circumstances, there remains the matching of the deed to the word. Becoming "doers of the word, and not hearers only" (James 1:22-25) requires more than passing from theory to practice. Moral courage must be exercised and appropriate actions must be energized if, to use an apostolic wordplay (Rom. 10:14-21), "hearing" *(akouē)* is to become embodied in "obedience" *(hup-akouē)*. It was "in his testimony before Pontius Pilate" that Christ Jesus "made the good confession" (1 Tim. 6:13), and some of

13. Lesslie Newbigin, *Proper Confidence: Faith, Doubt, and Certainty in Christian Discipleship* (Grand Rapids: Eerdmans, 1995), p. 93.

the followers of "the faithful and true witness" (Rev. 3:14) have "been slain for the word of God and for the witness they had borne" (Rev. 6:9). Martyrdom in the strong sense always remains in the outlook for prophetic witness.

What then must we do, corporately and individually, to exercise our prophetic office in Christ? I suggest we need continually to rediscple ourselves to our Master. Put rather simply and concretely, that will entail at least three things. First, a meditative study of the Scriptures. "Lord, to whom shall we go? You have the words of eternal life" (John 6:68). Our access to those words and their speaker is by way of the scriptural records. Second, a discernment of spirits. That itself is a prophetic charism. It is cultivated as we study our Lord in the Scriptures and seek communion with him in prayer. And third, we shall strive for a life of following and obedience, renewed by conscious reflection and deliberate decision, such that the habit of discipleship is built up in us and the theological virtues of faith, hope, and love increase in us and shape our character now and for eternity.

8

The Priestly Office

Alexander Nairne's classic essays and exposition on the Letter to the Hebrews were aptly entitled *The Epistle of Priesthood*.[1] While a sacrificial understanding of the person and work of Christ is not limited to Hebrews among the New Testament writings, it is there that we may suitably begin our discussion of his priestly office, the benefits we draw from it, and the share which Christians and the church are given in it. By a track analogous to that followed in the previous chapter, we shall move toward the practice of the church that is epitomized in the prayer borrowed by the Church of South India from the old Mozarabic liturgy:

> Be present, be present, O Jesus, thou good High Priest, as thou wast in the midst of thy disciples, and make thyself known to us in the breaking of the bread, who livest and reignest with the Father and the Holy Spirit, one God, world without end. Amen.[2]

1. Alexander Nairne, *The Epistle of Priesthood: Studies in the Epistle to the Hebrews* (Edinburgh: T. & T. Clark, 1913).
2. The Church of South India, *The Book of Common Worship, as Authorised by the Synod 1963* (London: Oxford University Press, 1963), p. 14.

1. THE CHRISTOLOGICAL USE

Hebrews 10:5-10 reads thus:

> When Christ came into the world, he said,
> "Sacrifices and offerings thou hast not desired,
> but a body hast thou prepared for me;
> in burnt offerings and sin offerings thou hast taken no pleasure.
> Then I said, 'Lo, I have come to do thy will, O God,'
> as it is written of me in the roll of the book."
> When he said above, "Thou hast neither desired nor taken plea-
> sure in sacrifices and offerings and burnt offerings and sin offerings"
> (these are offered according to the law), then he added, "Lo, I have
> come to do thy will." He abolishes the first in order to establish the
> second. And by that will we have been sanctified through the offering
> of the body of Jesus Christ once for all.

Cardinal Joseph Ratzinger perceptively remarks that the foregoing
passage makes of the incarnation a "prayer-event" between Father and Son.[3]
We catch a glimpse of that in the recorded occasions when Jesus prayed in
the Gospels. He prayed when he came up from the waters of his baptism
(Luke 3:21). Amid his busy ministry in Galilee, he withdrew before dawn to
a lonely place to pray (Mark 1:35; cf. Luke 5:16). He could spend all night
in prayer (Luke 6:12). After feeding the multitudes he went up on the
mountain by himself to pray (Matt. 14:23; Mark 6:46). He was praying
when his transfiguration took place (Luke 9:28f.). He could rejoice in the
Holy Spirit (Luke 10:21) and thank his Father for his own relationship as
Son and the knowledge it brought and allowed him to communicate (Luke
10:22; Matt. 11:25-27). It was Jesus' own praying that prompted his disciples
to ask for instruction in prayer (Luke 11:1). Jesus prayed before calling
Lazarus forth from the tomb, knowing that the Father always hears him
(John 11:41-43). On the night of his Last Supper, Jesus prayed for his
disciples in what has come to be called his "high priestly prayer" (John 17).
In the Garden of Gethsemane, he prayed three times (Matt. 26:36-44; Mark
14:32-39; cf. Luke 22:39-43); and it is there that we overhear his "Abba,
Father" addressed to the One who sent him and whose will he completely

---

3. Joseph Ratzinger, *Theologische Prinzipienlehre. Bausteine zur Fundamentaltheologie*
(Munich: Wewel, 1982), p. 20.

accepts to the point of passion and death (Mark 14:36). On the cross, Jesus prays, "Father, forgive them; for they know not what they do" (Luke 23:34), and with his last breath cries, "Father, into thy hands I commit my spirit!" (Luke 23:46).

The primitive Christian hymn in Philippians 2:5-11 presents the self-emptying of the divine Son in incarnation and earthly life as obedience to the heavenly Father even to the point of death. His life of obedience, in human form and for a fallen humanity, was necessarily one of sacrifice, from the cradle to the cross. Jesus was, in an old devotional phrase, "a priest to his fingertips" — the fingers that gripped his mother's hand as an infant and that were splayed out on the cross as the nails were driven in. Considering the bread and wine over which Jesus had said, "This is my body, given for you" and "This cup is the new covenant in my blood," Thomas Aquinas took the sacrificial elements as embracing the whole life of Christ: "The body of Christ represents the mystery of the incarnation, . . . while the blood of Christ represents in a sacramental way his passion."[4]

The Letter to the Hebrews gives the title of "great high priest" (4:14) to the Christ who, "although he was a Son, . . . learned obedience through what he suffered" (5:8), and who, in a once-for-all sacrifice, "offered up himself" (7:27) and with "his own blood" (9:12) entered the heavenly sanctuary, where he "always lives to make intercession" for "those who draw near to God through him" (7:25). The epistle makes clear the humanity of Christ, his ability to sympathize with his human brothers and sisters — and not only sympathize, for (as Oscar Cullmann writes) "he must be able to suffer *with* humans in order to suffer *for* them" (cf. Heb. 2:9, 14f., 17f.).[5] But ultimately it is *God* who provides the blood of sacrifice (cf. Lev. 17:11), and so the Letter to the Hebrews insists that Christ is no less than the Son of God (1:2-8; 3:6; 4:14; 5:5, 8; 6:6; 7:3, 28; 10:29). In Chalcedonian terms, the singleness of Christ's person, the second person of the Trinity, allows the "communication of properties" whereby a Charles Wesley can sing of "the incarnate God" and his "blood divine":

4. Thomas Aquinas, *Commentary on First Corinthians,* sixth lecture on the eleventh chapter (*Sancti Thomae Aquinatis Opera Omnia,* reprint of the Parma edition of 1852-73 [New York: Musurgia Publishers, 1948-49], 13:246).

5. Oscar Cullmann, *The Christology of the New Testament,* trans. S. C. Guthrie and C. A. M. Hall (Philadelphia: Westminster, 1959), pp. 83-107 (in particular p. 97).

How great the sin of Adam's race!
How greater still the Saviour's grace,
When God doth for his creature die![6]

The vicariousness of Christ's self-offering is unmistakable: he did for humankind what we could not do for ourselves. Yet its intention is inclusive in scope: its purpose is to sanctify us, so that we may follow our Forerunner into the presence of the Father. That brings us to the second use of the priestly office, its restoration to redeemed humanity.

2. THE BAPTISMAL USE

Hebrews 9:14 declares that "the blood of Christ, who through the eternal Spirit offered himself without blemish to God, [will] purify your conscience from dead works to serve the living God." That sounds like a baptismal reference, especially when taken in conjunction with Hebrews 10:22: "Let us draw near with a true heart in full assurance of faith, with our hearts sprinkled clean from an evil conscience and our bodies washed with pure water." The rhetorical parallelism of "hearts sprinkled clean" and "bodies washed" suggests the sacramental view of baptism as "an outward and visible sign of an inward and spiritual grace."[7] The priesthood of Christ, in which Christians are admitted to share by the baptism of faith, takes for Christians the forms of both prayer and consecrated conduct.

Suffering with Christ in order that we may also be glorified with him, Christians already are allowed the privilege of sons and daughters to address God, with Christ and in the Spirit, as "Abba! Father!" (Rom. 8:14-17). Having "a great high priest who has passed through the heavens, Jesus, the Son of God," Christians may "with confidence draw near to the throne of grace, that we may receive mercy and find grace to help in time of need" (Heb. 4:14-16). As part of their preparation for baptism in the rites of the early church, the candidates "received" the Lord's Prayer and then "gave it back" (a dual ceremony similar to the *traditio* and *redditio* of the creed). They were instructed in the meaning of the prayer that they would henceforth

6. John and Charles Wesley, *Hymns on the Lord's Supper* (Bristol, 1745), no. 45.
7. The Church of England Catechism in the *Book of Common Prayer.* The phrase has Augustinian roots, and the notion became a commonplace in the medieval West.

regularly use.[8] The recipient of Christians' prayers is the Holy One whose sovereign will we seek to see universally established; his paternal care of us includes provision for us here and hereafter, and he will see us through whatever lies between us and the final coming of his kingdom. As sinners we need his forgiveness, and so Christian prayer takes place through Jesus Christ our Redeemer. We hallow God's name by praying in the name of Jesus. The Mediator himself can be invoked, as in the ancient "Jesus Prayer" which Eastern Christians have allowed to set the very rhythm of their breathing: "Lord Jesus Christ, Son of God, have mercy on me." Love for our neighbors includes praying for them, and so we ourselves intercede for the removal of whatever is keeping them from enjoyment of God's reign.

The language of the cult is used by the apostle Paul to characterize the moral conduct expected of Christians. In Romans 12:1f. he writes:

> I appeal to you therefore, brethren, by the mercies of God, to present your bodies as a living sacrifice, holy and acceptable to God, which is your reasonable worship. Do not be conformed to this world but be transformed by the renewal of your mind, that you may prove what is the will of God, what is good and acceptable and perfect.

And, speaking of Christians as "members of Christ," he writes in 1 Corinthians 6:19f.:

> Do you not know that your body is a temple of the Holy Spirit within you, which you have from God? You are not your own; you were bought with a price. So glorify God in your body.

The consecration of our life to God can occur in many forms. The ancient monastic pattern, whether in solitude or in community, follows a

---

8. Patristic expositions of the Lord's Prayer can be found in the treatises of Tertullian and Cyprian devoted to it; in Origen, *On Prayer,* chaps. 18-30; in Augustine, *Sermons* 56-59; in John Chrysostom's *Nineteenth Homily on Matthew;* and in Gregory of Nyssa's *Five Sermons on the Lord's Prayer.* The Lord's Prayer figures in the catechisms of the Protestant and Catholic Reformations, and Teresa of Ávila used it to instruct her religious communities in *The Way of Perfection* (chaps. 27-42). Examples of twentieth-century expositions are Romano Guardini, *The Lord's Prayer,* trans. Isabel McHugh (New York: Pantheon Books, 1958); William Barclay, *The Plain Man Looks at the Lord's Prayer* (London: Collins Fontana, 1964); and one of the fragments of Karl Barth's *Church Dogmatics* IV/4, *The Christian Life,* trans. G. W. Bromiley (Grand Rapids: Eerdmans, 1981).

concentrated rhythm of prayer and work, in which work is also prayer and prayer is also work — for how else may one both "pray constantly" (1 Thess. 5:17) and "work night and day" (2 Thess. 3:8)?[9] All Christians, in fact, are enjoined by the apostle: "Whatever you do, in word or deed, do everything in the name of the Lord Jesus, giving thanks to God the Father through him" (Col. 3:17). That is why worldly occupations also allow the exercise of a vocation (a *Beruf*), as Luther and the Protestant Reformers could insist; and so George Herbert could pray:

> Teach me, my God and King,
> In all things Thee to see;
> And what I do in anything,
> To do it as for Thee.
>
> A man that looks on glass,
> On it may stay his eye;
> Or if he pleaseth, through it pass,
> And then the heaven espy.
>
> All may of Thee partake:
> Nothing can be so mean,
> Which with this tincture, *For Thy sake,*
> Will not grow bright and clean.
>
> A servant with this clause
> Makes drudgery divine;
> Who sweeps a room, as for Thy laws,
> Makes that and the action fine.
>
> This is the famous stone
> That turneth all to gold:
> For that which God doth touch and own,
> Cannot for less be told.[10]

9. See G. Wainwright, "*Ora et labora:* Benedictines and Wesleyans at Prayer and at Work," in his *Methodists in Dialogue* (Nashville: Abingdon Press/Kingswood Books, 1995), pp. 89-106.

10. George Herbert, "The Elixir," from *The Temple* (1633).

3. THE SOTERIOLOGICAL USE

In talking of the priestly office, it has been particularly difficult to reserve the soteriological theme for treatment after the christological and the baptismal. We have, however, now reached the midpoint of these five chapters and the very heart of the *munus triplex*. "Christ crucified" is the epitome of the apostolic gospel (1 Cor. 1:21; 2:2). The cross is the sign *par excellence* of Christianity. Special concentration is needed on Christ's sacrifice of himself and the Father's acceptance of his offering. Appropriately we may turn to Calvin for an exposition of Christ's work of salvation at this point — "the point on which our whole salvation turns" — and quote in full a passage from the final edition of the *Institutes* where the author writes in classic terms that would be just as recognizable to an Athanasius as to an Anselm.[11] Recognizing the depth of the predicament of fallen humanity in our separation from God, Calvin sets out the saving work of Christ in his sacrificial death and his ministry as heavenly intercessor and describes the benefits that accrue to believers:

> Now we must speak briefly concerning the purpose and use of Christ's priestly office: as a pure and stainless Mediator he is by his holiness to reconcile us to God. But God's righteous curse bars our access to him, and God in his capacity as judge is angry toward us. Hence, an expiation must intervene in order that Christ our priest may obtain God's favor for us and appease his wrath. Thus Christ to perform this office had to come forward with a sacrifice. For under the law, also, the priest was forbidden to enter the sanctuary without blood [Heb. 9:7], that believers might know, even though the priest as their advocate stood between them and God, that they could not propitiate God unless their sins were expiated [Lev. 16:2f.]. The apostle discusses this at length in the Letter to the Hebrews, from the seventh almost to the end of the tenth chapter. To sum up his argument: The priestly office belongs to Christ alone because by the sacrifice of his death he blotted out our own guilt and made satisfaction for our sins [Heb. 9:22]. God's solemn oath, of which he "will not repent," warns us what a weighty matter this is: "You

11. Since it is often alleged that reparatory accounts of the atonement are Western rather than Eastern, let me cite, for instance, Athanasius, *On the Incarnation of the Word*, chaps. 9, 20, 34.

are a priest forever after the order of Melchizedek" [Ps. 110:4; cf. Heb. 5:6; 7:15]. God undoubtedly willed in these words to ordain the principal point on which, he knew, our whole salvation turns. For, as has been said, we or our prayers have no access to God unless Christ, as our High Priest, having washed away our sins, sanctifies us and obtains for us that grace from which the uncleanness of our transgressions and vices debars us. Thus we see that we must begin from the death of Christ in order that the efficacy and benefit of his priesthood may reach us.

It follows that he is an everlasting intercessor: through his pleading we obtain favor. Hence arises not only trust in prayer, but also peace for godly consciences, while they safely lean upon God's fatherly mercy and are surely persuaded that whatever has been consecrated through the Mediator is pleasing to God. Although God under the law commanded animal sacrifices to be offered to himself, in Christ there was a new and different order, in which the same one was to be both priest and sacrifice. This was because no other satisfaction adequate for our sins, and no man worthy to offer to God the only-begotten Son, could be found. Now, Christ plays the priestly role, not only to render the Father favorable and propitious toward us by an eternal law of reconciliation, but also to receive us as his companions in this great office [cf. Rev. 1:6]. For we who are defiled in ourselves, yet are priests in him, offer ourselves and our all to God, and freely enter the heavenly sanctuary that the sacrifices of prayer and praise that we bring may be acceptable and sweet-smelling before God. This is the meaning of Christ's statement: "For their sake I sanctify myself" [John 17:19]. For we, imbued with his holiness in so far as he has consecrated us to the Father with himself, although we would otherwise be loathsome to him, please him as pure and clean — and even as holy.[12]

Using an Old Testament typology, Charles Wesley gives a graphic account of how Christ's believing people are carried by him into the presence of God. Our names are graven on the Lord's hands (cf. Isa. 49:16), inscribed on the precious stones that adorn the vestments of our Great High Priest (cf. Exod. 28:9-12, 21, 29):

12. John Calvin, *Institutes* II.15.6 (English translation: *Calvin: Institutes of the Christian Religion,* ed. John T. McNeill and Ford Lewis Battles, 2 vols. [Philadelphia: Westminster, 1960], 1:501f.

By thy divine oblation raised,
And on our Aaron's ephod placed
We now with thee in heaven appear.

The death exalts thy ransomed ones,
And sets us 'midst the precious stones,
Closest thy dear, thy loving breast;
Israel as on thy shoulders stands;
Our names are graven on the hands,
The heart of our eternal Priest.[13]

Precisely because there is no question of detracting from Christ's "grand oblation," we can, by "casting" ourselves on Christ (a favorite Wesleyan expression in this connection), render our souls and bodies to the Father:

On him, who all our burdens bears,
We cast our praises and our prayers,
Ourselves we offer up to God,
Implunged in his atoning blood.[14]

Father, on us the Spirit bestow,
Through which thine everlasting Son
Offered himself for man below,
That we, e'en we before thy throne
Our souls and bodies may present,
And pay thee all thy grace hath lent.[15]

While the eucharistic hymns of the Wesleys describe the sacramental "showing" of Christ to the Father and the believers' return of themselves to God in a way entirely consistent with classical Protestant doctrine, the manner of our participation in Christ's sacrifice has been deeply controversial in Christian history. Calvin ends his section on the priestly office of Christ with a sideswipe at Rome: "The more detestable is the fabrication of those who, not content with Christ's priesthood, have presumed to sacrifice him anew. The papists attempt this each day, considering the Mass

13. John and Charles Wesley, *Hymns on the Lord's Supper,* no. 117.
14. John and Charles Wesley, *Hymns on the Lord's Supper,* no. 137.
15. John and Charles Wesley, *Hymns on the Lord's Supper,* no. 150.

as the sacrificing of Christ."[16] That will oblige us to face the fourth, and eventually come to the fifth, aspect of the priestly office.

Meanwhile, we note that the benefits of Christ's priestly work may be expressed not only in the "upward" movement of our access to the Father through him but also in the "downward" movement of his gifts toward us. When the ascending Christ imparted his final blessing to his disciples (Luke 24:50f.), his raised hands were a kind of invocation of "the promise of my Father," the "power from on high" with which they would be clothed (Luke 24:49). The Holy Spirit, released at the Son's request (John 14:16f., 26; 15:26; Acts 2:33), is in fact Christ's fundamental and all-embracing gift. The Spirit is the personal form of that "grace and peace" with which the apostle Paul greets his addressees "from God our Father and the Lord Jesus Christ" (Rom. 1:7; 1 Cor. 1:3; 2 Cor. 1:2; Gal. 1:3f.; Eph. 1:2; Phil. 1:2; 1 Thess. 1:1; 2 Thess. 1:2; 1 Tim. 1:2; 2 Tim. 1:2; Titus 1:4). It is the descent of the Holy Spirit — invoked in the classical liturgies in Christ's name upon the assembly, their action, and the bread and wine — which allows Christians to receive the blessings of Christ's communion at the Lord's Table.

4. The Ministerial Use

There can be no doubt, historically, that priestly designations for bishops (first, and then also for presbyters) arose in connection with their presidency at the Eucharist, the "sacrifice of praise" offered by the entire Christian community.[17] It is important to note that all the classical forms of the Eucharistic Prayer remain aware that the offering is that of the whole people. The presider issues a summons: "*Let us* give thanks to the Lord our God." The rest of the assembly responds, "It is meet and right so to do." The presider voices the prayer in the "we" form. It is concluded by the congregational "Amen." In cases where specific ministers are called "priests," their office is not to exclude the priesthood of all Christians and of the Christian community as a whole; it is rather to help that priesthood to expression.

16. Calvin, *Institutes* II.15.6 (ET, 1:503).
17. See, for instance, Robert J. Daley, *The Origins of the Christian Doctrine of Sacrifice* (Philadelphia: Fortress, 1978), pp. 89f., 95-100, 127-34.

The matter is controversial in divided Christendom. Attempts have been made to find an account acceptable both to "catholic" churches which give a constitutive role to "priests" and to "protestant" churches jealous to maintain "the priesthood of all believers." A careful statement from an ecclesiastically diverse context is made in the "Ministry" section of the Lima text on *Baptism, Eucharist, and Ministry* of the Faith and Order Commission of the World Council of Churches. Paragraph 17, headed "Ordained Ministry and Priesthood," reads as follows:

> Jesus Christ is the unique priest of the new covenant. Christ's life was given as a sacrifice for all. Derivatively, the Church as a whole can be described as a priesthood. All members are called to offer their being "as a living sacrifice" and to intercede for the Church and the salvation of the world. Ordained ministers are related, as are all Christians, both to the priesthood of Christ and to the priesthood of the Church. But they may appropriately be called priests because they fulfil a particular priestly service by strengthening and building up the royal and prophetic priesthood of the faithful through word and sacraments, through their prayers of intercession, and through their pastoral guidance of the community.[18]

Ecumenically, the most promising line seems to me to be the development of the notion and practice of "representative" ministry, the term used in the commentary to paragraph 13 in the Lima text. It would help to break through the badly formulated alternative of a difference in *kind* or in *degree* between the ordained and the other members of the church. Precisely as *representatives* of Christ and his church, the ordained ministers are *distinct,* but *what* they represent is *not other* than the character and mission of the whole church; and this itself is *nothing else* than participation, by the grace of the Holy Spirit, in the ministry of Christ the Savior of the world and Head of the church. All members of the church retain their privileges and responsibilities as baptized believers.

---

18. *Baptism, Eucharist, and Ministry,* Faith and Order Paper no. 111 (Geneva: World Council of Churches, 1982), p. 23.

5. THE ECCLESIOLOGICAL USE

How is the church as a whole a priestly people in Christ? The First Epistle of Peter puts it this way (2:4f.):

> Come to him, to that living stone, rejected by men but in God's sight chosen and precious; and like living stones be yourselves built into a spiritual house, to be a holy priesthood, to offer spiritual sacrifices acceptable to God through Jesus Christ.

Eastern Orthodox theologians emphasize that by its very existence, its worship, and its consecration to God, the church is already fulfilling — representatively, on behalf of the world — the divine vocation addressed to the human race to serve as a priest of all creation. In *For the Life of the World*, Alexander Schmemann wrote thus:

> We know that we were created as *celebrants* of the sacrament of life, of its transformation into life in God, communion with God. We know that real life is "eucharist," a movement of love and adoration towards God, the movement in which alone the meaning and the value of all that exists can be revealed and fulfilled. We know that we have lost this eucharistic life and, finally, we know that in Christ, the new Adam, the perfect Man, this eucharistic life was restored to man. For He Himself was the perfect Eucharist; He offered Himself in total obedience, love and thanksgiving to God. God was His very life. And He gave this perfect and eucharistic life to us. In Him God became our life. And thus this offering to God of bread and wine, of the food that we must eat in order to live, is our offering to Him of ourselves, of our life and of the whole world. "To take in our hands the whole world as if it were an apple!" said a Russian poet. It is our Eucharist. It is the movement that Adam failed to perfect, and that in Christ has become the very life of man: a movement of adoration and praise in which all joy and suffering, all beauty and all frustration, all hunger and all satisfaction are referred to their ultimate End and become finally meaningful. . . . We offer the world and ourselves to God. But we do it *in Christ* and *in remembrance of Him*. We do it *in Christ* because He has already offered all that is to be offered to God. He has performed once and for all this Eucharist and nothing has been left unoffered. In Him was Life — and this Life of us all, He gave to God. The Church is all those who have

been accepted into the eucharistic life of Christ. And we do it *in remembrance of Him* because, as we offer again and again our life and our world to God, we discover each time that there is nothing else to be offered but Christ himself — the Life of the world, the fullness of all that exists.[19]

More activist Western Christians may think that such a quietly radiant view of the church does not do full justice to the proclamatory thrust inherent in the ensuing statement of 1 Peter (2:9):

You are a chosen race, a royal priesthood, a holy nation, God's own people, that you may *declare* the wonderful deeds of him who called you out of darkness into his marvelous light. (emphasis added)

The word here translated "declare" is *ex-angellō*, one of a series of related verbs in biblical Greek reflecting the Hebrew *higgid* (from *ngd*), which is how the psalmist speaks of the "publication" of God's name and deeds among the nations (Pss. 9:11; 40:5; etc.). In the New Testament, *kat-angellō* is used for proclaiming Christ (Acts 17:3; Phil. 1:17f.; Col. 1:28), the gospel (1 Cor. 9:14), the "word" (Acts 13:5; 15:36; 17:13). The gospel is "good news *(eu-angellion)*," for it tells of God's work in Christ for the world's salvation. The preaching of the gospel throughout the world is a prelude to the end (Matt. 24:14); it gives people in all nations an opportunity to "come to the knowledge of truth" as it is found in Christ Jesus, who "gave himself as a ransom for all" (cf. 1 Tim. 2:3-7) — and therein to find the destiny proposed by the Creator as the "chief end" of humankind, namely (in the words of the Westminster catechisms), to "glorify God and to enjoy him for ever."

Certainly the apostle Paul was what we would call today an "aggressive" evangelist; and he understood his evangelism in terms of priesthood and sacrifice. At the end of his life, he wrote to Timothy: "I am already on the point of being sacrificed; the time of my departure has come" (2 Tim. 4:6). The martyrdom Paul expected was but the culmination of an apostolate marked by "afflictions, hardships, calamities, beatings, imprisonments, tumults, labors, watching, hunger" (2 Cor. 6:4f.). He bore on his body the marks of Jesus (Gal. 6:17). In the trials of apostleship Paul

19. Alexander Schmemann, *For the Life of the World,* 2d ed. (Crestwood, N.Y.: St. Vladimir's Seminary Press, 1973), pp. 34f.

believed that he was "carrying in the body the death of Jesus": "While we live we are always being given up to death for Jesus' sake, so that the life of Jesus may be manifested in our mortal flesh. So death is at work in us, but life in you" (2 Cor. 4:7-12). The cultic roots of this sacramental language become unmistakable when the apostle writes: "Even if I am to be poured as a libation upon the sacrificial offering of your faith, I am glad and rejoice with you" (Phil. 2:17). The self-spending of the gospel preacher is part of the larger offering that includes the converts' faith. The modern spread of the gospel in, say, tropical Africa was dependent, under God, on the willingness of missionaries from Western Europe and North America to enter "the white man's grave": many African Christians always thankfully recognized that as a cause for rejoicing, whatever the ambiguities introduced by concomitant colonialism.

A further text from Saint Paul reads thus (Rom. 15:15f.):

> On some points I have written to you very boldly by way of reminder, because of the grace given me by God to be a minister *(leitourgon)* of Christ Jesus to the Gentiles in the priestly service *(hierourounta)* of the gospel of God, so that the offering *(prosphora)* of the Gentiles may be acceptable, sanctified by the Holy Spirit.

The offering of the Gentiles — it matters little here whether the genitive is objective or subjective — is their "obedience," which is "the obedience of faith" (Rom. 1:5). The offering of believers comes to ritual expression in the Eucharist. Grounded in the death of Christ, who made (in the traditional words of the Anglican *Book of Common Prayer*) "by his one oblation of himself once offered, a full, perfect, and sufficient sacrifice, oblation, and satisfaction, for the sins of the whole world, and did institute, and in his holy Gospel command us to continue, a perpetual memory of that his precious death, until his coming again," the congregation there makes "this our sacrifice of praise and thanksgiving" and, drawing by faithful communion on the "benefits of his passion," is able to "offer and present" unto the Lord "ourselves, our souls and bodies, to be a reasonable, holy, and lively sacrifice." The purpose of believers' testimony in the world is, according to the apostle Paul, to swell the eucharistic chorus: "We too believe, and so we speak, . . . so that as grace extends to more and more people it may increase thanksgiving, to the glory of God" (2 Cor. 4:13-15). Thus a purpose of the prophetic mission of the church is to bring others into its company as a priestly people, offering "a sacrifice of praise to God, that is, the fruit of lips that acknowledge his name" (Heb. 13:15). That the sacrifice is not limited to lip service is immediately made clear: "Do not neglect to do good and to share what you have, for such sacrifices are pleasing to God" (Heb. 13:16). That points to what Eastern Orthodox theologians have taken to calling "the liturgy after the Liturgy."

6. The Contemporary Hermeneutic

After what is, I hope, a fair scriptural and traditional description of the priestly office exercised by Christ and in which Christians are given a share, we come again to the question of contemporary interpretation. What is the human condition being addressed by this office, what human questions are being offered an answer? And what are the problems and possibilities for letting this answer be heard?

The aspect, state, or lot of humankind which Cardinal Newman saw represented here was that of suffering: he lists the slaves, the oppressed, the poor, the sick, the bereaved, the troubled in mind.[20] I think I am aiming in the same direction when I name the fundamental issue as alienation and reconciliation, as estrangement and atonement. What is wrongfully separated needs to be brought together. To go through Newman's list: oppression is political alienation, for the disenfranchised are deprived of the privileges and responsibilities that go with the human vocation to live in society; poverty is economic alienation, for the impoverished are cut off from their share in the fruit of the earth that humankind is charged by God to cultivate; sickness is physical alienation, and a troubled mind is psychological alienation, and both remove the sufferers from the flourishing existence which God envisioned for his human creatures; slavery is alienation of identity, the profoundest infraction of the dignity of every child of God; bereavement displays death as the alienation of humankind from the life of communion for which it was made. Christ entered into the alienation which is fundamental to all these aspects of the human predicament: he entered the condition of a humanity estranged from the living God. In the history of theology there is a narrow but distinguished line of thinkers who insist that the

20. John Henry Newman, *Sermons Bearing on Subjects of the Day* (London: Longmans, Green, new impression 1909), "The Three Offices of Christ," p. 54.

humanity which Christ assumed was not a humanity as it still was "before the fall" nor yet already a humanity as it will be in the definitive kingdom, but precisely a *fallen* humanity — though he himself remained without personal sin and was raised in glory at his resurrection. The line may begin with Gregory Nazianzen, with his "what had not been assumed would not have been healed," and certainly extends to Karl Barth and Hans Urs von Balthasar, who deliberately treated our question in the way we have posed it.[21]

The purpose of Christ's entry into the human condition of estrangement, and of his work within it, was precisely "atonement," a priestly work *par excellence*. The primary and basic achievement was the reconciliation of the world to God, so that human beings might be restored to the divine communion. The restored relationship to God has consequences for each individual who accepts it, and also consequences for relationships among human beings. The mental, physical, and spiritual conditions of mortals are placed in the hands of the healing Savior whose eternal purpose is good. And since God's love for humankind (the divine *"philanthrōpia"* of Titus 3:4) calls forth a corresponding love for one another among the brothers and sisters of Christ (the *"philadelphia"* of Romans 12:10), the church has the chance to experience and model a social life in which divisions are overcome through a practical, self-sacrificial love that embraces every member in the household of the faith and reaches out to every neighbor in need (cf. Gal. 6:10); fragmentation thereby gives way to community.

Various images, models, or patterns have been employed in the history of theology to describe Christ's saving work in terms of atonement.[22] Concentrating on the theme of sacrifice, Frances M. Young relates Christ's death to two perennially problematic areas: "the problem of evil, pain and suffering, the illogical and inexplicable way in which life treats

21. Gregory Nazianzen, *Epistle* 101 (Migne, *Patrologia Graeca* 37:181); Karl Barth, *Church Dogmatics* I/2, trans. G. T. Thomson and H. Knight (Edinburgh: T. & T. Clark, 1956), sec. 15.2, particularly pp. 149-59; Hans Urs von Balthasar, *Mysterium Paschale: The Mystery of Easter*, trans. A. Nichols (Grand Rapids: Eerdmans, 1993), in particular pp. 20-23 (explicitly p. 22). See Harry Johnson, *The Humanity of the Saviour* (London: Epworth Press, 1962); and Thomas G. Weinandy, *In the Likeness of Sinful Flesh: An Essay on the Humanity of Christ* (Edinburgh: T. & T. Clark, 1993).

22. See the surveys in Robert S. Paul, *The Atonement and the Sacraments* (Nashville: Abingdon, 1960); and Frederick W. Dillistone, *The Christian Understanding of Atonement* (Digswell Place, Hertfordshire: Nisbet, 1968).

people, often we feel undeservedly," and "the problem of guilt and sin, the inner conflicts and weaknesses of human beings."

She writes that Christians affirm in faith

> that the sacrifice of Christ on the cross is a guarantee that present appearances are not the ultimate. It is not just that God demonstrated his love to men. It is more than that; for God took upon himself the consequences of evil and sin. God accepted the terrible situation, demonstrating that he takes responsibility for evil in his universe, that he recognizes the seriousness of evil, its destructive effect, its opposition to his purposes; that it cannot be ignored, but must be challenged and removed; that it is costly to forgive; that he suffers because his universe is subject to evil and sin.[23]

And on the human side, Young continues:

> If we are realistic, we soon become conscious of human helplessness to create utopia; we are conscious, individually as well as by being members of society, of human failure to live up to ideals of love and justice to which the value systems of our culture subscribe. In this context, the sacrifice of Christ is relevant, because it faces up to and accepts the situation. It shames us into climbing down from our pillars of pride and self-sufficiency, into recognizing our inadequacy and the depths of our sin and guilt, into seeing our need for repentance; and having shamed us, it deals with the problem by offering unconditional forgiveness, by wiping away the guilt and alienation, by mending the estrangement. It can do this because in this sacrifice the tragic situation was unreservedly accepted and its terrible consequences drained to the dregs. The situation was not avoided or suppressed. The cup was not refused or passed on. Because Christ accepted it, we can know ourselves accepted in spite of consciousness of guilt, in spite of being unacceptable.[24]

We may take just one domain (and a vital one) in which the sharing by Christians in the priestly office of Christ requires contemporary exercise: the question of peace and reconciliation. As those who, in Christ, know

---

23. Frances M. Young, *Sacrifice and the Death of Christ* (London: SPCK, 1975), pp. 123-25.

24. Young, *Sacrifice and the Death of Christ*, pp. 127f.

themselves to be part of a world that has been "reconciled to God by the death of his Son" (Rom. 5:10f.; cf. 2 Cor. 5:18f.), Christians have been given a "ministry of reconciliation." As "ambassadors for Christ," we have to bring the "message of reconciliation" to a worldwide audience (2 Cor. 5:19f.). But we risk having received "the grace of God in vain" (2 Cor. 6:1), if we remain unreconciled among ourselves; for a common reconciliation to God entails peace among the beneficiaries of God's grace (Eph. 2:11-21). The task of uniting divided Christian communities makes of the modern ecumenical movement a priestly ministry. The case could be no more dramatic than in Northern Ireland, where there is a chance that water, bread, and wine could prove themselves more potent symbols than sashes, berets, and flags, and that hands lifted in prayer or laid on heads in forgiveness and healing could turn out closer to reality than hands that plant bombs or squeeze triggers.[25]

25. See G. Wainwright, "The Reconciliation of Divided Churches: A Witness to the Gospel," in *Studia Liturgica* 18 (1988): 75-95; and "Ecumenism and Reconciliation," in *Reconciliation in Religion and Society,* ed. Michael Hurley (Belfast: Institute of Irish Studies, 1994). pp. 72-88.

9

The Royal Office

An equivalent to the second article of the Nicene Creed, with its confession of the person of Christ and his work "for our salvation," is found in the ancient hymn, the Te Deum:

> Thou art the King of glory, O Christ.
> Thou art the everlasting Son of the Father.
> When thou tookest upon thee to deliver man,
> thou didst humble thyself to be born of a Virgin.
> When thou hadst overcome the sharpness of death,
> thou didst open the kingdom of heaven to all believers.
> Thou sittest at the right hand of God, in the glory of the Father.
> We believe that thou shalt come to be our judge.
> We therefore pray thee, help thy servants,
> whom thou hast redeemed with thy precious blood.
> Make them to be numbered with thy saints,
> in glory everlasting.

In this present acclamation of the living Christ are interwoven the themes of his identity, his dignity, and his work. For the sake of analysis, we shall try to sort out the strands in our accustomed way.

I. THE CHRISTOLOGICAL USE

"Thou art the King of glory, O Christ": that is a statement about his eternal being. It *was* so, from all eternity: "Thou art the everlasting Son of the Father." It *will be* so, to all eternity: "Thou sittest at the right hand of God, in the glory of the Father." It would not be quite right to ask, "But what happened in between?" For when he stooped to "deliver man," being born of a virgin and tasting the sharpness of death, he was not stripped of his glory. Rather, it was shown in a new light; or even better, it transformed an old darkness. The wise men brought to the infant Jesus the royal gift of gold: "Gold I bring to crown him again. . . ." Yet in Eastern Orthodox iconography of the nativity scenes, the swaddling clothes are also the grave clothes, and the face of the Christ child is already that of the Man of Sorrows. The One whom the Magi sought as "king of the Jews" at his birth (Matt. 2:2) had his title acknowledged by Pilate at his death: "Jesus of Nazareth, the King of the Jews" (John 19:19). At the baptism of Jesus, the voice from heaven proclaimed from the royal psalm, "Thou art my beloved Son" (cf. Ps. 2:7), yet with the immediate addition from the songs of the suffering servant: "in whom I am well pleased" (cf. Isa. 42:1).

Pointers to the paradoxical royalty of Christ are found during the course of his earthly ministry. When a crowd thronged to join him in a desert place, Jesus "had compassion on them, because they were like sheep without a shepherd"; and having taught them many things, he exercised messianic largesse by feeding them also from the loaves and fish (Mark 6:30-44). In Saint John's account, they then tried "to make him king" (John 6:15). Jesus' final entry into Jerusalem was modeled, according to Saint Matthew, on the prophecy of Zechariah 9:9:

> "Tell the daughter of Zion,
> Behold, your king is coming to you,
> humble, and mounted on an ass,
> and on a colt, the foal of an ass." (Matt. 21:1-9)

The crowds that went before him and that followed him shouted, "Hosanna to the Son of David! Blessed is he who comes in the name of the Lord! Hosanna in the highest!" — or, in Saint Luke's version, "Blessed is the King who comes in the name of the Lord! Peace in heaven and glory in the highest!" (Luke 19:38). From the fourth century onward, the church has celebrated, and even reenacted, the triumphal entry into Jerusalem on Palm Sunday; but, the procession over, the traditional readings at the Eucharist on that day are from Philippians 2:5-11 as the Epistle, where Christ "emptied himself" and remained obedient unto death, death on a cross, before he was "highly exalted" by the Father; and from Matthew 26 and 27 as the Gospel, the story of the passion.

The cross of Christ is itself the beginning of his "elevation," his "glorification," as the vocabulary of the Fourth Gospel shows (John 3:14; 7:39; 8:28, 54; 12:16, 23, 28, 32-35; 13:31f.; 17:1-5). Or, in Luke's Gospel: the robber hanging beside him recognizes Jesus as King. Commenting on Luke 23:42, Calvin can say that the penitent thief "adores Christ as King while on the gallows, celebrates his kingdom in the midst of fearful and unspeakable abasement, and proclaims him, at the hour of his death, the Author of life."[1] In medieval sculptures and illuminations, Christ was often depicted on the cross with his outstretched arms upholding on the one side the sun and on the other the moon. "The love which moves the sun and the other stars" — as Dante calls it — bled on Calvary. "The Lord reigned from a tree," as the Old Latin version of Psalm 95(96):10 puts it, echoed in the Passiontide hymn "The Royal Banners Forward Go" *(Vexilla regis):*

> Fulfilled is all that David told
> In true prophetic song of old:
> Amidst the nations, God, saith he,
> Hath reigned and triumphed from the tree.[2]

The royal dignity of Christ, his participation as Son in the divine sovereignty of the Trinity, consists in self-giving love, now displayed, amidst fallen humanity, in human form. "Love unknown," in the words of Samuel Crossman's poem, "love to the loveless shown. . . ."[3] Christ's resurrection by the Father in the Spirit is the confirmation of the sovereignty of the God who is Love.

1. See, in the translated series "Calvin's Commentaries," *A Harmony of the Gospels Matthew, Mark, and Luke,* trans. A. W. Morrison, vol. 3 (Grand Rapids: Eerdmans, 1980), pp. 202f.

2. "Vexilla regis prodeunt" is a hymn by the sixth-century Venantius Fortunatus. The translation is by John Mason Neale.

3. Samuel Crossman (ca. 1624-83), "My Song is Love Unknown" (from his *The Young Man's Meditation, or Some Few Sacred Poems upon Select Subjects and Scriptures* [London, 1664]).

Christ had never ceased to reign. During his earthly ministry Jesus was, in Origen's term, *autobasileia,* the kingdom of God in person.[4] The demons knew that, and Jesus made it quietly explicit in the so-called Beelzebul controversy (Mark 3:22-27; cf. Matt. 12:24-29; Luke 11:15-22):

> And the scribes who came down from Jerusalem said, "He is possessed by Beelzebul, and by the prince of demons he casts out the demons." And [Jesus] called them to him, and said to them in parables, "How can Satan cast out Satan? If a kingdom is divided against itself, that kingdom cannot stand. And if a house is divided against itself, that house will not be able to stand. And if Satan has risen up against himself and is divided, he cannot stand, but is coming to an end. But no one can enter a strong man's house and plunder his goods, unless he first binds the strong man; then indeed he may plunder his house."

But the exorcisms performed by Jesus were no sheer display of naked power. He remained Son of God in hard-won obedience to the Father. That is the meaning of the temptation stories (Matt. 4:1-11; Mark 1:12f.; Luke 4:1-13), of the agony in Gethsemane ("Yet not what I will, but what thou wilt," Mark 14:36), and of the saying in Hebrews that "although he was a Son, he learned obedience through what he suffered" (Heb. 5:8). To receive being directly from the being of God the Father (*ek tēs ousias tou Patros,* as the Council of Nicea put it): that is the being of God the Son. To be loved, and to love: that is the being of God the Son in the Holy Trinity. And that is what, at the level of the creatures, the incarnation, passion, death, and resurrection of the Son have made possible for fallen — and redeemed — humanity: adoption as God's children in Christ, enabled by the Spirit to return the Father's love in an obedience that gives victory over all that separates us from God.

2. THE BAPTISMAL USE

According to Colossians 1:13f., God the Father "has delivered us from the dominion of darkness and transferred us to the kingdom of his beloved Son,

---

4. Origen, *Commentaria in Matthaeum* XIV.7, on Matt. 18:23, referring also to Matt. 5:3 (Migne, *Patrologia Graeca* 13:1197).

in whom we have redemption, the forgiveness of sins." In Christ, believers are therefore given a share in God's kingdom. Polemically put, that means that we are to rule over sin: "Let not sin therefore reign in your mortal bodies," says the apostle Paul to the Romans, who had been baptized into Christ's death, so that as Christ was raised from the dead by the glory of the Father, they too might "walk in newness of life" (Rom. 6:1-4). The Eastern Orthodox rite of baptism includes a twofold ceremony, known as the *apotaxis* and the *syntaxis,* in which the candidates turn westward, the direction of darkness, in order to renounce the devil and his works, and then are turned toward the east, where the sun rises for a new day, in order to join the ranks of God by their professing faith in Christ and the Holy Trinity.

We have already heard John Chrysostom on the rule of Christians over sin and their being clothed and crowned with God's truly regal gifts.[5] Calvin puts it this way:

> Our King will never leave us destitute, but will provide for our needs until, our warfare ended, we are called to triumph. Such is the nature of his rule, that he shares with us all that he has received from the Father. Now he arms and equips us with his power; adorns us with his beauty and magnificence, enriches us with his wealth. These benefits, then, give us the most fruitful occasion to glory, and also provide us with confidence to struggle fearlessly against the devil, sin, and death. Finally, clothed with his righteousness, we can valiantly rise above all the world's reproaches; and just as he himself freely lavishes his gifts upon us, so may we, in return, bring forth fruit to his glory.[6]

To rule over sin is, positively put, to serve God. And to serve God is to reign in royal dignity. So an old Latin prayer, from the Gelasian and Gregorian Sacramentaries, addresses God, "cui servire est regnare" ("whom to serve is to reign").[7] Or in the paraphrase of the Anglican *Book of Common Prayer:*

---

5. See above, p. 112.

6. John Calvin, *Institutes* II.15.4 (English translation: *Calvin: Institutes of the Christian Religion,* ed. John T. McNeill and Ford Lewis Battles, 2 vols. [Philadelphia: Westminster, 1960], 1:499; hereafter cited as ET).

7. "Deus, auctor pacis et amator . . ."; see L. C. Mohlberg, *Liber Sacramentorum Romanae Aeclesiae: Sacramentarium gelasianum* (Rome: Herder, 1960), p. 214 (prayer no. 1476); Jean Deshusses, *Le sacramentaire grégorien: ses principales formes d'après les plus anciens manuscrits,* vol. 1 (Fribourg: Éditions universitaires, 1971), p. 444 (prayer 1345).

O God, who art the author of peace and lover of concord,
in knowledge of whom standeth our eternal life,
whose service is perfect freedom:
Defend us thy humble servants in all assaults of our enemies;
that we, surely trusting in thy defense,
may not fear the power of any adversaries,
through the might of Jesus Christ our Lord. Amen.[8]

"Whose service is perfect freedom": despite the very opposite accusation of Marxists and Freudians who seek to "emancipate" people from "God," there is no contradiction between the kingdom of God and human salvation. Rather, with Saint Irenaeus, "Gloria Dei, vivens homo" ("The glory of God is man alive").[9]

The paradox of a sovereign service, grounded in love, is well expressed in the twin theses of Martin Luther's *Freedom of a Christian:*

A Christian is a perfectly free lord of all, subject to none.
A Christian is a perfectly dutiful servant of all, subject to all.

Luther cites the apostle Paul: "For though I am free from all men, I have made myself a slave to all" (1 Cor. 9:19), and "Owe no one anything, except to love one another" (Rom. 13:8); and ultimately refers to Christ, who, "although he was Lord of all, was 'born of a woman, born under the law' [Gal. 4:4], and therefore was at the same time a free man and a servant, 'in the form of God' and 'of a servant' [Phil. 2:6f.]."[10]

Such is the royal dignity now afforded the followers of the Son of Man who came not to be served but to serve, and to give his life as a ransom for many (cf. Mark 10:42-45; Luke 22:25-27).

8. This is "the second collect, for peace" in the office of Morning Prayer of the 1662 Prayer Book.

9. Irenaeus, *Against the Heresies* IV.20.7 (Migne, *Patrologia Graeca* 7:1037).

10. Quoted from the American translation of *Luther's Works,* vol. 31, ed. H. J. Grimm (Philadelphia: Fortress Press, 1957), p. 344.

3. The Soteriological Use

The royal character of Christ's saving work emerged already during his earthly ministry. By his exorcisms and his healings as well as by his preaching, Jesus announced the coming of the divine kingdom. Jesus summoned people to enter the dawning reign of God by repentance and faith (Mark 1:15), concretely by way of following himself (Mark 1:16-20; 8:34-38; Matt. 8:18-22 = Luke 9:57-62). His disciples formed the nucleus of what would become his church, the body of which he is the Head. He provided his community with ministers in the shape of his apostles (Matt. 10:1-4 = Mark 3:13-18 = Luke 6:13-16; Matt. 16:18f.; Luke 22:31f.; cf. John 20:19-23; 21:15-19). On the eve of his passion and in the sequel of his resurrection, he instituted what were to be the sacraments of the community's continuing life and of new admissions to its membership: Eucharist (Matt. 26:26-29; Mark 14:22-25; Luke 22:17-20; 1 Cor. 11:23-26) and baptism (Matt. 28:16-20).[11]

The constitution of the church of Jesus Christ could be completed only with the redemptive work of his death: a traditional interpretation of John 19:34 sees the church as born with the water and the blood from Christ's riven side.[12] The Te Deum proceeds to describe Christ's redemptive work and its results in this way:

> When thou hadst overcome the sharpness of death,
> thou didst open the kingdom of heaven to all believers. . . .
> We believe that thou shalt come to be our judge.
> We therefore pray thee, help thy servants,
> whom thou hast redeemed with thy precious blood.
> Make them to be numbered with thy saints,
> in glory everlasting.

The royal themes in that text may be made explicit.

11. Krauss notes that anti-Roman concerns impeded traditional Protestant recognition of the "community-building" aspect of the royal office of Christ (A. Krauss, "Das Mittlerwerk nach dem Schema des munus triplex," *Jahrbücher für deutsche Theologie* 17 [1872]: 631). For a more ecumenical approach, see Robert Newton Flew, *Jesus and His Church: A Study of the Idea of the Ecclesia in the New Testament* (London: Epworth Press, 1938).

12. Augustine, *De civitate Dei* XXII.17 (Migne, *Patrologia Latina* 41:778-79); for other patristic references, see E. C. Hoskyns, *The Fourth Gospel*, 2d ed., ed. F. N. Davey (London: Faber, 1947), pp. 534f.

First, as to Christ's death and resurrection. "Jesus of Nazareth, the King of the Jews" is what Pontius Pilate wrote on the title of the cross (John 19:19-22); and this descendant of "David according to the flesh" was, in the words of the apostle Paul, marked out as "Son of God in power according to the Spirit of holiness by his resurrection from the dead, Jesus Christ our Lord" (Rom. 1:3f.). The royal nature of Christ's saving work through his death and resurrection is often described in Scripture and Tradition in terms of a mighty victory over the enemies of humankind, that is, the devil and his works of sin and death; and in a psalm applied in the church's liturgy to Christ's ascension, the "King of glory" is hailed as "the LORD, strong and mighty, the LORD, mighty in battle!" (Ps. 24:8). The champion has "disarmed the principalities and powers and made a public example of them, triumphing over them in the cross" (Col. 2:15).[13] The strong Son of God died, so that "through death he might destroy him who has the power of death, that is, the devil, and deliver all those who through fear of death were subject to lifelong bondage" (Heb. 2:14f.). Our Savior Christ Jesus "abolished death and brought life and immortality to light through the gospel" (2 Tim. 1:10). "The Lion of the tribe of Judah, the Root of David, has conquered" (Rev. 5:5); the inscription he now bears is "King of kings and Lord of lords" (Rev. 19:16). "Fear not," he says, "I am the first and the last, and the living one; I died, and behold I am alive for evermore, and I have the keys of Death and Hades" (Rev. 1:17f.). His victory, says Saint Paul in Romans 8:31-39, is made over to us: if Christ Jesus "died," "was raised from the dead," "is at the right hand of God," and "intercedes for us," then "who shall separate us from the love of Christ?" No, "we are more than conquerors through him who loved us," and nothing "in all creation, will be able to separate us from the love of God in Christ Jesus our Lord."

Secondly, then, Christ's royal office toward us extends to his continued protection and equipment of us for our salvation. Christ indeed, says Calvin, "rules more for our own sake than for his."[14] "Protected by Christ's hand," we are "furnished with the gifts of the Spirit"; and, "relying on the power of the same Spirit," we need "not doubt that we shall always be victorious over the devil, the world, and every kind of harmful thing."[15] For the remaining stages in a war whose cosmic outcome is already certain,

13. Taking *en autō* as "in it" rather than "in him."
14. Calvin, *Institutes* II.15.4 (ET, 1:498f.).
15. Calvin, *Institutes* II.15.3f. (ET, 1:498f.).

we are exhorted to be "strong in the Lord and in the strength of his might"; we have at our disposal "the whole armor of God": the belt of truth, the breastplate of righteousness, the shield of faith, the helmet of salvation, and the sword of the Spirit, which is the Word of God (cf. Eph. 6:10-17). According to Calvin again, Christ's declaration that his "kingship is not of this world" (cf. John 18:36) should arouse us "to the hope of a better life" and "to await the full fruit of this grace in the world to come."[16]

Third, however, the royal functions of Christ include judgment: "We believe that thou shalt come to be our judge." The apostle Paul declares that "we must all appear before the judgment seat of Christ, so that each one may receive good or evil, according to what he has done in the body" (2 Cor. 5:10). The judge is also "our Savior." Taking off from Romans 8:1 (and landing at 2 Timothy 4:8), Charles Wesley anticipates the scene:

> No condemnation now I dread;
> Jesus, and all in him, is mine!
> Alive in him, my living Head,
> And clothed in righteousness divine,
> Bold I approach the eternal throne,
> And claim the crown, through Christ, my own.[17]

It will not be the works of believers that save them; but, being "created in Christ Jesus for good works," we shall not be saved without the works which "God prepared beforehand, that we should walk in them" (Eph. 2:8-10); for works are the sign and fruit of a living faith (cf. James 2:17f.). Christ must, therefore, rule in us if we are to persevere to the end; and the prayer remains necessary and appropriate, "Help thy servants, whom thou hast redeemed with thy precious blood," if we are to be "numbered with thy saints, in glory everlasting."

Calvin viewed the Last Judgment as the final act of Christ's rule before he would, as the loyal Son, deliver the kingdom to the Father. These are the consequences which Calvin drew for the godly and the ungodly:

> All the more reason, then, is there that we should one and all resolve
> to obey, and to direct our obedience with the greatest eagerness to the

---

16. Calvin, *Institutes* II.15.3 (ET, 1:498).

17. The hymn "Free Grace," from John and Charles Wesley, *Hymns and Sacred Poems* (London, 1739).

divine will! Now Christ fulfills the combined duties of king and pastor for the godly who submit willingly and obediently; on the other hand, we hear that he carries a "rod of iron to break them and dash them all in pieces like a potter's vessel" [cf. Ps. 2:9]. We also hear that "he will execute judgment among the Gentiles, so that he fills the earth with corpses, and strikes down every height that opposes him" [Ps. 110:6]. We see today several examples of this fact, but the full proof will appear at the Last Judgment, which may also be properly considered the last act of his reign.[18]

In expecting the Last Judgment, the church expresses its confidence that the divine kingdom will finally come in all its fullness. All that presently opposes its achievement will be removed, whether by conversion or by destruction. Given the lengths to which God has gone to redeem the world in Christ, we may hope in God's patience and mercy toward ourselves and toward others, while waiting "with eager longing" for the day when God will be "all in all" (cf. Rom. 8:19-25; 1 Cor. 15:24-28).

4. The Ministerial Use

Calvin spoke of Christ as "king and pastor." Nowhere in the New Testament or in the Christian Tradition are special ministers within the church called "kings." Ephesians 4:11, however, speaks of "pastors," and this became a characteristic designation for a particular ministry. In biblical Israel, rulers were seen, under God (Pss. 23; 80:1; Isa. 40:11; Ezek. 34:11-16), as shepherds of the people (2 Sam. 5:2; 1 Chron. 11:2; Jer. 3:15; 23:4). Under Christ as "the chief Shepherd," Christian elders are to "tend the flock of God" (1 Pet. 5:1-4). Rule within the church must be pastoral in nature, after the model of the one Good Shepherd who laid down his life for the sheep (John 10:11-18). Only insofar as they, in a strong sense, "spend their lives" in the service of the congregation do Christian pastors have real authority. The injunction and example of Jesus are quite explicit in this regard (Mark 10:42-45):

18. Calvin, *Institutes* II.15.5 (ET, 1:501).

You know that those who are supposed to rule over the Gentiles lord it over them, and their great men exercise authority over them. But it shall not be so among you; but whoever would be great among you must be your servant, and whoever would be first among you must be slave of all. For the Son of man also came not to be served but to serve, and to give his life as a ransom for many.

This is not a point for a Christian minister, with a risk of false humility, to expatiate upon. The papal title — *servus servorum Dei*, "servant of the servants of God" — must suffice as, at one and the same time, a statement of the ideal, a warning against the ease of self-deception in this matter, and finally (perhaps) a hint of God's gracious power to make Christian ministry authentic in spite of human unworthiness.

The tasks of a Christian pastor are to gather, to guide, to guard, to nourish, and to build up. Gathering includes the search for the lost, whether those who have never yet been introduced to the fold or those who have strayed from it (cf. Luke 15:3-7). Clear-sighted guidance is needed to avoid pitfalls (cf. Matt. 15:14) and maintain a steady course and firm direction (cf. Eph. 4:14). The flock needs guarding against wolves, both those that attack directly from outside and those that don sheep's clothing or even a shepherd's garb (cf. Matt. 10:16; John 10:12f.; Acts 20:28f.; 2 Pet. 2:1-3). In the name of Christ, the true pastor provides nourishment from the pulpit and at the Table, through dispensing "the milk of the word *(to logikon gala)*" (1 Pet. 2:2, KJV) and through stewardship of the body and blood of the Lord who serves at the Meal he himself provides (cf. Luke 22:14-21, 27). It is a pastoral task to "equip the saints for the work of ministry, for building up the body of Christ, until we all attain to the unity of the faith and of the knowledge of the Son of God, to mature manhood, to the measure of the stature of the fulness of Christ" (Eph. 4:11-13). The institutional forms and structures of pastoral ministry have been, and remain, controversial in a divided Christendom, especially between churches which claim an "historic episcopate" and those which do not; but, as the Lima text of Faith and Order shows, all Christian communities recognize the need in one shape or another for a ministry exercised in the name of the Christ who is "the Shepherd and Guardian *(poimēn kai episkopos)*" of their souls (1 Pet. 2:25).[19]

19. See *Baptism, Eucharist, and Ministry,* Faith and Order Paper no. 111 (Geneva: World Council of Churches, 1982), pp. 20-32 ("Ministry").

The role of servant does not remove but rather strengthens the responsibility of pastors for the discipline, order, and unity of the community. Precisely for the good of the community, pastors are not permitted to evade the duty of vigilance or "oversight." In the name of Christ, pastors are called upon to dispense justice, always according to the teaching of the Lord (Matt. 16:19; 18:15-22; John 20:22f.), and to coordinate the various gifts and ministries that are distributed throughout the membership. Their institutional authority is most effective when matched by the moral authority that is recognized to a life lived in conformity to Christ (cf. 1 Cor. 4:16; 11:1).

5. The Ecclesiological Use

According to Calvin, the communal aspect of Christ's kingly rule is displayed in his present and final protection against all adversaries:

> Therefore, whenever we hear of Christ as armed with eternal power, let us remember that the perpetuity of the Church is secure in this protection. Hence, amid the violent agitation with which it is continually troubled, amid the grievous and frightful storms that threaten it with unnumbered calamities, it still remains safe. David laughs at the boldness of his enemies who try to throw off the yoke of God and his Anointed, and says: "The kings and people rage in vain . . . , for he who dwells in heaven is strong enough to break their assaults" [Ps. 2:2-3]. Thus he assures the godly of the everlasting preservation of the Church, and encourages them to hope, whenever it happens to be oppressed. Elsewhere, speaking in the person of God, David says: "Sit at my right hand, till I make your enemies your footstool" [Ps. 110:1]. Here he asserts that, no matter how many strong enemies plot to overthrow the Church, they do not have sufficient strength to prevail over God's immutable decree by which he appointed his Son eternal King. Hence it follows that the devil, with all the resources of the world, can never destroy the Church, founded as it is on the eternal throne of Christ.[20]

20. Calvin, *Institutes* II.15.3 (ET, 1:497f.).

Thus the church's royal status in the world resides, in a passive sense, in its being under the protection of Christ the eternal King.

Based on the promise of Jesus that "the gates of Hades shall not prevail against it" (Matt. 16:18), all Christian communities confess that the church will stand forever: "Una Sancta Ecclesia perpetuo mansura est," as the Confession of Augsburg puts it in article 7. But that church is differently identified according as it is concretely located by the confessors along a number of axes: In what sense is it composed of "the elect"? What definition and weight are given to "heresy" and "schism," and what judgments are rendered in particular cases? What factors are considered constitutive of ecclesial unity and continuity? At its best, the modern ecumenical movement has been a struggle on the part of many in a divided Christendom to discern the rule of Christ among those who profess his name. The ecumenical pioneer W. A. Visser 't Hooft wrote thus:

> A church which takes the kingship of Christ seriously is one which seeks to restore the unity of the Church of Christ. If there is only one King, if salvation means to be part of the one Body, no church can accept the fact that the people of God are scattered and that the Body is broken. It is not for the sake of greater efficiency in its practical tasks, not for the sake of a common front against common enemies, it is for the sake of keeping faith with the King, whose kingdom cannot be divided against itself, that the churches must enter upon the difficult pilgrimage toward visible and tangible unity. But precisely because the only unity which is in line with the specific mission of the Church is unity *in Christ,* the search for unity can never be separated from the obedient following of his will.`. . . . Christian unity is only found as churches turn together to their common Lord. . . . And true unity can, therefore, never be bought at the expense of that truth which is manifested in Christ himself.[21]

21. W. A. Visser 't Hooft, *The Kingship of Christ* (New York: Harper, 1948), pp. 113f.; cf. G. K. A. Bell, *The Kingship of Christ: The Story of the World Council of Churches* (Harmondsworth, Middlesex: Penguin Books, 1954). Alas, the World Council of Churches no longer stands for the classical ecumenism of a W. A. Visser 't Hooft; see the programmatic statement of the general secretary of the WCC since 1992, Konrad Raiser, *Ecumenism in Transition: A Paradigm Shift in the Ecumenical Movement?* (Geneva: WCC Publications, 1991), and my critical review of it in *Mid-Stream* 31 (1992): 169-73. Theologically, the classical line is now better represented in the series of bilateral dialogues among the Christian communions.

If the church benefits from Christ's rule over the world, may it also be said that the church, properly defined, actively shares in that rule of Christ? The thought is enough to make Lutherans — with their doctrine of the two sharply distinguished "kingdoms," the spiritual and the temporal — shudder. But Calvinists — with their doctrine that Christ rules precisely *by his word* — are more inclined to a theocratic view. The best answer I know is that of Karl Barth, with his notion of the analogical relation between *Bürgergemeinde* and *Christengemeinde,* "community of citizens" and "community of Christians." Barth's position is that the church knows by faith the life of God's kingdom — justice, peace, freedom, and so on — in a deep, abiding, and definitive way; and that it is the church's task to bear witness to those realities before the world, where they should find at least a provisional, outward, and imperfect expression in the social and political realm.[22]

A sacramental, and particularly a eucharistic, nuance may be given to that position. At the Last Supper, Jesus said to his disciples (Luke 22:28-30):

> You are those who have continued with me in my trials. As my Father appointed a kingdom for me, so do I appoint for you that you may eat and drink at my table in my kingdom.

Now the Eucharist has traditionally been seen as a foretaste of the messianic meal in the final kingdom. To illuminate the question of the church's rule in the world, let us put that eucharistic fact together with Saint Paul's statement in Romans 14:17 that "the kingdom of God is *not* food and drink but righteousness and peace . . . in the Holy Spirit" (emphasis added). The context of the apostle's remark is disputes over meat eating and wine drinking: he rebukes those who, "for the sake of food, destroy the work of God." According to Saint Luke, the Lord will at the Judgment reject the claim of the "workers of iniquity" to have eaten and drunk in his presence (Luke 13:25-27). Yet the kingdom of God is pictured as a feast: "And [people] will come from east and west . . . and sit at table in the kingdom of God" (Luke 13:29). It would capture the gist of biblical teaching concerning the messianic banquet if

22. Karl Barth, *Against the Stream: Shorter Post-War Writings, 1946-1952,* ed. R. G. Smith (New York: Philosophical Library, 1954), pp. 13-50 ("The Christian Community and the Civil Community," 1946).

we were to paraphrase the apostle thus: The kingdom of God is food and drink *only insofar as* eating and drinking express justice, peace, and joy in the Holy Spirit.[23]

When any creature of God is received with thanksgiving (cf. 1 Tim. 4:3-5), its use becomes thereby an occasion and medium of communion with God. In the eucharistic liturgy, in what occurs with bread and wine over which thanks are given, exemplary use is made of food and drink as a medium of communion with God in Christ in which we cannot make abstraction of communion with fellow human beings (cf. 1 John 4:7-21). Moreover, the general way in which people use all food is itself a test of the way in which they are living before the triune God and among themselves. Since the Eucharist is representative of all meals, and since all food and drink is representative of the totality of human life, the sacrament should be so celebrated that it shows the kingdom of God to be food and drink *only upon condition that* their use embodies justice, peace, and joy in the Holy Ghost. To look at those three in turn:

First, justice. A responsibly celebrated Eucharist exemplifies justice because grateful people are all equally welcomed by the merciful Lord into his table fellowship, and all together share in the fruits of redemption and in the foretaste of the new heavens and the new earth in which right will prevail (cf. 2 Pet. 3:13).

Second, peace. The Eucharist, responsibly celebrated, exemplifies peace, because reconciled people are there at peace with God and with one another (cf. Matt. 5:23f.).

Third, joy. The Eucharist, responsibly celebrated, exemplifies joy in the Holy Ghost, because there we "do not get drunk with wine," but rather the cup of blessing conveys to all who partake of it a taste of that "sober intoxication" which the Spirit gives (cf. Eph. 5:18).

Having learned and experienced all this in the paradigm of the Lord's Supper, the church is committed to an everyday witness in word and deed which will give the opportunity for all the material resources of creation and all occasions of human contact to become the medium of that communion with God and among human beings which is marked by justice, peace, and joy in the Holy Spirit, and in which the kingdom of God and of his Christ consists.

---

23. This use of Rom. 14:17 was first developed in my book *Eucharist and Eschatology* (London: Epworth Press, 1971), pp. 59, 148-50.

6. The Contemporary Hermeneutic

I have tried, again, to give a fair scriptural and traditional description of the royal office exercised by Christ and in which Christians are given a share. But again we must return a bit more explicitly to contemporary interpretation. What is the human condition being addressed by this office? What human question is being offered an answer? And what are the problems and possibilities for letting this answer be heard?

The fundamental issue being addressed by the royal office is that of power and authority. Many interpreters of culture see the modern West, and indeed the modern world, as the age of human autonomy — what the theologian Dietrich Bonhoeffer called humankind's "coming of age."[24] The phenomenon stretches, at different paces in different places, from the emancipation of serfs and slaves — through revolution against colonial and imperialist powers — to the assertion of a free spirit of inquiry in all matters of science. The thrust toward liberty has found some of its driving force in the biblical tradition, in ways argued by the so-called secular theologians of the 1960s and still by some third-world theologians today. In part, however, secularization and liberation have meant turning against the institutional church — and that is understandable insofar as the historic church, against its vocation and true nature, has been an instrument of oppression. But radical assertions of human autonomy have extended their attack to God and to the Christ who reveals God. Humanity will never be free, it is claimed, until the illusion of God has been overcome, the "God" who has been used by the holders of power to legitimate their own authority and to keep the oppressed deprived. The preaching of a suffering Christ, it is claimed, has served to dignify a condition of wretchedness and so keep the dispossessed acquiescent in their place. A "superior humanity" can arise, it was Nietzsche's message, only by an overturning of Christian values.

Now as Christians we must be sensitive to criticism that may help us to purge the idols. But we may not abandon the truth of faith, not only for our own sake but for the sake of the world before which we are entrusted to represent it. In particular, we must beware of those theological tendencies within our own company which strike at the sovereignty of the God who created the world, who sustains it from moment to moment,

24. Dietrich Bonhoeffer, *Letters and Papers from Prison*, enlarged ed., ed. E. Bethge (New York: Macmillan, 1972).

and who stands personally revealed in the Jesus confessed by his followers as Christ and Lord. While visiting the chapel of the College of William and Mary in Virginia, I was told of the American worthy who, at the time of the Revolutionary War, refused to speak of "the kingdom of God" and would talk only of "God's republic." Naïvely amusing as it is, that political quip may reflect, at the theological level, a deism that removes any divine action and rule from the world. More sophisticatedly, contemporary theologians can be found rejecting what they call the "monarchical metaphor" for God's relations with the world, either on philosophical grounds (such as that of "closed causality")[25] or on ideological grounds (such as an alleged linkage with a reprehensible "patriarchy").[26] In my judgment, Christians should be very wary about welcoming "the collapse of the house of authority," bringing down the Scriptures, creeds, liturgies, and institutions of the admittedly imperfect historic church.[27]

As illustrations, let me take two cases where the royal office of Christ remains vital to Christian faith and life, and therefore to the witness that we bear in the midst of the world. First there is the issue of what I will call "cultural freedom" in West European and North American societies, and most sharply perhaps in the United States. There is a tendency in some quarters to replace the first commandment with the First Amendment — and that in a sense that would have astonished at least some of the founders of the United States. The First Amendment is extended, or rather distorted, to mean the absolute right of self-expression, however appalling the self to be expressed. In an individualism gone rife, everyone does what is right in his or her own eyes. In a Christian perspective, however, the neighbor is (negatively put) the limit of my freedom — or (positively put) a personal call to service. We enjoy true freedom under the *lex Christi*, "the law of Christ." That third use of the law, to give it its Reformed name, becomes possible when, by the first use of the law, sufficient stability has been achieved in political society for persons to be brought, by the second use of the law, to conviction of sin and acceptance

---

25. Edward Farley, *Ecclesial Reflection* (Philadelphia: Fortress, 1982); but see my review in *Theology Today* 40 (1983-84): 200-204.

26. See Sallie McFague, *Metaphorical Theology: Models of God in Religious Language* (Philadelphia: Fortress, 1982), and later writings. A more recent swearword among such critics is "kyriarchal," which shows that the issue is that of the divine sovereignty.

27. The "collapse of the house of authority" is what Farley describes and seeks to hasten.

of the gospel — and so to the faith that works by love. That love, Christ shows us, will be self-sacrificial. It will be exercised in the discipline of a covenant community.[28]

Second, there is the question of "ultimate hope." Of course, the preaching of a future life must not be allowed to detract from the amendment of inhuman conditions on earth. To that extent, we must heed Marxist critiques. But if we were *not* to preach "the life of the world to come," we should be cheating the poor once again. As Christians, we believe that every tear will be wiped dry, and that the peace and plenty of God's kingdom is intended for people of every time and place. Even such a left-leaning theologian as Helmut Gollwitzer argued, and indeed powerfully, against his Marxist friends that all hopes are groundless without a transcendent realm beyond death in which a community drawn from every generation will dwell securely.[29] The Christian faith is that the exaltation of Christ has "opened the kingdom of heaven to all believers."

28. See the writings of John Howard Yoder, such as those gathered in *The Priestly Kingdom* (Notre Dame, Ind.: University of Notre Dame Press, 1984) and in *The Royal Priesthood: Essays Ecclesiological and Ecumenical,* ed. Michael G. Cartwright (Grand Rapids: Eerdmans, 1994).

29. Helmut Gollwitzer, *Krummes Holz, aufrechter Gang. Zur Frage nach dem Sinn des Lebens* (Munich: Kaiser, 1970).

The Threefold Office in Prospect

To speak of a theological or practical prospect for the threefold office is something of a wager. Many perhaps would consider that the categories of prophet, priest, and king belonged already to a bygone age. Certainly there are few *kings* left in the world; yet the perdurance of an occasional monarchy, and the fascination which a royal family can still hold, especially for foreigners, suggests that the "divinity that doth hedge a king" may not quite have vanished from the face of the earth. The very term *priestcraft* as a synonym, and worse, for superstition and obscurantism may have practically disappeared from our "enlightened" world; yet a certain mystery attaches to science and technology as they discover and master the secrets of the universe. There may be few *prophets* for stoning, but gurus attract followers searching for deep wisdom. If we were to grant, however, that the terms *prophet, priest,* and *king* were relatively unfamiliar to the modern world, it might well be that therein resides precisely their chance. Perhaps the rather archaic quality they now possess would precisely allow them to function as archetypes. Let us examine what would be the necessary conditions for that to happen, and what its value might be.

In his interesting and influential book entitled *The Nature of Doctrine,* George Lindbeck has proposed to understand Christianity as a cultural and linguistic tradition.[1] While it would be a mistake to bracket the ontological reference of doctrines in favor of reducing them to a set of speech-rules (as

---

1. George A. Lindbeck, *The Nature of Doctrine: Religion and Theology in a Postliberal Age* (Philadelphia: Westminster, 1984).

many saw Lindbeck doing), his fundamental insight is valid that Christianity entails a complex of language-use interwoven with perceptions, habits, and skills which can only be appropriated by disciplined participation; membership in the ecclesial community requires learning one's way into the verbal and practical tradition. There is no reason to expect that its content and forms should be immediately accessible to the outsider. There is therefore nothing untoward about our maintenance — or, if it has been forgotten, retrieval — of the language of prophet, priest, and king, provided three conditions are met. First: the reference of prophet, priest, and king should have some relevance to the human condition. While the "cult of relevance" is deplorable, it would be a betrayal to think that the gospel were *ir*relevant to human needs and possibilities, properly understood. Second: prophet, priest, and king would need to suit the person and work of the Savior and the nature of the salvation experienced in him. Here it is necessary to test whether our triad matches other scriptural and traditional ways of describing Christ and Christian existence. Third: prophet, priest, and king would have to retain or regain a living context in the devotional and liturgical life of the church, for it is in image and rite that archetypes dwell, persist, and exercise their power.

1. KNOWLEDGE, POWER, AND REDEMPTIVE MEDIATION

As to the first requirement, the relevance of our triad to the human condition: I will recall the way each of the previous chapters ended. First I invoked John Henry Newman on "the three principal conditions of mankind," namely, "suffering," "work," and "study," which were for him matched by the priestly, regal, and prophetic offices of Christ respectively. In the three subsequent chapters, I found my own equivalents. The prophetic office of Christ addresses the human questions of knowledge and meaning. The priestly office of Christ deals with human alienation and estrangement by providing a divine reconciliation and atonement. The royal office of Christ addresses the human questions of power and authority. What remains is briefly to indicate the connections among these themes of knowledge, power, and redemptive mediation.

Proverbially, knowledge is power; and some late-twentieth-century epistemologists have called attention to the reverse dynamic: rather benignly, J. Habermas has pointed to the "interests" which guide our acquisition of knowledge; in more sinister fashion, M. Foucault sought to show that power holders control what counts as knowledge. Without knowledge, power would be blind; without power, knowledge would be ineffective. Combined, knowledge and power give opportunity for good or for ill. In the fallen condition of humankind, wisdom can (apparently) be overpowered; and legitimate authority can (apparently) be ignored. Even worse, power and knowledge together can be used to express, produce, or maintain alienations between the possessors and the deprived in every sphere of human existence. Into this situation, Jesus Christ comes redemptively. Grounded in the reality of divine wisdom and sovereignty, Christ offers the vision and the possibility of a relationship between knowledge and power that is characterized by love. Freely undertaken at cost to self and for the good of all, Christ's sacrificial service bears the moral authority to invite human beings to enter in repentance and faith, through the liberating Spirit, into that life of communion which God purposes for his creatures. There, knowledge comes through love of the other; and love of the other informs the exercise of power. And because the God revealed in Christ is the creator of all things and their redeemer, there is the real prospect that they will finally find their consummation in him. "To crown all," said John Wesley in harmony with the classic Christian Tradition, "there will be a deep, an intimate, an uninterrupted union with God; a constant communion with the Father and his Son Jesus Christ, through the Spirit; a continual enjoyment of the Three-One God, and of all the creatures in Him."[2]

2. THE SAVIOR AND THE SALVATION

Let us move on to the second set of conditions: Does the threefold office touch all bases as a description of the Savior and his work? On its own terms, it avoids the inadequacy of taking any one of its facets singly. W. A. Visser 't Hooft put the dangers of the respective unilateralisms this way:

> A one-sided emphasis on the prophetic ministry leads inevitably to moralism and rationalism: Christ becomes a great teacher of ideas and

2. Sermon 64, "The New Creation," in *The Works of John Wesley*, vol. 2, ed. Albert C. Outler (Nashville: Abingdon, 1985), pp. 500-510 (here p. 510).

principles, but his work, past, present and future, disappears from the horizon. An exclusive emphasis on the priestly function leads to pietism and mysticism: Christ is the Lamb of God, but his piercing word and his victory over sin and death are not taken seriously. The full concentration on the kingship of Christ leads to utopianism and apocalypticism: Christ is the glorious King, but it is forgotten that his victory is the invisible victory of the word and that in this world the road to glory is the way of the cross.[3]

Positively, it must be tested whether the threefold office appropriately covers the same area as is described by other intentionally comprehensive formulae for salvation in Christ. Not all triads are theologically significant. "Three strikes, you're out" is not necessarily of divine inspiration, nor even the three stumps that make up a wicket. But let us try out our triad in relation to two other familiar tripartite formulations. Jesus said: "I am the way, and the truth, and the life" (John 14:6). For Saint Paul, the three abiding graces were "faith, hope, love" (1 Cor. 13:13). For bringing these two other triads into comparison with our own, I am indebted to suggestions by the Roman Catholic Walter Kasper in the first case, and the Presbyterian George Stroup in the second.[4]

The Way, the Truth, and the Life

In calling himself "the way, the truth, and the life," the Johannine Christ was describing his own saving work in relation to humankind. He is the way to be followed; he is the revealer of truth; he is the source of abundant life.

First, truth. The revelation of truth belongs to the prophet and teacher. "The question of truth," says Kasper, "is a radical human question." It was also Pilate's question: "What is truth?" (John 18:38). The truth of Christ is a key category of the Fourth Gospel. Truth is the removal of a veil, *a-lētheia*, letting reality be seen as it is in God's eyes. Only so can one get one's bearings and live authentically. "Light," says Kasper, "is

3. W. A. Visser 't Hooft, *The Kingship of Christ* (New York: Harper, 1948), p. 17.
4. Walter Kasper, *Jesus the Christ,* trans. V. Green (New York: Paulist Press, 1976), in particular pp. 259-66; George W. Stroup, *Jesus Christ for Today* (Philadelphia: Westminster, 1982), in particular pp. 88-106.

therefore a symbol of salvation. But where is there a dependable light among the many will-o'-the-wisps and the deceitful glitter of the world?" The Old Testament speaks of the Lord himself as light (Ps. 27:1; Isa. 60:19); his law is a lamp to the feet and a light to the path (Ps. 119:105). The Fourth Gospel calls Christ "the light of the world" (John 8:12; cf. 1:9; 12:46). He opposed lies and darkness, which are the consequence of sin (John 1:5; 3:19; 8:44; cf. 1 John 3:8). At Christmas and Epiphany we celebrate Christ as the *sol invictus*, "the unconquered sun." In the Easter Vigil we hail "the light of Christ," the *lumen Christi*. These are traditionally seasons of baptism, the sacrament of faith, which the early church called "enlightenment."[5]

Second, life. The giving of life belongs to the priestly office. "Life," says Kasper, "is always more than the purely biological; life includes man and his question about life, about authentic, fulfilled, true life. Life longs for the light of life, and that light is an essential factor in life itself. But since life is constantly threatened by decay and death, the question of true life includes the question of abiding, eternal life." In the Old Testament, God is the fount and lord of life (1 Sam. 2:6; Job 12:9f.; Deut. 32:39; Ps. 104:29). God's life has appeared in Jesus Christ (John 1:4; 5:26; 11:25; 1 John 1:1; 5:11). Christ is sent to bring life to the world (John 3:15f.; 10:10). Christ sealed the gift of life by loving "his own . . . to the end" (John 13:1) and making his redemptive passover on the cross (John 19:28-37; 1 Cor. 5:7). "By giving his life, his self-sacrifice, Jesus is both sacrificial victim and sacrificing priest" (Kasper). Only then is his flesh given for the life of the world (John 6:51c); and "he who eats my flesh and drinks my blood has eternal life, and I will raise him up at the last day" (John 6:54). The Eucharist becomes the bread of life to the believer. By the rite which Christ instituted on Maundy Thursday, we commemorate the unrepeatable sacrifice of Good Friday, in continuing dependence on the heavenly intercession upon which Christ entered at his ascension.

Third, the way. The way of truth and life is a royal road; and direction belongs to the king, guidance to the shepherd. In the Old Testament, the Lord is Israel's king (Exod. 15:18; Pss. 95–99; 145; 146) and shepherd (Gen. 49:24; Ps. 23:1). In the Fourth Gospel, Jesus is "the good shepherd," who "lays down his life for the sheep" (John 10:11-18); he is "the King of the Jews," who "bear[s] witness to the truth" (John 18:33-37). As the

---

5. So already Justin Martyr, *First Apology*, 61 and 65 (Migne, *Patrologia Graeca* 6:421 and 428; hereafter cited as *PG*).

"pioneer of [our] salvation" (Heb. 2:10; 12:2; cf. Acts 3:15; 5:31), he has gone ahead to prepare a place for his followers, that where he is, there they may be also (John 14:2f.). Lifted up, he is drawing all people to himself (John 12:32). One theme of Ascension Day is the theme of the sovereignty of Christ, celebrated in the liturgical application of Psalm 47 to him. In 1925, Pope Pius XI instituted the feast of Christ the King, in order to reaffirm the universal rule of Christ in an increasingly secular age. Now moved from the last Sunday in October to the Sunday before Advent, it has been adopted into the calendar of many other churches also.

Faith, Hope, and Love

According to the apostle Paul, faith, hope, and love are the three gifts of God that last throughout the course of human salvation. Each of the triad rests upon the person and work of Christ.

First, faith. Jesus Christ is "the faithful prophet" (G. Stroup). Toward the God he calls "Abba," his trust is unreserved, and his obedience complete. Prefaced by "Amen" ("Verily, verily . . ."), his teaching testifies to the faithfulness *('emeth)* of God. Indeed, he himself is the Amen of all the promises of God, and "that is why we [in turn] utter the Amen through him, to the glory of God" (2 Cor. 1:20). And that Amen of ours is the prayerful expression of all the trust and obedience that faith includes.

Second, love. What Stroup calls "the priest's cross" is grounded in the love of God. However inadequate the so-called Abelardian theory may be when it views Christ and his cross solely in terms of a "moral example and influence," no other account of the atonement — whether military, satisfactory, or penal — can claim to capture an aspect of the redemption unless it begins and ends, as Abelard did, in God's love. The human expression of that love was Christ's "having loved his own . . . to the end" (John 13:1). Christ's self-sacrifice invites his disciples to "take up [their] cross" (Matt. 16:24). To confess Jesus Christ in the flesh is inseparable, says the First Letter of John, from "love of the brethren," which itself is a test of love toward God.

Third, hope. If Christ is "the source of hope," says Stroup, it is because "Jesus reigns . . . [and] is also yet to reign." Death could not hold him, and the "last enemy" is therefore radically defeated. Through Christ "we are more than conquerors": Nothing "in all creation, will be able to separate us from the love of God in Christ Jesus our Lord" (Rom. 8:37-39).

The way, the truth, and the life; faith, hope, and love: the brevity of my remarks may have left an impression of artificiality; but I hope I have done enough at least to suggest the correspondence in substance and pattern between the threefold office of Christ and those other two triads that the Christian Tradition has also sensed to be comprehensive statements of the person and work of the Savior and the nature of the salvation experienced in him. The third and final condition for prophet, priest, and king to continue as an archetypical triad was that it should retain or regain a vital place in the church's worship.

3. The Vital Continuum

The liturgical assembly functions in the life of the church as a hermeneutical continuum, where the repertory of scriptural images and themes is transmitted and their interpretation encouraged. Moreover, the liturgical assembly brings to significant expression, at the level of rite and symbol, the roles of Christ and of his church in the salvation of humankind; and it is, in particular, the focal occasion and instance of participation by Christians and the church in Christ's threefold office. In this connection, let me make three sets of remarks, in reference to (1) the structure of the Sunday service, (2) the liturgical calendar, and (3) verbal imagery in worship.

First, the structure of the Sunday service. One of the most remarkable ecumenical convergences in the twentieth century has been the recovery by the modern liturgical movement of the principle, and (with varying success) the practice, of the Sunday service as a service of word and sacrament. From different starting points, the Roman Catholic Church has created a new lectionary from which many other churches also benefit,[6] and Catholic preachers are now setting fine examples in the exposition of Scripture; while slowly but (I trust) surely, Protestant churches are learning that the reduction of their worship to the spoken word alone was an unwanted accident rather than a Reformation principle, since at least

6. The Roman lectionary was prepared to accompany the Missal of Paul VI (1969). Ecumenical work in North America by the Consultation on Common Texts has adapted the Roman schedule of readings to form a "Common Lectionary" which is now widely used in Anglican and Protestant churches of the English-speaking world.

Luther, Calvin, and Cranmer desired a full service of word and sacrament, Sunday by Sunday. Let me suggest that the deep structure of the Christian rite, simply as a liturgical order, matches the threefold office of Christ. In the reading and exposition of the Scriptures, which is the core of the first part of the Sunday liturgy, we are apt to find our hearts burning within us as Christ the Word himself prophetically interprets the word which testifies to him. Then, the great Easter Vigil suggests, the proper place for baptisms is after Scriptures and sermon, for baptism is a response to the proclamation of the gospel; and if on some Sundays we have no baptisms, then at least the saying of the creed can remind us of our own baptismal confession of faith. Baptism may be, as the Danish Lutheran Regin Prenter argued, the royal sacrament *par excellence:* we confess Christ as Lord and are made over to his sovereignty and given a share in his reign.[7] The Sunday service then moves into Eucharist and Communion, where, breaking bread at Christ's command, we celebrate his priestly work and receive the benefits of his sacrifice.

Second, the liturgical calendar. The yearly round cannot simply be an annual commemoration of certain events in the life of Jesus in the chronological sequence in which they occurred over the entire period of his earthly ministry. That is because the incarnate One, the events of whose life are commemorated in the church's festivals, was and is the eternal Son of God. The constancy of his Person through the states of humiliation and exaltation — which allows also the "communication of properties" between his divine and human natures — means that whenever we celebrate Christ, it is his whole mystery that we celebrate: incarnate, crucified, risen, ascended, glorified, and indeed awaited. He is Prophet, Priest, and King throughout his history; and it is as Prophet, Priest, and King that we worshipfully receive him and his ministry at every service. Nevertheless, a certain concentration of attention may shift throughout the Christian year.

In that case, it is not inappropriate to focus at Christmas on the incarnation of the Word, and to follow — especially in our Gospel lectionaries — through Epiphany and Lent Christ's ministry of proclamation in word and deed: the prophetic office. In Lent, however, we see him already in the shadow of the cross, and the priestly office reaches its most poignant moment on Good Friday, although its climax comes only with the entry into the heavenly sanctuary, a theme of the ascension. Already a king on

7. Regin Prenter, *Connaître Christ* (Neuchâtel: Delachaux & Niestlé, 1966), pp. 39-74 (especially pp. 72f.).

the cross, Christ's majesty was displayed on Easter Day, and the great fifty days up to Pentecost are a royal season (in the ancient church, Christians did not kneel but only stood to pray during that period of the year). Thus the liturgical calendar can after all serve to express the threefold office, provided its "sequential" character be firmly held within a comprehensive grasp of the entire mystery of Christ's person and work.

Third, verbal imagery. I am not suggesting that Christians at worship should at every turn of phrase mouth the words "prophet, priest, and king," "prophet, priest, and king." That would be to risk falling into the particularly Protestant temptation of didacticism in liturgy. But on the structural basis of Sunday worship as I have described it, and with the festal coloring of the Christian year as I have evoked it, it should be possible to use language that expresses, sometimes directly, sometimes more subtly, the threefold office of Christ. We shall call him Prophet, Priest, and King, but not use those words in isolation, as though throwing them at him or at the congregation in order to make a point. Much rather, they will have their rich scriptural and traditional content restored to them through their association with the biblical readings, the broader language of praise and prayer, the liturgical structures and rites, the unfolding of the Christian festivals — and insofar as the terms and the offices need direct exposition and interpretation, it will be done, at least in the context of the worship assembly, primarily in a kerygmatic way, and only secondarily in a doctrinal way.

Those, then, are the conditions for a renewed emphasis on the threefold office of Christ: it must be related to the human condition; it must match other comprehensive descriptions of the person and work of Christ and of the salvation found in him; it must have a vital context in the worship of the church. If those conditions are met, then I think there is great value in the threefold office of prophet, priest, and king as archetypes. The value is, in the one direction, christological; in the other, ecclesiological.

4. CHRISTOLOGY: DOXOLOGY AND DOGMA

To speak of Christ in terms of the threefold office has the value of uniting doxology and dogma in his regard.

The title Prophet is, at first sight, perhaps the most modest of the three, yet it gets filled with the majesty of God: the man from Nazareth is the eternal Word of God incarnate, the transcendent Wisdom of God in human expression. The title King is the grandest of the three, yet the Lord became a servant, so that finally we might share in his reign: "For you know the grace of our Lord Jesus Christ, that though he was rich, yet for your sake he became poor, so that by his poverty you might become rich" (2 Cor. 8:9). The title Priest captures the heart of Christ's mediatorial role, which in the face of human sin needed to be redemptive; in him, God reconciled the world to himself and restores humankind to the divine image.

From the earliest days, it appears that Christians have also *worshiped* the One who *mediates* God to us and our access to God, and who is himself the *pattern* of our communion with the Father.[8] This doxological practice constituted for the early church a basis and context for dogmatic reflection. Against Arianism, Athanasius established the godhead of the Son on the twin grounds that Christ received worship and that only God could reveal God and save humankind, our reception of revelation and salvation in him being precisely what motivates our worship of him.[9] Against Apollinarianism, Gregory Nazianzen established the full humanity of Christ on the ground that "what had not been assumed would not have been healed,"[10] and it was left to Cyril of Alexandria, as T. F. Torrance has shown, to bring out the necessary role of the human mind of Christ if we are to bring our "reasonable worship" *(logikē latreia)* to God.[11] The Council of Chalcedon recognized that both the divine and the human natures of Christ are grounded in the one *hypostasis* of God the Son. One way the Council expressed that was to say that the Son, now and forever incarnate, receives "a single worship" *(mia latreia).*

Within that dogmatically established regulative framework, to speak of Christ as Prophet, Priest, and King is to take a step in the direction of that more pictorial and affective language which is appropriate to doxology and kerygma. It was, in the first place, the practice of the church in proclamation and worship that helped the Councils of Nicea, Ephesus,

8. See G. Wainwright, *Doxology: The Praise of God in Worship, Doctrine, and Life* (New York: Oxford University Press, 1980), pp. 45-86.

9. Athanasius, *Letter to Adelphius,* 3f. (Migne, *PG* 26:1074-77); *Letters to Serapion* I.29f. (Migne, *PG* 26:597-600).

10. Gregory Nazianzen, *Epistle* 101 (Migne, *PG* 37:181).

11. T. F. Torrance, "The Mind of Christ in Worship: The Problem of Apollinarianism in the Liturgy," in his *Theology in Reconciliation* (London: Chapman, 1975), pp. 139-214.

and Chalcedon to the dogmatic recognition of Christ's deity and the unity of his Person in the two natures of divinity and humanity. That dogma itself is meant as a permanent service to worship and preaching.

Having briefly shown the suitability to christology of the combination of prophet, priest, and king, I want now to show the value for ecclesiology of the threefold office in and under the one Christ.[12]

5. ECCLESIOLOGY: BEFORE GOD AND IN THE WORLD

The *munus triplex* in its threefold unity can assist the church's self-understanding and practice both in its internal life and in its mission for the sake of the world.

Down the years, John Henry Newman, with a continual ringing of the changes in terminology and perhaps with some development in this thought, drew on the threefold office in order to expound the nature and structures of the church. Christianity, he said, for instance, is "at once a philosophy, a political power, and a religious rite." Or again, it is a "passion" (the priestly office), a "fellowship" (the royal office), and a "science" (the prophetic office). Or yet again: "Christianity is dogmatical [the prophetic office], devotional [the priestly], practical [the royal] all at once."[13] The health of the church depends on these three functions being

12. For the threefold office as a continuing link between christology and ecclesiology in a Reformed context, see, in firmly trinitarian perspective, Philip W. Butin, *Reformed Ecclesiology: Trinitarian Grace according to Calvin,* Studies in Reformed Theology and History 2/1 (Princeton, N.J.: Princeton Theological Seminary, 1994), in particular pp. 29-42.

13. Besides Newman's 1840 Anglican sermon on "The Three Offices of Christ," his other most sustained writing on the theme is found in the preface he wrote in 1877 as a Roman Catholic to the third edition of his old *The Via Media of the Anglican Church* (London: Longmans, Green), vol. 1, pp. xlvi-xciv. In the introduction to his edition of that work, H. D. Weidner writes: "Newman owes his idea of the nature of Christ's offices to the Evangelicals, but he applied them to the nature of the Church more boldly than they were prepared to do. . . . The doctrine of the incarnation was the key to Newman's ecclesiology. The church shared in the extension of Christ's body in the world and in his mission expressed in the triple office" (*The "Via Media" of the Anglican Church by John Henry Newman* [Oxford: Clarendon Press, 1990], pp. li, lviii). For the whole subject in Newman, see Nicholas Lash, *Theology on Dover Beach* (London: Darton, Longman and Todd, 1979), pp. 89-108 ("Life, Language and Organization: Aspects of the Theological

kept in proper balance. Their upsetting allows one to deduce from Newman what Maurice Nédoncelle has called "a theology of the abuses of the
Church."[14] Positively put, "the prophetical, priestly and royal offices constitute," in the words of Nicholas Lash, "a 'triangle of forces' that is in
principle . . . an *equilateral* triangle." At least, each of the three offices is
"reshaped by its coincidence with the others." Each qualifies, and is
qualified by, the others; and so all together are transformed. The equi-
librium is precarious, because, as Newman recognizes, "in man as he is,
reasoning tends to rationalism; devotion, to superstition; and power, to
ambition and tyranny." So, says Lash, with the state of the Roman Catholic   Lash
Church after Vatican II in view: "Theological rationalism [needs to be]
held in check by the theologian's engagement in and sensitivity to the
particular circumstances, experience and suffering of the worshipping community to which he belongs. . . . The theologian's work requires the corrective influence not only of the context of worship but also of what I
have called 'the operation of catholicity,' expressed (in part) through the
practical instruments of the Church's administration." Similarly: "The
characteristic tendency of church authorities prematurely to 'order' the life
of the Church through the exercise of power requires corrective pressure
both from the exigencies of worship and life in particular places, and also
from the requirements of sound scholarship and good argument." Other
churches might conduct a similar exercise of self-examination. Lash recognizes, of course, that "the ultimate ground and guarantee of [the] equi-
librium, which is not under our control, is the abiding presence of the
Spirit of the risen Christ."

Turning now to the place and role of the church in the world and
before God, it is possible to sketch the interlocking functions of the *munus
triplex* in terms of a triad that has found much favor in the modern
ecumenical movement: *leitourgia, martyria,* and *diakonia.*

First, *leitourgia.* With Karl Barth and the Swiss Reformed theologian

---

Ministry"), and "Catholic Theology and the Crisis of Classicism," in *New Blackfriars* 66
(1985): 279-87. Lash's own phrases in the next few sentences are taken from the two
sources just indicated. Another study placing Newman's use of the *munus triplex* in the
context of subsequent developments in Roman Catholic theology of the church is Avery
Dulles, "The Threefold Office in Newman's Ecclesiology," in *Newman after a Hundred
Years,* ed. I. Ker and A. G. Hill (Oxford: Clarendon Press, 1990), pp. 375-99.

14. M. G. Nédoncelle, "Newman, théologien des abus de l'Église," in *Oecumenica:
An Annual Symposium of Ecumenical Research, 1967,* ed. F. W. Katzenbusch and V. Vajta
(Minneapolis: Augsburg, 1967), pp. 116-32.

of worship Jean-Jacques von Allmen, we can see Christian worship as also a "public service" (corresponding to the Greek etymology of liturgy), which the church offers to God on behalf of a world that is *not yet* willing or able to render praise and prayer.[15] The church in Christ intercedes for the conversion of the world and the needs of humankind — grounded in the redemption which God has wrought and the church now celebrates.

Second, *martyria*. By its proclamation, the church testifies to the wonderful works of God and so seeks to bring the world also into God's marvelous light (cf. 1 Pet. 2:9), where spiritual sacrifices may be offered — both of praise and of doing good (cf. Heb. 13:15f.).

Third, *diakonia*. Although, for instance, in almsgiving, our left hand should not know what our right hand is doing, yet the witness of our good works should bring the world to the worship of God: "Let your light so shine before men, that they may see your good works and give glory to your Father who is in heaven" (Matt. 5:16).

Once again, the proportion and combination is important: *leitourgia, martyria, diakonia;* worship, witness, ministry; the threefold office of priesthood, prophecy, and royal service.

And now the end is in sight, and not only of these chapters; for "salvation is nearer to us now than when we first believed" (Rom. 13:11).

6. THE ESCHATOLOGICAL OUTLOOK

The entire exercise of the threefold office has been geared toward the end. As Prophet, Christ reveals the will and pleasure of God, which includes for humankind a salvation in which we attain our "chief end," namely, "to glorify God and enjoy him for ever" (to speak with the Westminster Catechism). As Priest, Christ removes the guilt of fallen humanity and restores our access to God, which is the condition of our salvation. As King, Christ preserves believers in our salutary communion with God by helping us to overcome the power of sin and bestowing on us the riches of his grace. The church is the company of those who already receive the

15. Jean-Jacques von Allmen, *Worship: Its Theology and Practice,* trans. H. Knight and W. F. Fleet (New York: Oxford University Press, 1965), e.g., pp. 16, 70; cf. Karl Barth, *Church Dogmatics* IV/2, trans. G. W. Bromiley (Edinburgh: T. & T. Clark, 1958), pp. 638-41, 695-710, and IV/3 (1962), pp. 865f., 883f.

benefits of Christ's threefold mediation and actively share, in Christ, in its further extension to the dimensions God has in view.

For a glimpse into the end, we may turn to the book of Revelation, where the historic offices of Christ and our participation in them are not forgotten but eternally transfigured.

In the end, as envisioned in the book of Revelation, the prophetic scroll is unsealed, and proclamation turns to sheer praise of the Savior and the glorification of God:

> And between the throne and the four living creatures and among the elders, I saw a Lamb standing, as though it had been slain . . . ; and he went and took the scroll from the right hand of him who was seated on the throne. And when he had taken the scroll, the four living creatures and the twenty-four elders fell down before the Lamb, each holding a harp, and with golden bowls full of incense, which are the prayers of the saints; and they sang a new song, saying,

> "Worthy art thou to take the scroll and to open its seals,
> for thou wast slain and by thy blood didst ransom men for God
> from every tribe and tongue and people and nation,
> and hast made them a kingdom and priests to our God. . . ."
>   (Rev. 5:6-10)

> "Amen! Blessing and glory and wisdom and thanksgiving and honor and power and might be to our God for ever and ever! Amen."
>   (Rev. 7:12)

In the end, as envisioned in the book of Revelation, the priestly sacrifice has prepared the wedding banquet, in which the blessed rejoice with the Savior and find enjoyment in God:

> Then I heard what seemed to be the voice of a great multitude, like the sound of many waters and like the sound of many thunderpeals, crying,
>   "Hallelujah! For the Lord our God the Almighty reigns.
>   Let us rejoice and exult and give him the glory,
>   for the marriage of the Lamb has come,
>   and his Bride has made herself ready;
>   it was granted her to be clothed with fine linen, bright and
>   pure" —

for the fine linen is the righteous deeds of the saints.

And the angel said to me, "Write this: Blessed are those who are invited to the marriage supper of the Lamb." And he said to me, "These are true words of God." (Rev. 19:6-9)

In the end, as envisioned in the book of Revelation, the royal glory of "him who sits upon the throne" is shared by the Lamb; and his faithful servants who bear his name will reign with him:

Then I looked, and I heard around the throne and the living creatures and the elders the voice of many angels, numbering myriads of myriads and thousands of thousands, saying with a loud voice, "Worthy is the Lamb who was slain, to receive power and wealth and wisdom and might and honor and glory and blessing!" And I heard every creature in heaven and on earth and under the earth and in the sea, and all therein, saying, "To him who sits upon the throne and to the Lamb be blessing and honor and glory and might for ever and ever!" And the four living creatures said, "Amen!" and the elders fell down and worshiped. (Rev. 5:11-14)

The throne of God and of the Lamb shall be in [the city], and his servants shall worship him; they shall see his face, and his name shall be on their foreheads. And night shall be no more; they need no light of lamp or sun, for the Lord God will be their light, and they shall reign for ever and ever. (Rev. 22:3-5)

And as the Handelian choruses of "Hallelujah" and "Amen" resound, we can meanwhile only say, "Come, Lord Jesus!" (Rev. 22:20).